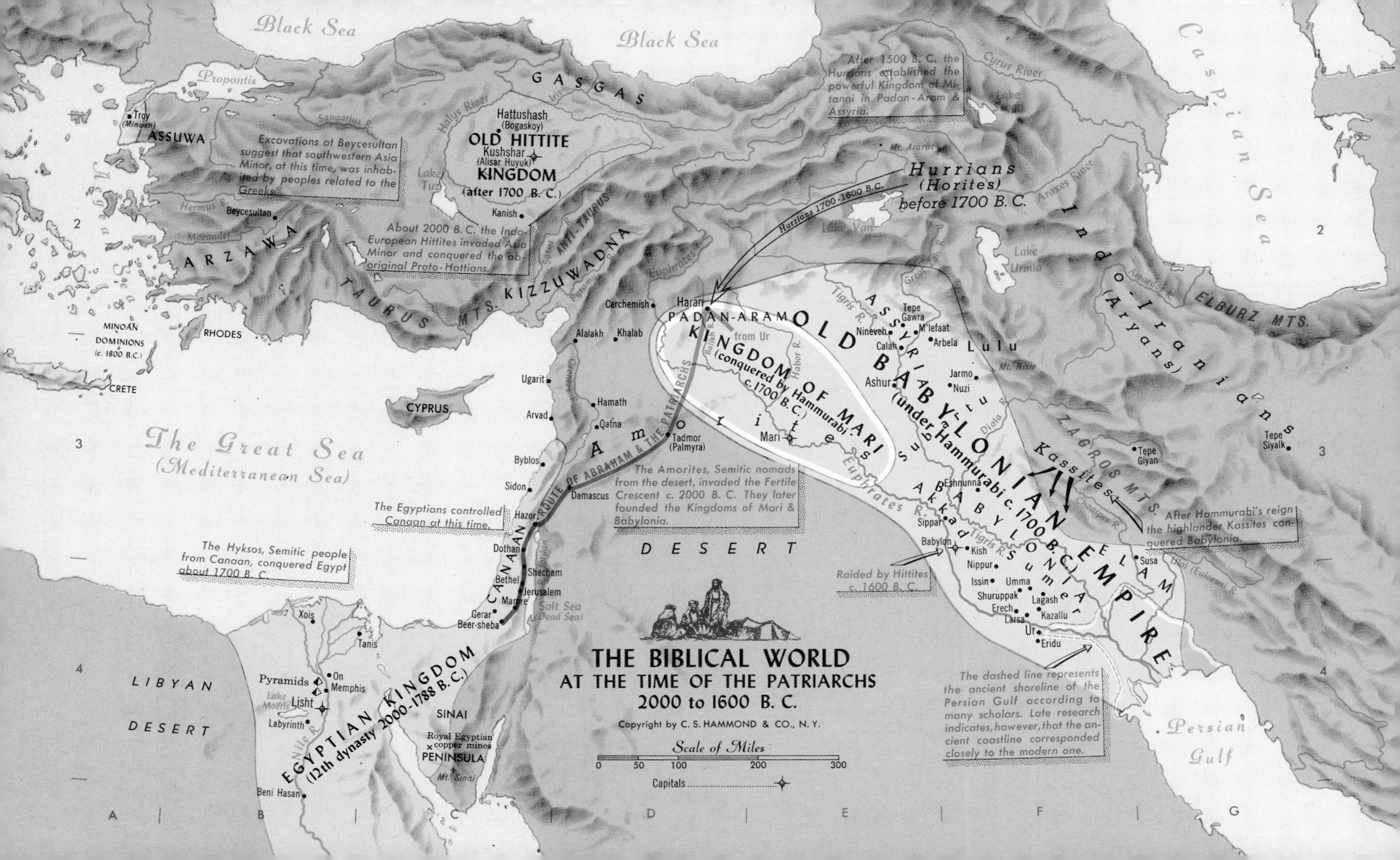
THE BIBLICAL WORLD
AT THE TIME OF THE PATRIARCHS
2000 to 1600 B. C.
Copyright by C. S. HAMMOND & CO., N. Y.
Scale of Miles
0 50 100 200 300
Capitals
Black Sea
Black Sea
Caspian Sea
The Great Sea
(Mediterranean Sea)
Aegean Sea
Persian Gulf
Propontis
GASGAS
ASSUWA
ARZAWA
TAURUS MTS.
KIZZUWADNA
ANTI-TAURUS
OLD HITTITE KINGDOM (after 1700 B. C.)
Hattushash (Bogaskoy)
Kushshar (Alisar Huyuk)
Kanish
Beycesultan
Troy (Minoan)
MINOAN DOMINIONS (c. 1800 B.C.)
RHODES
CRETE
CYPRUS
Excavations at Beycesultan suggest that southwestern Asia Minor, at this time, was inhabited by peoples related to the Greeks.
About 2000 B. C. the Indo-European Hittites invaded Asia Minor and conquered the aboriginal Proto-Hattians.
After 1500 B. C. the Hurrians established the powerful Kingdom of Mitanni in Padan-Aram & Assyria.
Hurrians (Horites) before 1700 B. C.
Hurrians 1700-1600 B.C.
Indo-Iranians (Aryans)
ELBURZ MTS.
ZAGROS MTS.
Kassites
After Hammurabi's reign the highlander Kassites conquered Babylonia.
Lulu
Mt. Ararat
Lake Van
Lake Urmia
Mt. Nisir
Cyrus River
Araxes River
Halys River
Sangarius R.
Hermus R.
Maeander R.
Iris R.
Euphrates R.
Tigris R.
Habor R.
Balikh R.
Diala R.
Choaspes R.
Ulai (Eulaeus) R.
Orontes R.
Jordan R.
Nile R.
Lake Tuz
PADAN-ARAM
Haran
from Ur
Carchemish
Alalakh
Khalab
Ugarit
Arvad
Hamath
Qatna
Byblos
Sidon
Hazor
Damascus
Tadmor (Palmyra)
Mari
KINGDOM OF MARI (conquered by Hammurabi c. 1700 B. C.)
OLD BABYLONIAN EMPIRE (under Hammurabi c. 1700 B. C.)
ASSYRIA
AKKAD
BABYLONIA
SUMER
ELAM
Amorites
Nineveh
Tepe Gawra
M'lefaat
Calah
Arbela
Ashur
Jarmo
Nuzi
Eshnunna
Sippar
Babylon
Kish
Nippur
Issin
Umma
Shuruppak
Lagash
Erech
Larsa
Kazallu
Ur
Eridu
Susa
Tepe Giyan
Tepe Siyalk
Raided by Hittites c. 1600 B. C.
The dashed line represents the ancient shoreline of the Persian Gulf according to many scholars. Late research indicates, however, that the ancient coastline corresponded closely to the modern one.
ROUTE OF ABRAHAM & THE PATRIARCHS
The Amorites, Semitic nomads from the desert, invaded the Fertile Crescent c. 2000 B. C. They later founded the Kingdoms of Mari & Babylonia.
DESERT
The Egyptians controlled Canaan at this time.
CANAAN
Dothan
Shechem
Bethel
Jerusalem
Mamre
Gerar
Beer-sheba
Salt Sea (Dead Sea)
The Hyksos, Semitic people from Canaan, conquered Egypt about 1700 B. C.
EGYPTIAN KINGDOM (12th dynasty 2000-1788 B. C.)
Xois
Tanis
On
Memphis
Pyramids
Lisht
Lake Moeris
Labyrinth
Beni Hasan
LIBYAN DESERT
SINAI PENINSULA
Royal Egyptian copper mines
Mt. Sinai
A B C D E F G
2 3 4

CANAAN BEFORE THE CONQUEST
Copyright by C. S. HAMMOND & CO., N. Y.
Scale of Miles
0 5 10 20 30 40
Perennial Rivers
Seasonal Rivers & Streams
Capitals
Phoenicians from the cities of Sidon and Tyre traded throughout the Mediterranean.
Canaan at this time was an Egyptian province organized on a city-state system. The local kings were only required to pay tribute and to furnish labor for Egyptian royal projects.
The 13th and 12th century kingdoms of Bashan, Ammon, Moab and Edom displaced the Rephaim, Zuzim, Emim and Horites respectively.
The destroyed cities of Sodom and Gomorrah are believed to be beneath the shallow waters of the Dead Sea which now cover the Vale of Siddim (shaded portion).
The Great Sea
(Mediterranean Sea)
HITTITE EMPIRE
Ubi
Damascus
Sidonians (Phoenicians)
MOUNT LEBANON
MT. HERMON
Sidon
Zarephath
Tyre
Kanah
Laish (Dan)
Kedesh
Misrephoth-maim
Achzib
Hazor
Merom
BASHAN (KINGDOM OF OG)
Karnaim
Ashtaroth
Accho
Achshaph
Chinnereth
Madon
Sea of Chinnereth
Yarmuk R.
MT. CARMEL
Kishon
Shimron
Mt. Tabor
Jokneam
Dor
Edrei
Megiddo
Taanach
Canaanites
Beth-shan
Ham
Ramoth-gilead
Ibleam
Pella
Dothan
Jabesh-gilead
Mahanaim
Plain of Sharon
Sochoh
Tirzah
Mt. Ebal
Shechem
Jacob's Well
Mt. Gerizim
Succoth
Jabbok R.
Penuel (Peniel)
Jordan
Aphek
Tappuah
Adam
Joppa
Ono
Lod
Hivites
Amorites
KINGDOM OF SIHON
Jazer
Rabbath-ammon
AMMON
Bethel
Ai
Beeroth
Gezer
Gibeon
Jericho
Gilgal
Ekron
Chephirah
Jebusites
Kirjath-jearim
Plains of Moab
Heshbon
Mt. Nebo (Pisgah)
Jerusalem (Jebus, Salem)
Beth-shemesh
Ashdod
Makkedah
Jarmuth
Medeba
Libnah
Bethlehem
Ashkelon
Adullam
Jahaz
Gath
Lachish
Mamre
Salt Sea (Dead Sea)
Gaza (Azzah)
Eglon
Kirjath-arba (Hebron)
Kiriathaim
Dibon
Aroer
Kirjath-sepher (Debir)
Hazeon-tamar (En-gedi)
Gerar
Arnon R.
Hittites
Raphia
Sharuhen
Besor
Beer-sheba
Arad
Ar
Hormah
Kir-moab (Kir-hareseth)
MOAB
Amalekites
Kenites
Rehoboth
Zoar
Ascent of Akrabbim
River of Egypt
Wilderness of Zin
Zered R.
Arabah
MT. SEIR
Bozrah
Kadesh-barnea (En-mishpat)
Oboth
EDOM
Punon
A B C D E
1 2 3 4 5 6 7

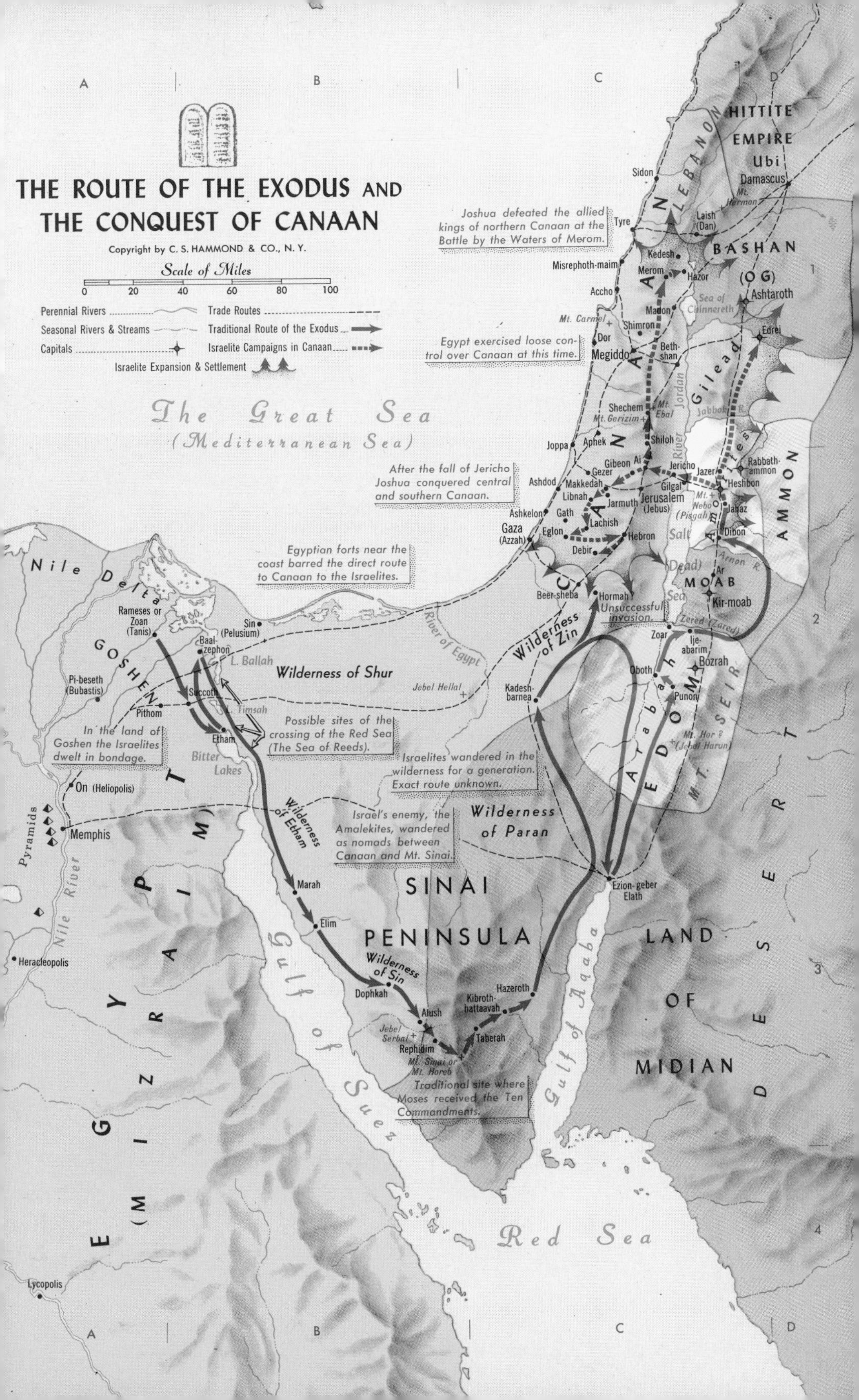
THE ROUTE OF THE EXODUS AND THE CONQUEST OF CANAAN
Copyright by C. S. HAMMOND & CO., N. Y.
Scale of Miles
0 20 40 60 80 100
Perennial Rivers
Seasonal Rivers & Streams
Capitals
Trade Routes
Traditional Route of the Exodus
Israelite Campaigns in Canaan
Israelite Expansion & Settlement
The Great Sea
(Mediterranean Sea)
HITTITE EMPIRE
Ubi
Damascus
Mt. Hermon
Sidon
LEBANON
Tyre
Laish (Dan)
Joshua defeated the allied kings of northern Canaan at the Battle by the Waters of Merom.
Kedesh
BASHAN
(OG)
Misrephoth-maim
Merom
Hazor
Accho
Ashtaroth
Sea of Chinnereth
Madon
Mt. Carmel
Shimron
Edrei
Dor
Megiddo
Beth-shan
Egypt exercised loose control over Canaan at this time.
Gilead
Jordan
Jabbok R.
Shechem
Mt. Ebal
Mt. Gerizim
CANAAN
Joppa
Aphek
Shiloh
River
Rabbath-ammon
Gibeon
Ai
Jericho
Jazer
After the fall of Jericho Joshua conquered central and southern Canaan.
Gezer
Ashdod
Makkedah
Gilgal
Heshbon
AMMON
Libnah
Jerusalem (Jebus)
Jarmuth
Mt. Nebo (Pisgah)
Jahaz
Ashkelon
Gath
Lachish
Gaza (Azzah)
Eglon
Hebron
Salt
Dibon
Debir
Arnon R.
(Dead)
Ar
Nile Delta
Egyptian forts near the coast barred the direct route to Canaan to the Israelites.
MOAB
Beer-sheba
Hormah
Unsuccessful invasion.
Sea
Kir-moab
Rameses or Zoan (Tanis)
Sin (Pelusium)
Wilderness of Zin
Zered (Zared)
Zoar
GOSHEN
Baal-zephon
L. Ballah
River of Egypt
Ije-abarim
Wilderness of Shur
Oboth
Bozrah
Pi-beseth (Bubastis)
Jebel Hellal
Kadesh-barnea
Succoth
L. Timsah
Punon
Pithom
Possible sites of the crossing of the Red Sea (The Sea of Reeds).
Arabah
EDOM
SEIR
In the land of Goshen the Israelites dwelt in bondage.
Etham
Mt. Hor? (Jebel Harun)
Bitter Lakes
Israelites wandered in the wilderness for a generation. Exact route unknown.
On (Heliopolis)
MT. SEIR
Israel's enemy, the Amalekites, wandered as nomads between Canaan and Mt. Sinai.
Wilderness of Paran
Pyramids
Memphis
Wilderness of Etham
Nile River
Marah
SINAI
Ezion-geber Elath
Elim
PENINSULA
LAND OF MIDIAN
DESERT
Heracleopolis
Wilderness of Sin
Dophkah
Gulf of Suez
Gulf of Aqaba
Hazeroth
Kibroth-hattaavah
Alush
Jebel Serbal
Rephidim
Taberah
Mt. Sinai or Mt. Horeb
Traditional site where Moses received the Ten Commandments.
EGYPT
(MIZRAIM)
Red Sea
Lycopolis
A
B
C
D
1
2
3
4

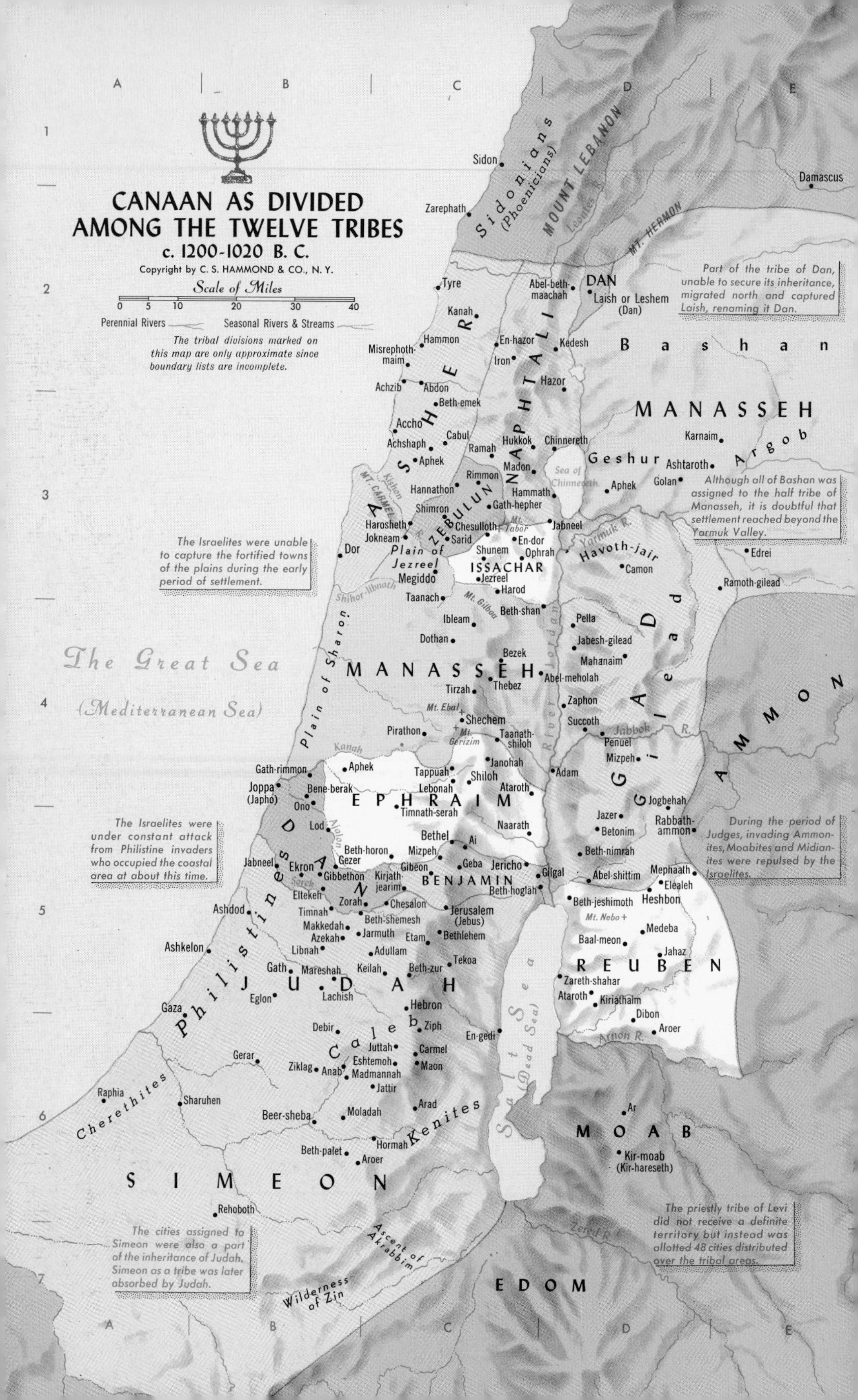
CANAAN AS DIVIDED
AMONG THE TWELVE TRIBES
c. 1200-1020 B. C.
Copyright by C. S. HAMMOND & CO., N. Y.
Scale of Miles
0 5 10 20 30 40
Perennial Rivers
Seasonal Rivers & Streams
The tribal divisions marked on this map are only approximate since boundary lists are incomplete.
The Israelites were unable to capture the fortified towns of the plains during the early period of settlement.
The Israelites were under constant attack from Philistine invaders who occupied the coastal area at about this time.
The cities assigned to Simeon were also a part of the inheritance of Judah. Simeon as a tribe was later absorbed by Judah.
Part of the tribe of Dan, unable to secure its inheritance, migrated north and captured Laish, renaming it Dan.
Although all of Bashan was assigned to the half tribe of Manasseh, it is doubtful that settlement reached beyond the Yarmuk Valley.
During the period of Judges, invading Ammonites, Moabites and Midianites were repulsed by the Israelites.
The priestly tribe of Levi did not receive a definite territory but instead was allotted 48 cities distributed over the tribal areas.
The Great Sea
(Mediterranean Sea)
Sidonians (Phoenicians)
MOUNT LEBANON
Leontes R.
MT. HERMON
Damascus
Sidon
Zarephath
Tyre
Abel-beth-maachah
DAN
Laish or Leshem (Dan)
Kanah
Hammon
Misrephoth-maim
Achzib
Abdon
Beth-emek
Accho
Achshaph
Cabul
Aphek
ASHER
NAPHTALI
En-hazor
Iron
Kedesh
Hazor
Ramah
Hukkok
Chinnereth
Madon
Rimmon
Sea of Chinnereth
Hammath
Hannathon
Gath-hepher
Shimron
ZEBULUN
Harosheth
Jokneam
Chesulloth
Sarid
Mt. Tabor
Jabneel
Kishon
MT. CARMEL
Dor
Plain of Jezreel
Megiddo
Shunem
En-dor
Ophrah
ISSACHAR
Jezreel
Harod
Shihor-libnath
Taanach
Mt. Gilboa
Beth-shan
Ibleam
Dothan
Bashan
MANASSEH
Karnaim
Argob
Geshur
Ashtaroth
Golan
Aphek
Yarmuk R.
Havoth-jair
Camon
Edrei
Ramoth-gilead
Pella
Jabesh-gilead
Mahanaim
GAD
Gilead
AMMON
Plain of Sharon
MANASSEH
Bezek
Abel-meholah
Thebez
Tirzah
Zaphon
Mt. Ebal
Shechem
Mt. Gerizim
Succoth
Jabbok R.
Penuel
Pirathon
Taanath-shiloh
Kanah
River Jordan
Mizpeh
Gath-rimmon
Aphek
Tappuah
Janohah
Shiloh
Adam
Joppa (Japho)
Bene-berak
Lebonah
Ataroth
Ono
EPHRAIM
Timnath-serah
Jogbehah
Jazer
Betonim
Rabbath-ammon
Lod
Aijalon
DAN
Naarath
Bethel
Ai
Beth-horon
Mizpeh
Beth-nimrah
Jabneel
Ekron
Gezer
Gibeon
Geba
Jericho
Gilgal
Abel-shittim
Mephaath
Gibbethon
Kirjath-jearim
BENJAMIN
Beth-hoglah
Elealeh
Sorek
Eltekeh
Heshbon
Beth-jeshimoth
Ashdod
Zorah
Chesalon
Jerusalem (Jebus)
Mt. Nebo
Timnah
Beth-shemesh
Makkedah
Azekah
Jarmuth
Etam
Bethlehem
Medeba
Baal-meon
Ashkelon
Libnah
Adullam
Jahaz
Philistines
Gath
Mareshah
Keilah
Beth-zur
Tekoa
REUBEN
JUDAH
Zareth-shahar
Eglon
Lachish
Ataroth
Kiriathaim
Gaza
Hebron
Salt Sea (Dead Sea)
Dibon
Debir
Ziph
En-gedi
Aroer
Caleb
Arnon R.
Juttah
Carmel
Gerar
Eshtemoh
Maon
Ziklag
Anab
Madmannah
Raphia
Jattir
Cherethites
Sharuhen
Arad
Beer-sheba
Moladah
Kenites
Ar
MOAB
Hormah
Beth-palet
Aroer
Kir-moab (Kir-hareseth)
SIMEON
Rehoboth
Ascent of Akrabbim
Zered R.
Wilderness of Zin
EDOM
A B C D E
1 2 3 4 5 6 7

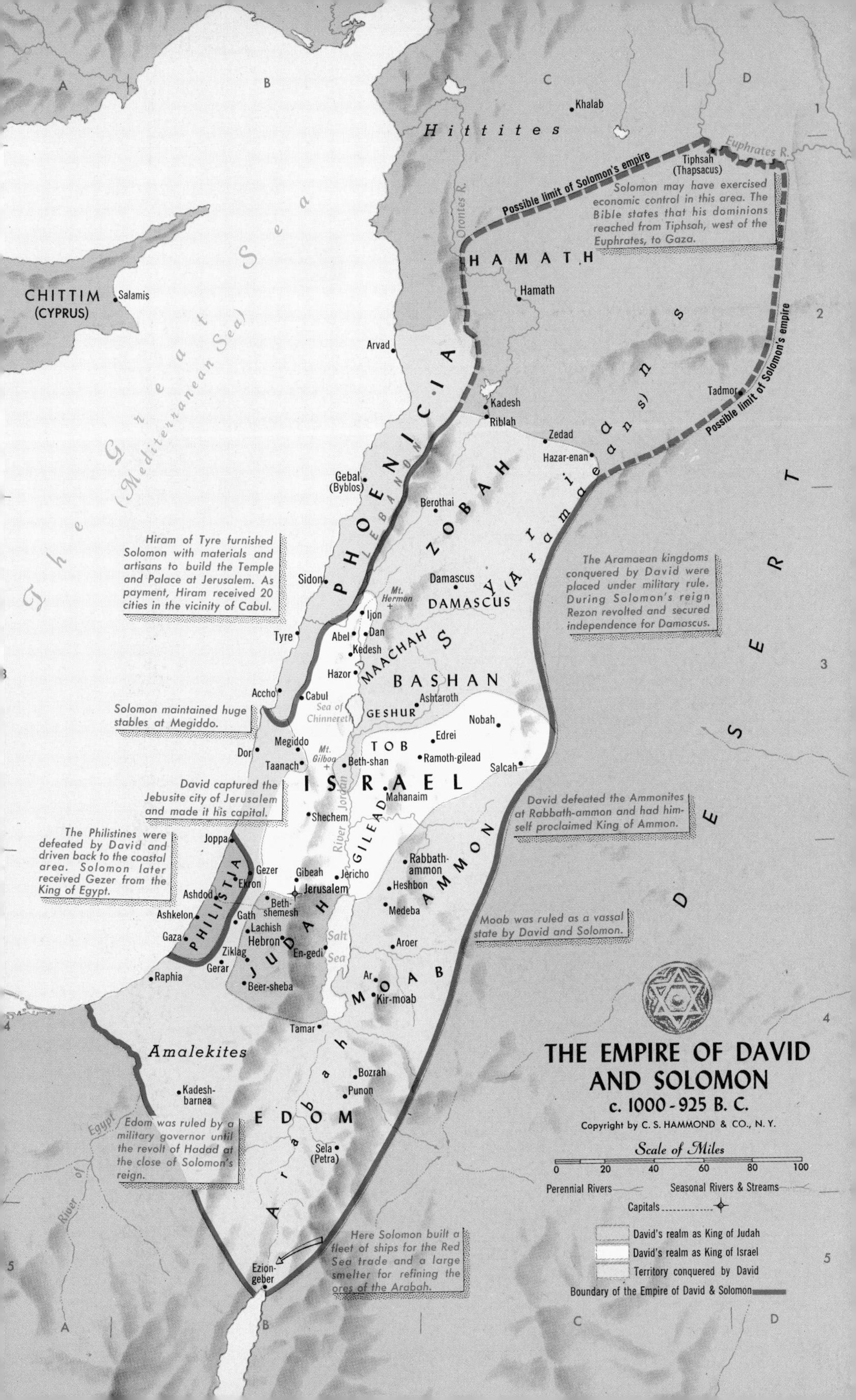
THE EMPIRE OF DAVID AND SOLOMON
c. 1000 - 925 B. C.
Copyright by C. S. HAMMOND & CO., N. Y.
Scale of Miles
0 20 40 60 80 100
Perennial Rivers
Seasonal Rivers & Streams
Capitals
David's realm as King of Judah
David's realm as King of Israel
Territory conquered by David
Boundary of the Empire of David & Solomon
Hittites
Khalab
Tiphsah (Thapsacus)
Euphrates R.
Possible limit of Solomon's empire
Solomon may have exercised economic control in this area. The Bible states that his dominions reached from Tiphsah, west of the Euphrates, to Gaza.
Orontes R.
HAMATH
Hamath
CHITTIM (CYPRUS)
Salamis
The Great Sea (Mediterranean Sea)
Arvad
PHOENICIA
LEBANON
Kadesh
Riblah
Zedad
Hazar-enan
Tadmor
Syria (Aramaeans)
ZOBAH
Gebal (Byblos)
Berothai
DESERT
Hiram of Tyre furnished Solomon with materials and artisans to build the Temple and Palace at Jerusalem. As payment, Hiram received 20 cities in the vicinity of Cabul.
Sidon
Mt. Hermon
Damascus
DAMASCUS
The Aramaean kingdoms conquered by David were placed under military rule. During Solomon's reign Rezon revolted and secured independence for Damascus.
Ijon
Tyre
Abel
Dan
Kedesh
MAACHAH
Hazor
BASHAN
Accho
Cabul
Ashtaroth
Solomon maintained huge stables at Megiddo.
Sea of Chinnereth
GESHUR
Nobah
Megiddo
Edrei
TOB
Dor
Mt. Gilboa
Beth-shan
Ramoth-gilead
Taanach
Salcah
David captured the Jebusite city of Jerusalem and made it his capital.
ISRAEL
Mahanaim
David defeated the Ammonites at Rabbath-ammon and had himself proclaimed King of Ammon.
Shechem
River Jordan
GILEAD
The Philistines were defeated by David and driven back to the coastal area. Solomon later received Gezer from the King of Egypt.
Joppa
Gezer
Gibeah
Jericho
Rabbath-ammon
Ekron
Jerusalem
Heshbon
AMMON
Ashdod
Beth-shemesh
Medeba
Ashkelon
Gath
PHILISTIA
Lachish
JUDAH
Moab was ruled as a vassal state by David and Solomon.
Gaza
Hebron
Salt Sea
Aroer
Ziklag
En-gedi
Gerar
Raphia
Beer-sheba
Ar
MOAB
Kir-moab
Tamar
Amalekites
Bozrah
Punon
Kadesh-barnea
EDOM
Arabah
Egypt
Edom was ruled by a military governor until the revolt of Hadad at the close of Solomon's reign.
Sela (Petra)
River of
Here Solomon built a fleet of ships for the Red Sea trade and a large smelter for refining the ores of the Arabah.
Ezion-geber

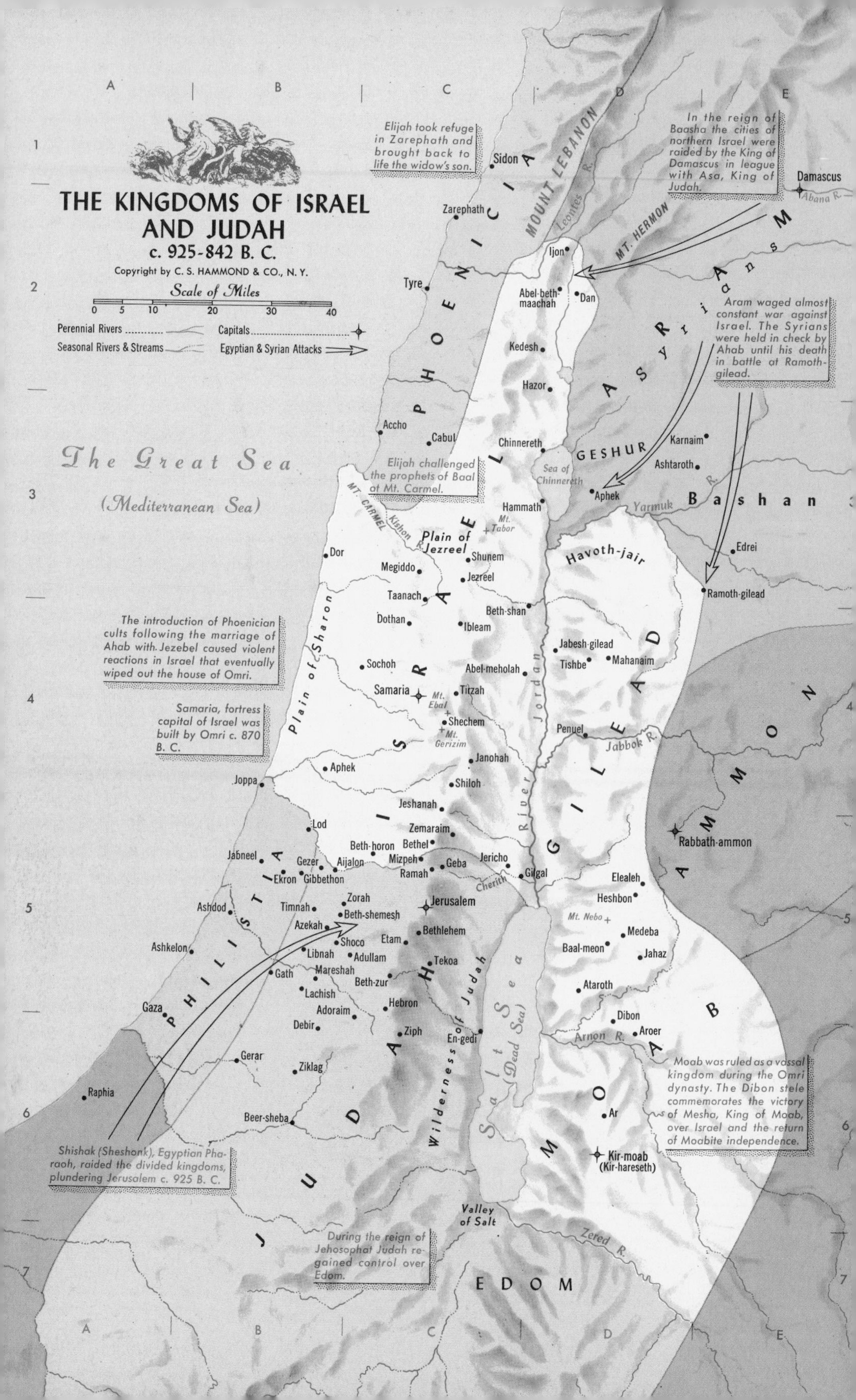

THE KINGDOMS OF ISRAEL AND JUDAH
c. 925-842 B. C.
Copyright by C. S. HAMMOND & CO., N. Y.
Scale of Miles
0 5 10 20 30 40
Perennial Rivers
Seasonal Rivers & Streams
Capitals
Egyptian & Syrian Attacks
The Great Sea
(Mediterranean Sea)
Elijah took refuge in Zarephath and brought back to life the widow's son.
In the reign of Baasha the cities of northern Israel were raided by the King of Damascus in league with Asa, King of Judah.
Aram waged almost constant war against Israel. The Syrians were held in check by Ahab until his death in battle at Ramoth-gilead.
Elijah challenged the prophets of Baal at Mt. Carmel.
The introduction of Phoenician cults following the marriage of Ahab with Jezebel caused violent reactions in Israel that eventually wiped out the house of Omri.
Samaria, fortress capital of Israel was built by Omri c. 870 B. C.
Moab was ruled as a vassal kingdom during the Omri dynasty. The Dibon stele commemorates the victory of Mesha, King of Moab, over Israel and the return of Moabite independence.
Shishak (Sheshonk), Egyptian Pharaoh, raided the divided kingdoms, plundering Jerusalem c. 925 B. C.
During the reign of Jehosophat Judah regained control over Edom.
PHOENICIA
MOUNT LEBANON
MT. HERMON
Aram Syrians
ISRAEL
GESHUR
Bashan
Havoth-jair
GILEAD
AMMON
MOAB
PHILISTIA
JUDAH
EDOM
Wilderness of Judah
Salt Sea (Dead Sea)
Plain of Sharon
Plain of Jezreel
Sidon
Zarephath
Tyre
Damascus
Abana R.
Leontes R.
Ijon
Abel-beth-maachah
Dan
Kedesh
Hazor
Accho
Cabul
Chinnereth
Sea of Chinnereth
Karnaim
Ashtaroth
Aphek
Yarmuk R.
Hammath
Mt. Tabor
MT. CARMEL
Kishon R.
Dor
Shunem
Megiddo
Jezreel
Edrei
Ramoth-gilead
Taanach
Beth-shan
Dothan
Ibleam
Jabesh-gilead
Tishbe
Mahanaim
Sochoh
Abel-meholah
Samaria
Mt. Ebal
Tirzah
Shechem
Mt. Gerizim
Penuel
Jabbok R.
Jordan River
Janohah
Aphek
Joppa
Shiloh
Jeshanah
Lod
Zemaraim
Rabbath-ammon
Beth-horon
Bethel
Jabneel
Gezer
Aijalon
Mizpeh
Geba
Jericho
Ramah
Gilgal
Ekron
Gibbethon
Cherith
Elealeh
Heshbon
Ashdod
Timnah
Zorah
Beth-shemesh
Jerusalem
Azekah
Mt. Nebo
Shoco
Etam
Bethlehem
Medeba
Ashkelon
Libnah
Adullam
Tekoa
Baal-meon
Jahaz
Mareshah
Gath
Beth-zur
Ataroth
Lachish
Hebron
Gaza
Adoraim
Dibon
Debir
Ziph
En-gedi
Arnon R.
Aroer
Gerar
Ziklag
Raphia
Beer-sheba
Ar
Kir-moab (Kir-hareseth)
Valley of Salt
Zered R.
A
B
C
D
E
1
2
3
4
5
6
7

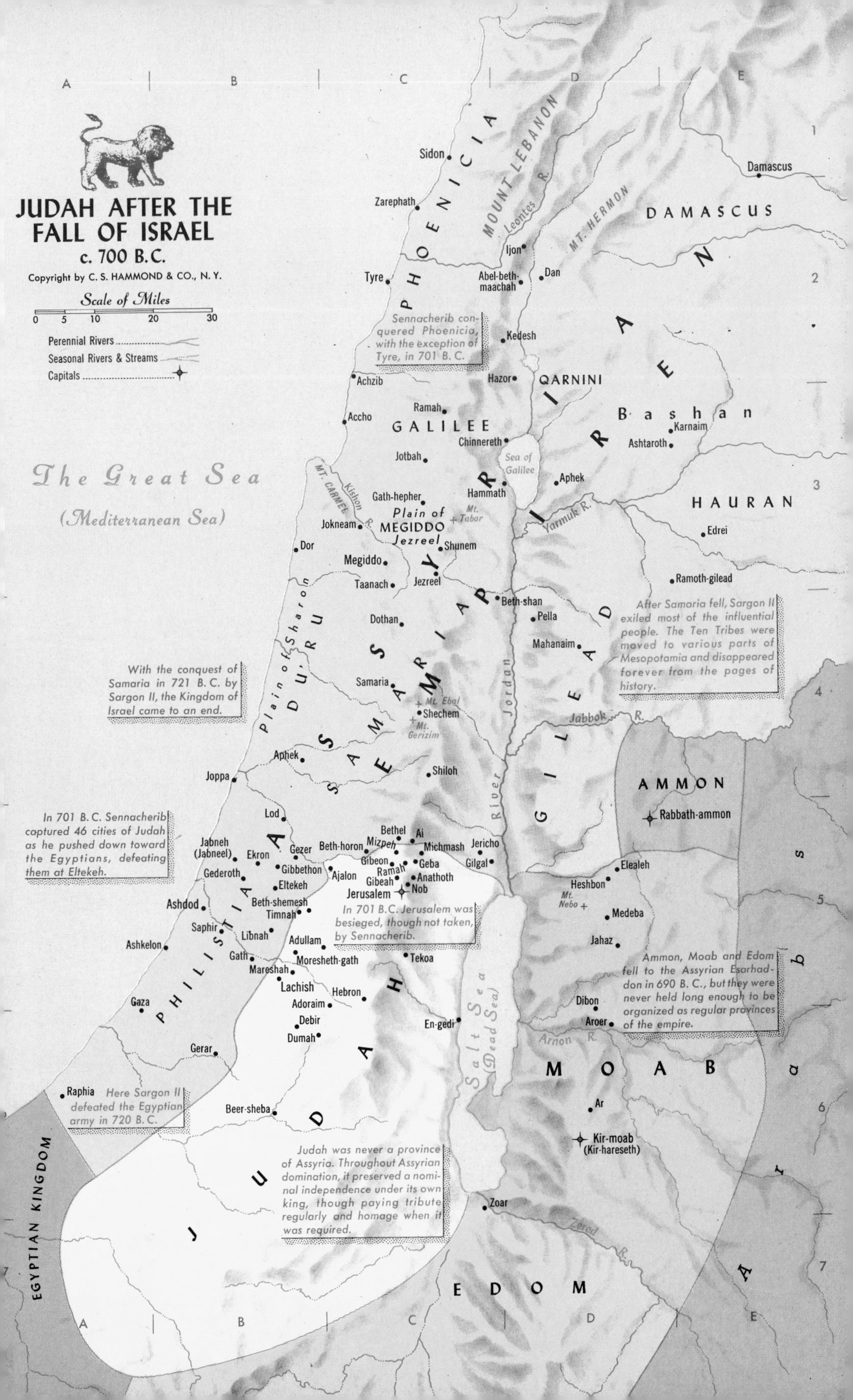
JUDAH AFTER THE FALL OF ISRAEL
c. 700 B.C.
Copyright by C. S. HAMMOND & CO., N. Y.
Scale of Miles
0 5 10 20 30
Perennial Rivers
Seasonal Rivers & Streams
Capitals
The Great Sea
(Mediterranean Sea)
Sennacherib conquered Phoenicia, with the exception of Tyre, in 701 B.C.
With the conquest of Samaria in 721 B.C. by Sargon II, the Kingdom of Israel came to an end.
In 701 B.C. Sennacherib captured 46 cities of Judah as he pushed down toward the Egyptians, defeating them at Eltekeh.
In 701 B.C. Jerusalem was besieged, though not taken, by Sennacherib.
After Samaria fell, Sargon II exiled most of the influential people. The Ten Tribes were moved to various parts of Mesopotamia and disappeared forever from the pages of history.
Ammon, Moab and Edom fell to the Assyrian Esarhaddon in 690 B.C., but they were never held long enough to be organized as regular provinces of the empire.
Here Sargon II defeated the Egyptian army in 720 B.C.
Judah was never a province of Assyria. Throughout Assyrian domination, it preserved a nominal independence under its own king, though paying tribute regularly and homage when it was required.
PHOENICIA
MOUNT LEBANON
MT. HERMON
DAMASCUS
QARNINI
Bashan
GALILEE
HAURAN
Plain of MEGIDDO
Jezreel
DU'RU
Plain of Sharon
SAMARIA
ASSYRIAN EMPIRE
GILEAD
AMMON
PHILISTIA
JUDAH
MOAB
EDOM
EGYPTIAN KINGDOM
Arabs
The Great Sea
Sidon
Zarephath
Tyre
Ijon
Dan
Abel-beth-maachah
Damascus
Kedesh
Achzib
Hazor
Accho
Ramah
Karnaim
Ashtaroth
Chinnereth
Sea of Galilee
Jotbah
Aphek
Hammath
Gath-hepher
Mt. Tabor
Yarmuk R.
Edrei
Jokneam
Shunem
Dor
Megiddo
Taanach
Jezreel
Ramoth-gilead
Beth-shan
Dothan
Pella
Mahanaim
Samaria
Mt. Ebal
Shechem
Mt. Gerizim
Jabbok R.
Aphek
Shiloh
Joppa
Jordan River
Rabbath-ammon
Lod
Bethel
Ai
Jabneh (Jabneel)
Ekron
Gezer
Beth-horon
Mizpeh
Michmash
Jericho
Gibeon
Geba
Gilgal
Gederoth
Gibbethon
Ajalon
Ramah
Anathoth
Elealeh
Eltekeh
Gibeah
Nob
Heshbon
Jerusalem
Ashdod
Beth-shemesh
Mt. Nebo
Timnah
Medeba
Saphir
Libnah
Ashkelon
Adullam
Jahaz
Gath
Moresheth-gath
Tekoa
Mareshah
Lachish
Hebron
Gaza
Adoraim
Dibon
Debir
En-gedi
Aroer
Dumah
Salt Sea (Dead Sea)
Arnon R.
Gerar
Raphia
Beer-sheba
Ar
Kir-moab (Kir-hareseth)
Zoar
Zered R.
Leontes R.
Kishon R.
MT. CARMEL

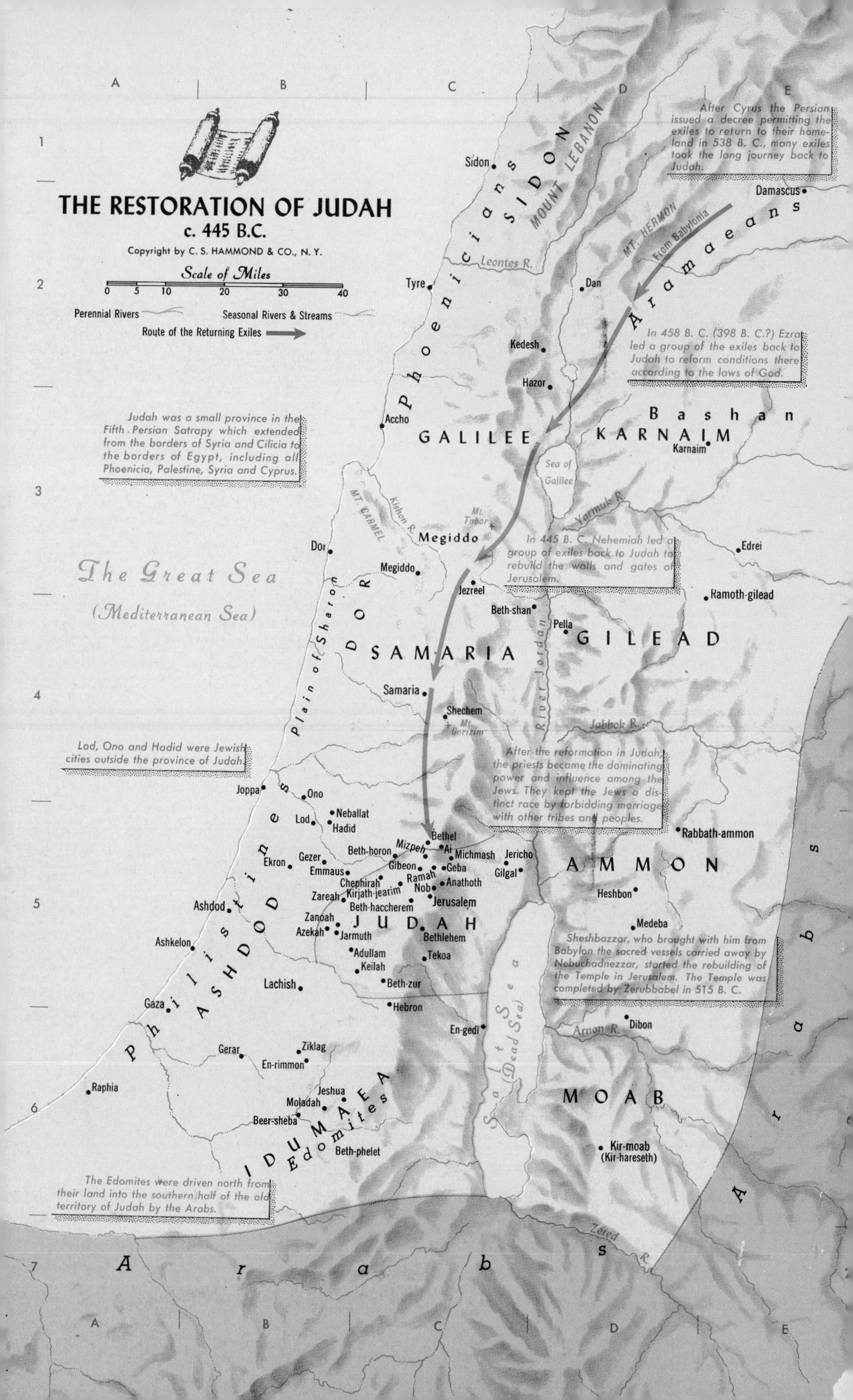
THE RESTORATION OF JUDAH
c. 445 B.C.
Copyright by C. S. HAMMOND & CO., N. Y.
Scale of Miles
0 5 10 20 30 40
Perennial Rivers
Seasonal Rivers & Streams
Route of the Returning Exiles
After Cyrus the Persian issued a decree permitting the exiles to return to their homeland in 538 B. C., many exiles took the long journey back to Judah.
In 458 B. C. (398 B. C.?) Ezra led a group of the exiles back to Judah to reform conditions there according to the laws of God.
Judah was a small province in the Fifth Persian Satrapy which extended from the borders of Syria and Cilicia to the borders of Egypt, including all Phoenicia, Palestine, Syria and Cyprus.
In 445 B. C. Nehemiah led a group of exiles back to Judah to rebuild the walls and gates of Jerusalem.
Lod, Ono and Hadid were Jewish cities outside the province of Judah.
After the reformation in Judah, the priests became the dominating power and influence among the Jews. They kept the Jews a distinct race by forbidding marriage with other tribes and peoples.
Sheshbazzar, who brought with him from Babylon the sacred vessels carried away by Nebuchadnezzar, started the rebuilding of the Temple in Jerusalem. The Temple was completed by Zerubbabel in 515 B. C.
The Edomites were driven north from their land into the southern half of the old territory of Judah by the Arabs.
The Great Sea
(Mediterranean Sea)
SIDON
MOUNT LEBANON
Phoenicians
Aramaeans
From Babylonia
MT. HERMON
Sidon
Tyre
Damascus
Leontes R.
Dan
Kedesh
Hazor
Accho
GALILEE
Bashan
KARNAIM
Karnaim
Sea of Galilee
Yarmuk R.
MT. CARMEL
Kishon R.
Mt. Tabor
Megiddo
Dor
Edrei
Jezreel
Ramoth-gilead
Beth-shan
Pella
DOR
Plain of Sharon
SAMARIA
GILEAD
River Jordan
Samaria
Shechem
Mt. Gerizim
Jabbok R.
Joppa
Ono
Neballat
Lod
Hadid
Bethel
Ai
Mizpeh
Beth-horon
Michmash
Jericho
Gezer
Ekron
Gibeon
Geba
Gilgal
Emmaus
Ramah
Anathoth
Chephirah
Nob
Kirjath-jearim
Zareah
Jerusalem
Beth-haccherem
Rabbath-ammon
AMMON
Heshbon
Ashdod
Zanoah
JUDAH
Medeba
Azekah
Jarmuth
Bethlehem
Ashkelon
Adullam
Tekoa
Keilah
ASHDOD
Lachish
Beth-zur
Philistines
Gaza
Hebron
En-gedi
Salt Sea
(Dead Sea)
Dibon
Arnon R.
Gerar
Ziklag
En-rimmon
Raphia
Jeshua
Moladah
MOAB
Beer-sheba
IDUMAEA
Edomites
Beth-phelet
Kir-moab
(Kir-hareseth)
Arabs
Zered R.
A B C D E
1 2 3 4 5 6 7

THE BIBLE STORY LIBRARY

THE BIBLE STORY LIBRARY

The Holy Scriptures retold in story form for the young and as an explanation and commentary for all, based on traditional texts and illustrated with the most famous Biblical art.

VOLUME ONE

From Creation To David

Edited by TURNER HODGES
with the assistance of ELIZABETH MACLEAN
Designed and produced by DONALD D. WOLF
with the assistance of MARGOT L. WOLF

THEODORE AUDEL & CO.

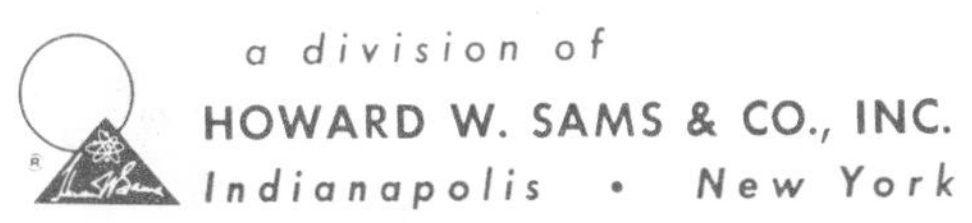

a division of
HOWARD W. SAMS & CO., INC.
Indianapolis • New York

ACKNOWLEDGMENTS

THIS WORK HAS BEEN SUBMITTED to clergymen of all faiths, and the publishers and editors are most grateful for the uniformly favorable comment on its fidelity to the Scriptures. They wish especially to acknowledge the gracious commendation of the following:

The Rev. Father ALBAN BAER, O.S.B., of the Priory, Portsmouth, who scrutinized the full work from the standpoint of the Catholic reader.

The Rev. Dr. DANIEL S. POLING, Editor of *The Christian Herald,* who wrote, "What you have done will be, I think, universally acceptable to our churches."

The Rev. Dr. LEROY A. MARTIN, President of Tennessee Wesleyan College, who wrote, "I congratulate you on doing an outstanding job."

The Very Rev. JUVENAL D. LALOR, O.F.M., of Christ the King Seminary, then President of St. Bonaventure University, who graciously praised the faithful "but oh, so clear" presentation.

Rabbi EPHRAIM S. KOLATCH of Temple Beth-el, New York, who commended the publishers' "great service to our children in presenting the Bible stories in one of the most attractive fashions I have ever observed."

PRINTED IN THE UNITED STATES OF AMERICA

Introduction

In this work the Holy Scriptures have been retold in story form and have been divided into individual stories of convenient length so that the substance of the Bible can be learned or consulted on a regular schedule; for example, one story each day, or one or more stories to be read on each Sabbath day, or the entire work to be read within one year.

As sources, the editors have used not only the authorized translations of the Scriptures into the English language but also the various special translations into not only English but other modern languages. Such special translations often reflect the most recent scholarship and are especially helpful in finding apt words to clarify the intended meaning of the original text. It must be remembered that the entire Bible was written in three different languages over a period of more than one thousand years and that some words used in the early translations are difficult to understand in their intended meanings today.

There have been many worthy books of Bible Stories. The editors have selected and used the best parts of the traditional books of this kind. In the retelling of a story it is necessary to use some degree of imaginative writing, such as the use of conversation in modern language, but the editors have been careful not to present invented material as though it were Scriptural. All conversation made part of these stories is either given in the Scriptures or is implied there.

The Purpose of This Work

This work has several purposes, but primarily the following:

1. For young readers: To acquaint them with the Bible so that they can read the Bible itself with understanding and with pleasure; for one cannot pleasurably read what one does not understand.

2. For adult readers: To interpret and explain the meanings of many

words and passages that may be difficult to understand in the original. The adult reader will often find this work an enlightening commentary on Biblical passages about which he is in doubt.

This work is not intended to replace the reading of the original Scriptures. In fact, the editors urge every reader of this work to read also the original, as soon as (in the case of young readers) he reaches an age at which he finds that the original can be readily understood. For this reason, the Table of Contents on pages ix to xv lists the books, chapters and verses where the reader can find the original text from which these stories were written.

Pronunciations of Names

The editors did not give the pronunciations of names wherever they appear in the stories, because they felt this method to be confusing to the reader. By turning to the last pages of the set the reader can find the pronunciation of any name he encounters in the book.

The Illustrations Used

The Art Director of this work has endeavored to make the illustrations accomplish two purposes:

1. To give the reader a visual understanding of the persons, places and events about which the Bible tells.
2. To introduce the reader to great Biblical art.

Many of the paintings and engravings are not technically faithful to the Scriptural text. Artists throughout the ages have had a tendency to portray Biblical scenes in terms of their own countries and times. Thus, an Italian artist of the 16th century would show Biblical characters dressed in clothing typical of 16th-century Italy; a Flemish artist would show them in Flemish dress and with a background of typical European cities or houses; and so on. Often the artist has not fully understood the Biblical text or has even invented characters and scenes of his own to accompany those drawn from the Scriptural account. Nevertheless, the works of art reproduced in the following pages are worthy of space because of their fame, their beauty, and the fact that their originals appear in the greatest cathedrals, churches and museums of the world. The explanations appearing with the illustrations invariably call attention to any inconsistency between the artist's interpretation and the Biblical text.

By far the most famous series of Biblical illustrations ever made was that of the French engraver, Gustave Doré, which he made in the second half of the 19th century. Literally tens of millions of copies of this series have been distributed, either in the form of prints or as reprinted in books and Bibles. In this work, outstanding examples of the Doré series have been included; but whereas Doré's originals appeared only in black-and-white, this work presents them with color skillfully added by the artist James Chapman.

A list of the color plates used to illustrate the Old Testament appears on page viii.

The reader may note with interest the fact that despite the strong roots of Christianity in Judaism, and the adherence of Jesus to the Jewish Scriptures (the Old Testament) virtually all the art in this work was executed by Christians. There is a little-known reason for this. In strict Jewish theology, such illustrations would violate the Commandment (Exodus 20:4) that says, "Thou shall not make any graven image, or any likeness of anything that is in heaven above, or in the earth beneath, or in the water under the earth . . ." In fact, Jews have traditionally retained Christian artists to illustrate one of their holiest books, the Haggadah (the story of the Exodus, read at the Passover feast).

THE PUBLISHERS

List of Color Illustrations

NOTE: The original paintings of these reproductions are, in order of their listing above, in the following museums: Louvre, Paris—Uffizi, Florence—Brera, Milan—Metropolitan Museum of Art, New York—Kunsthalle, Hamburg—Kunsthalle, Bremen—Royal Museum of Fine Arts, Copenhagen—Kunsthalle, Hamburg—Staedtische Kunstsammlung, Duesseldorf—Louvre, Paris—Staatliche Kunsthalle, Karlsruhe—Prado, Madrid—Royal Museum of Fine Arts, Copenhagen—Castle Celle, Germany—Borghese, Rome—Castle Celle, Germany—Uffizi, Florence—Louvre, Paris—Royal Academy, Denmark—Schack Gallery, Munich—Manchester City Art Gallery, England—Louvre, Paris—Staedtische Kunstsammlung, Duesseldorf—Borghese, Rome.

Contents

The table of contents for the stories of the New Testament can be found preceding page 545.

1

The story of how God made the world

IF YOU LOOK UP INTO THE SKY, you see the bright sun in the daytime and the moon and the many stars at night, and all around them the air and empty space reaching forever into the distance. We call this part of the world the *heavens*.

If you look around you, you see the land we live upon, and the waters that make rivers and lakes and great oceans. On this land and in these waters there are so many different kinds of plants and animals that you could not begin to count them all. We call this part of the world the *earth*.

God made the heavens and the earth, just as God made you and every other living thing. God did this at the beginning of time.

It took God six days to make the heavens and the earth and all living things.

The history of the creation of the world is given in the first book of the Bible. This book is called "Genesis," which means, in Greek, "the beginning." This first book of the Bible tells how God made the earth and sea, the sun and moon, and the first man and woman, Adam and Eve, who were intended to live happily in the garden of Eden but disobeyed the commands of God and so brought sin into the world. They were punished by being driven out of the garden and were made to earn their food by hard labor, their sorrow being made greater by the wickedness of their son Cain.

First day. More years than you can count have passed since God created the earth. At first the world was without regular form. Earth and water were mingled; there were no trees or flowers, and no living creatures. All was darkness; there was no firm land, no sea, no stars or moon, no sound to break the silence.

Then God said, "Let there be light."

The sun and moon were not made at first, but there was a bright light that shone for a time, and then again came darkness.

God divided the light from the darkness, calling the light day, and the darkness night. And that great act of God's power marked the first of the six days of creation.

Second day. When that first night had passed away, and there was again light on the face of the earth, God made the "firmament," that is, the sky. He divided the waters that were above, the moist clouds, from the waters that were below, which were the oceans. So there was a sky above with the many forms and colors of passing clouds on the clear blue. Then night came again, and the work of the second day of creation was done.

Third day. Then God said, "Let the waters below the sky be gathered into one place so that the dry land may appear!"

On this third day, the vapors and mists having been lifted up on high, the waters were collected together, and the great seas were formed, into which flowed rivers, rising from springs that flowed together and so made wide and flowing streams of water. As the waters were thus collected together, the earth was left dry. Mountains and hills, the tops of which were almost hidden in the clouds, appeared; and rocks, against which beat the great waves of the newly created sea. But the hills and valleys were bare; no grass or flowering plants were there, no forests, none of the beautiful blossoms that now exist.

Then God said,

"Let the earth produce vegetation, seed-bearing plants and the various kinds of trees that bear fruit containing their seed!"

Thus God completed the work He had begun on this day. The same Power that made the waves of the sea, that made the rivers to flow through the valleys and the earth to stand dry in the midst of the waters, now commanded grass to grow, flowers to bloom, sweet fruit to ripen, and lofty trees to cover the hills and make the valleys green.

In three days the earth, which was at first dark and "without form, and void," had been shone upon by a great light; the sky had been created; seas and rivers had been made; grass had grown, herbs "whose seed was in itself"—stone fruit and fruit such as apples and oranges—were there. And with that the third day's work was ended.

Fourth day. On the fourth day the sun and moon were created, "two great lights, the greater light to rule the day, and the lesser light to rule the night." The stars also were made and gave light upon the earth. The light of the first day was divided from the darkness, and when night came there was no light; but now there was a lesser light of the moon and the stars to shine, so that the night was not quite dark.

And God showed that there were to be other uses for these greater and lesser lights. He said:

"Let them serve for signs, to fix times and days and years." Ever since, men have used these great lights to guide their calendars and to know the time of day.

Fifth day. The fifth day was a very wonderful day. Sun and moon and stars had been made, the waters had been divided from the land, and on the land were grass and trees and fruit. Now the time had come for the creation of animal life. At God's command fishes came to be in the rivers and birds flew about in the air. Great whales swam in the ocean, along with other great monsters of the deep.

And God said to all the creatures he had created,

"Be fruitful and multiply—that is, have many children—and fill the waters in the seas; and let the birds multiply on the earth."

That was the fifth day's work, but as yet there were no animals on the land. The sea and the air were full of living creatures, some very large and some very small, but the earth had none.

Sixth day. But on the next day, the sixth day, God made animals to live on the dry land; all those large creatures that are so wonderful; the cattle that feed in the fields, and many small animals and insects described in the Bible as "everything that creepeth upon the earth."

Then God looked at the world He had created, with its fresh and plentiful vegetation and its abundant animal life, and He was pleased.

How God made the first man

Still His work was not complete. Although everything He had thus far created was perfect in every way, there was no creature with a mind to think and reason, and therefore no one to worship the God who was the Creator. Then it was that God made man. God said,

"Let Us make man in Our image, after Our likeness, and let him have

The Creation of Light! And God said, Let there be light.

dominion (the power to rule) over the fish of the sea and the birds of the air, the domestic animals, the wild beasts, and all the land reptiles!"

And God did exactly that. He made Adam, the first man, in His own "image and likeness," and He gave Adam power to rule over the living things of the world.

Seventh day. God completed His work of creation in six days, and on the seventh day He rested. The seventh day of the week, called the Sabbath, has been observed as a day of rest ever since.

2

The story of the Garden of Eden

THE PLACE WHERE MAN WAS MADE was named Eden, and in one part of it was a garden, a beautiful place where grew flowers and trees, which bore fruit fit for the food of man.

Adam was placed in this garden and God told him he might eat freely of all the fruits that grew there so abundantly. There was one exception. In the garden was a single tree from which Adam might not eat the fruit.

"From every tree in the garden you are free to eat," God told Adam. "But from the Tree of the Knowledge of Good and Evil you must not eat; for the day that you eat of it you shall certainly know death."

After giving Adam possession of the garden, God made every kind of bird, animal, and reptile go before Adam, and Adam gave each of them a name.

Although there were so many animals of every kind, Adam himself had no companion. So God completed His work by making the first woman, whose name was Eve. She was a "help meet," or suitable companion, for Adam; that is, a wife to be always with him, to love him, and be loved by him better than anything else in the world.

Then God blessed Adam and Eve, and He looked on everything that He had made and all was very good.

God did not intend Adam and Eve to be idle, for He knows that work is necessary to happiness. He told Adam to work in the garden, to keep it in order, and to attend to the growth of the vegetables and fruits that gave him food. He reminded Adam and Eve that they must not touch the fruit of the Tree of Knowledge, or they would know death.

That must have seemed very terrible to Adam and Eve, even though they

At God's command Adam gives names to all the animals in the Garden of Eden.

did not yet know what death meant; for as yet there was nothing in the world but happy life, and the death of anything was unknown. But no doubt they knew that God would be very angry if they did not obey Him, and that His anger would make them very unhappy.

For a short time Adam and Eve were obedient and happy. Adam worked in the garden, and Eve helped him, and they enjoyed the sweet fruits for food.

Among the living things in the garden was a serpent, or snake, which, we are told in the Bible, was "more subtle (that is, clever) than any beast of the field," and it was able to speak. None of the other animals that had been created could do that. But many people believe that this serpent was really an evil spirit, the one that in other parts of the Bible is named Satan and often called a serpent. The evil spirit was able to take the form of a serpent and to go near Eve and whisper to her.

How Eve was tempted by the serpent

"Were you really told not to eat the fruit of this tree?" the serpent asked.

"Indeed we were," Eve replied. "We were told that we would both surely die if we did not obey God's command about this fruit."

The serpent was wicked and did not care whether or not God's commands were obeyed.

"That is not true," the serpent said. "God told you not to eat because the fruit of this tree would give you wisdom. You would then be as wise as God Himself, and He does not want that."

The woman foolishly believed the serpent. Besides, the fruit looked delicious and there was a great deal of it on the tree. Also, she thought it might be pleasant to have great wisdom.

So Eve allowed the serpent to persuade her, and she tasted the fruit; and Adam, who saw what she had done, forgot the command he had received and the punishment he had been told would follow disobedience, and he also ate of the forbidden fruit.

No sooner had they eaten than they were changed creatures, no longer good, but feeling ashamed of themselves. They knew the Lord was near, and for the first time they felt afraid to have Him see them. They heard His voice calling,

"Adam, where are you?"

Eve hands the forbidden fruit to Adam.

Adam answered, "I was afraid, and hid myself."

God knew He had been disobeyed, but He asked Adam if he had eaten fruit of the tree he had been told not to touch.

Adam tried to excuse himself.

"The woman You gave me tempted me," he said. "She tempted me, and I ate."

Eve was ashamed, and afraid because she had disobeyed God, and she did not even attempt to excuse herself.

"Yes, the serpent tempted me, and I yielded to the temptation. I ate the fruit we were told not to eat," she said.

God's curse on the serpent, Adam, and Eve

Then God laid a curse upon the serpent, saying that forever after it would have to crawl in the dust and that it would always be the enemy of woman and her offspring. Adam and Eve probably did not understand the Lord's full meaning at that time, but since then His words have been interpreted in connection with the words of prophets who lived thousands of years later: That mankind would always have to struggle against the devil, or powers of evil, represented by the serpent; that the offspring of woman would be represented by the promised Christ, or Messiah; so by the woman was meant the Virgin Mary, of whom, in fulfillment of the prophecies, Christ would be born.

Adam and Eve were both punished for their disobedience. They were told that sorrow and pain would be theirs all the days of their life; that they must live by hard work; that they would die, and would return to the dust from which they had come.

Adam and Eve were driven from the garden in which they had been placed, and at the entrance of Eden God placed angels and a sword of fire to be a guard so that the wicked Adam and Eve could never return again. They had lost the right to dwell in the beautiful garden, to eat the fruit and be happy and good; they had brought sin into the world, and, with sin, they had brought pain and shame.

Adam would thereafter be forced to labor in the fields and earn his food by the sweat of his brow. Instead of the perpetual joy and everlasting life that they might have had, God afflicted both Adam and Eve with sorrow. Also He doomed them and their descendants to death, which they had never known before. They had not even known what it was!

3

The story of the murder of Abel

After Adam and Eve were driven out of Eden, they began to cultivate the soil. It was difficult work, because there were many weeds and briers, but by laboring hard they were able to grow plenty to eat.

God soon gave them two sons. The one born first was called Cain. His younger brother was called Abel. As they grew up, Cain became a "tiller of the soil"—that is, a farmer—and Abel looked after the flocks of sheep, so that both were able to be of great help to their parents.

Although Adam had been severely punished by God, he did not lose the love and reverence he held for his Heavenly Father. After leaving Eden, Adam still worshiped God. He did this, as men did long ago, by offering sacrifices to God. A sacrifice might be fine fruits from the orchard, or vegetables from the field, or a lamb or sheep from the flock. The sacrifice was placed on an altar while men worshiped.

Cain and Abel were taught to worship also, and to make sacrifices that showed their devotion to the Lord.

On one such occasion, as the brothers were working in the fields, Abel made an offering of a fine lamb, giving grateful thanks to God for all His mercies. This sacrifice was pleasing to God, because it was made in a reverent and grateful spirit.

Cain, at the same time, grudgingly made an offering of some of the grains and grasses of his crop. Cain did not make his offering in the same spirit of loving gratitude that had inspired Abel, and God knew this. Because of the different manners in which the two sacrifices were offered, God found Abel's offering pleasing to him, but Cain's He did not.

Cain became very angry, and jealous of his brother. God spoke to Cain, saying:

"Why are you angry? If you had been doing right, would you not be happy?"

Cain would not listen to reason, even when the Lord spoke, but was angry at his brother and jealous because his brother had found more favor with God. Cain quarreled with his brother Abel and became so angry that he struck Abel. Abel fell dead at Cain's feet.

That was the first death of a man that had been known in the world, and the first death was a murder; not a quiet death, such as good men meet, with prayer on their lips and loving friends around, but a sudden, violent death. The only one near to see the dying youth give up his breath was his own brother, who ought to have loved and taken care of him, but who, in a fit of anger, had struck the blow that killed him.

Cain was filled with horror when he saw his brother lying dead at his feet; but he was sullen. Instead of asking forgiveness for what he had done,

Cain (at the left) and Abel build altars and make sacrifices to God.

God's curse on Cain

he tried to hide the deed, even from the Lord, Who sees everything and knows every thought.

God spoke, and how awful his voice must have sounded in Cain's ear!

"Where is your brother Abel?" God asked, giving Cain a chance to answer Him truthfully and honestly, although God already knew what had happened.

"I don't know," said Cain, which was of course a wicked lie. And then he added unfeelingly, "Am I my brother's keeper?"—meaning, "Am I supposed to take care of my brother?"

He was partly, at least, his brother's keeper, for he was the elder, and no doubt Adam and Eve trusted him to protect with his greater strength the younger and more gentle Abel.

Then God spoke again to Cain.

"Your brother's blood is crying to me from the ground!" He said, meaning that God knew full well that Cain had slain his own brother, and that it was impossible to conceal this from God's all-seeing eye.

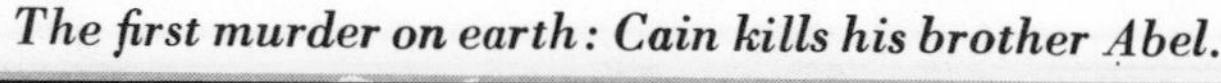
The first murder on earth: Cain kills his brother Abel.

God's punishment of Cain was severe. He did not kill Cain, as He might have done, but placed a curse on him. From that day forth, Cain would have to wander homeless through the world, an outcast and a wanderer. No longer would the ground yield bountiful crops where Cain tilled the soil.

God did not say that Cain would at once starve, or that the earth would not give some fruit for his food, but only that it would not yield bountifully, that it would give him only a little fruit. Cain would never have much but would be always poor and a wanderer from place to place.

Cain knew what a punishment this was. He had no hope to cheer him, nothing but the thought that for the rest of his life he would be homeless and wretched. He feared that he himself might meet as violent and sudden a death as his brother did.

He need not have been afraid of being killed. None would kill him, for God set a mark upon him that he might be known, and God threatened vengeance on any who might slay Cain.

"My punishment is too much to bear!" cried Cain, nevertheless. He doubtless realized that with a murderer's mark on him, people everywhere he went would shun him and hate him for what he had done. Another thought added to his misery.

"And never again shall I see the face of the Lord!" he wept. He knew that his happy life was over, and that from then on he would always be sad. His peace of mind was gone, lost to him because of his great crime.

Cain builds the first city

Sadly, he wandered from the land where he had lived with his parents and his brother and settled in the Land of Nod, where he took a wife. Their first son was named Enoch, and Cain built an entire city which he named after his son.

Cain had many children, grandchildren, and great-grandchildren. Among them were Jubal, who invented music and musical instruments; Tubal-Cain, who worked in metals and made the first tools of iron and brass; and Jabal, who gathered together flocks and herds and led a wandering life. Jabal was, as the Bible expresses it, "the father of all such as dwell in tents, and of such as have cattle."

After Abel's death and Cain's banishment, Adam and Eve had another son, whom they named Seth. Eve hoped that he would grow up to be like

Enoch is taken to heaven. He was the first human being so favored by God.

the good Abel whom Cain had killed. She believed that this son was the gift of God, to take the place of the dear child she had lost, for neither Adam nor Eve forgot the Lord and His goodness. They believed that He still watched over them as a Father, although they had sinned so greatly.

"God has given me another son, to take the place of Abel," said Eve.

Adam was one hundred and thirty years old when Seth was born, for people lived to be very old in those days. The Bible does not tell us how many more children Adam and Eve had in their lives, but probably they had a great many, for they had many, many grandchildren.

Since people lived for hundreds of years, a single person could easily have more than a hundred children, so it is not hard to understand how the population of the world increased very rapidly indeed.

When Seth was a hundred and five years old, he had a son named Enos. By that time there were a great many people in the world, and men had learned to pray to God. Possibly Adam himself told his children, and his grandchildren, and their grandchildren, of the time when he and Eve had lived in the Garden of Eden. He would explain why they had been driven out, and warn all against yielding to the temptation of sin. Adam could have so spoken to the great-great-great-grandchildren of his great-great-great-grandchildren, and even more, because he lived to the age of nine hundred and thirty years.

Adam's grandson Enos, the son of Seth, became the father of Cainan. Cainan became the father of Mahalaleel, Mahalaleel the father of Jared, and Jared the father of Enoch. Each of these men had many other sons, and they had daughters as well. Enoch was a very holy man, and he was the father of Methuselah, who lived longer than any other man the world has ever known. Methuselah lived for nine hundred and sixty-nine years.

Enoch was such a holy man that he did not die as most men have died since the first sin of Adam and Eve. Instead, God took him directly to heaven when he was three hundred and sixty-five years old. One day Enoch went out walking and, as the Bible tells us, he was seen no more, for God took him.

Although Enoch was a holy and righteous man, his children and grandchildren were not, and eventually they became so wicked that God grew discouraged with man.

The giants who lived on earth

Among the people on the earth at that time were many men with great physical strength and power. These were the giants of ancient times—the men about whom great stories were told. But probably they were not good men, but were warriors who used their power to conquer and oppress other men.

Also, God was displeased because the descendants of Seth, though they worshiped God, began to marry women who were descended from Cain and had wholly or partly stopped worshiping God.

At about this time, God said,

"My spirit must not remain in man forever. Man is not an angel but is only flesh. Accordingly, I will allow the present population of the earth only one hundred and twenty years more."

By this statement God predicted the great flood that He would send to cover the earth. For God had grown tired of the wickedness of man. The giants were famous for their power and courage, but they were violent and wicked, had bad thoughts in their hearts, and forgot the Lord in Whom their fathers had believed. God, we are told, was sorry that He had made man; all the people were so wicked He determined to destroy them, and not only them, but the animals that He had made, "man, and beast, and the creeping things, and the fowls of the air."

4

The story of Noah and the Great Flood

THE WORLD WAS SO FILLED WITH WICKEDNESS that God had decided to destroy every living thing. He was angry with the evil of men and determined that no trace should be left on earth of the sin and corruption that had grown up in the beautiful world of His creation.

There was one man who still loved God and was a good man. His name was Noah, and the Lord decided to save him and his family.

Noah was the grandson of Methuselah, the oldest man who ever lived.

For Noah's sake, God decided to save also two of every kind of living thing. God had determined to send a great flood upon the earth, and He spoke to Noah.

"I have resolved on the extermination of all mortals, for the earth is full of wrongdoing through them; I am going to exterminate them from the earth," said God to Noah. "Make yourself an ark, or ship, of wood; make the ark with cabins, and smear it with pitch inside and out." (Pitch is the same black, tarry substance that we often call asphalt or bitumen.)

And God instructed Noah exactly as to how the ark, or ship, must be built. It must be large—large enough to contain not only Noah, his wife, his three sons, and their wives, but also many thousands of animals, birds, and reptiles.

Then, after the flood was over, there would be enough animals of all kinds to repopulate the earth with them. God instructed Noah to take with him two of every "unclean" beast (that is, animals not fit for food), and seven pairs of every "clean" beast (animals from which good meat could be had). This would make it possible for them all to reproduce their kind. God also instructed Noah to take seven pairs, a male and a female each, of all the birds of the air.

The instructions for building the ark were very clear. It was to be a large, covered ship, with a doorway and a window on the side and with three decks or stories—a lower, a middle, and an upper story. It was to have many rooms—or cabins—and it was to be coated inside and out with pitch, to waterproof it. It was called an ark, which means box, because of its shape.

How the ark was built

The ark was the first ship that had ever been made, for the people in those days had, perhaps, scarcely seen the sea. If they had seen it, they would have been afraid, strong and bold as they were, to venture upon it, for they did not know how to build a boat to float safely, much less a ship large enough to hold a great number of persons.

People must have wondered what Noah and his sons were making, and, perhaps, laughed at him. If Noah had told them that a great flood was coming, which would cover the earth and destroy all living things except those that God had chosen to save, they were so unbelieving and wicked, and had so forgotten what they might have been told of the power of God, that they would probably not have believed him.

The ark is built while Noah watches. It was 500 feet long, 75 wide, and 50 high.

Noah, his family and the animals entering the ark.

But God said to Noah,

"I am about to bring a flood upon the earth, to destroy every mortal thing under the heavens, who has the breath of life in him; everything that is on the earth shall perish."

The next words of the Lord, however, must have been very comforting and reassuring to Noah, for God said:

"But with you I will make a covenant (an agreement, or promise): You shall enter the ark, accompanied by your sons, your wife, and your sons' wives. Also, of all living creatures, of all animals, you must have two of every kind enter the ark, to keep them alive with you. Take also some of every kind of edible food, and store it by you, to be food for yourself and them."

Noah did just as God had commanded him, for Noah trusted in the Lord.

Noah went on working until the great ship, or ark, was finished. Then, still obeying the command of God, Noah found a pair of every living thing, and enough food for them and himself and family. When all was ready, he placed the beasts and birds and creeping things in the ark. He and his wife, and his sons, whose names were Shem, Ham, and Japheth, and their wives, went into the ark and waited for the flood which they knew the Lord would send.

He did send it. The Bible tells of it in words that are very dramatic, both in the original Hebrew and in the translation that we read. "The fountains of the deep" burst forth; the windows or "floodgates" of heaven were opened.

The flood that destroyed the earth

You have, no doubt, seen heavy rain come down suddenly, pouring from the sky, and you may have seen small streams quickly become like great rivers, as if all at once new springs of water had broken forth. But never since has there been such rain known as that which then fell upon the earth. Very heavy rain, even in the countries where there is most rain, seldom lasts more than a few hours, and although we have wet seasons, some rain perhaps every day for a month or even more, yet the rain sometimes ceases and sometimes comes down gently. But Noah saw from the ark the rain coming down like a great torrent for forty days and forty nights. It did not slacken or stop.

At first the little streams and great rivers rose and covered the fields. Then the waters rose higher and higher, drowning the cattle and wild animals that fled into caves.

Men and women, trembling with fright, climbed the hills for safety. They knew now how great was the power of the Lord Whom they had forgotten, and how truly Noah had spoken when he told them why the ark was built.

But still the waters rose higher and higher. The valleys became one great sea; the smaller hills were covered. People who were too weak to climb were swept away by the great rush of waters, and others sought safety on the lofty mountains. But the rain poured down the sides of the highest hills, and men and women were carried away to death by the force of the waters.

Then came the time when the mountain tops were covered and there was nothing but a great raging sea. The towns that the mighty men had built, all the work they had done, were hidden beneath the waters. Still the

The Great Flood: The interpretation of the French engraver Gustave Doré. The ark can be seen in the background. It is not known why Doré (and some other artists) showed the people without clothes on. They were probably clothed.

When the ark landed Noah built an altar and gave thanks to God.

ark floated safely, for it was upheld by the power of the Lord, and in it was all that was left of the life that had been upon the earth.

For a hundred and fifty days the waters were at their height, but Noah and those with him were safe. Then the flood abated, and the ark rested on the mountain of Ararat.

The landing on Ararat

It was on the seventeenth day of the seventh month that the ark struck ground at the top of Mount Ararat. The waters continued to go down for two months longer, and on the first day of the tenth month, the tops of some of the earth's mountains became visible. This was the first dry land that those in the ark had seen for many a long day, and their joy at the sight is impossible to describe.

Noah had a window in the side of the ark, and forty days after the rain had ended Noah released a raven from that window. It went flying back and forth seeking a place where the earth had again become dry, so that man might once again live on the land. Since the raven merely kept on flying, Noah could not learn a great deal from it, and so he next released a dove.

The dove could find no dry resting place on which to perch, so it flew back to the dryness of the ark. A week later Noah sent the dove out again, and this time it flew back with a symbol of hope for those in the ark. It bore an olive leaf in its mouth, which meant that somewhere it had found a spot where vegetation could exist, and therefore the ground was no longer flooded.

Now Noah knew that there must be some lessening of the waters on the earth. After waiting seven days he let the dove fly again, and it did not come back. Noah knew then that there must be dry land. Removing the covering of the ark, he looked out and once again saw the earth. The Lord had sent a great wind, which drove the waters back and soon dried the land.

Then God told Noah to leave the ark, with his wife and sons and their wives, and all the living things that were with him.

At this time, Noah was six hundred years old. Altogether he had spent a year and two months in the ark, with his wife, his sons, their three wives, and all the pairs of animals, birds, and reptiles that God had commanded him to preserve with himself.

That is the wonderful story of the flood as told in the Bible; and scientists called archaeologists have dug up records, engraved on baked clay, from ruins thousands of years old, which tell nearly the same story.

When Noah was once again on the dry land, he built an altar and thanked God for His mercy, and God promised that the world would never again be destroyed by a flood.

"The rainbow in the clouds," said the Lord, "will be a witness of this promise forever."

The Lord said He would never again destroy every living thing, but that so long as the earth remained the seasons would come in regular order; there would be seed-time and harvest-time, cold and heat, summer and winter, day and night. And we may see how He has kept His promise ever since. Every year the leaves come upon the trees at the same time, the grass grows, the corn ripens and is ready for reaping, winter and summer come every year, every day the sun gives us light, and every night darkness comes.

The meaning of the rainbow

Whenever we see the rainbow in the clouds—and we may very often see it after a heavy rain storm—we should remember how once God destroyed the wicked people of the world, all but a few righteous men and their families, and how he preserved these few because Noah believed in Him and did as God commanded. Let us remember, too, that God promised Noah, and, through him, promised us, that He would not again destroy the world with a flood of water.

The great flood, the story of which we have just read, happened many thousands of years ago, but not a year has passed since without the rainbow, with all its beautiful colors, being seen in the clouds to remind us of God's power and goodness.

God blessed Noah and his sons, and told them He gave them power over beasts, birds, and fishes—that "every moving thing that lives" would be food for them. He commanded them, too, that they must take care of each other. Noah, no doubt, had told his children the shocking story of the murder of Abel by his brother Cain; and now the Lord again warned them against the sin of murder, saying, "Whoever sheds man's blood, by man shall his blood be shed; for man was made in the image of God."

The great flood is often referred to as "the deluge," and the time before it is called "antediluvian times," meaning all the years of creation before the flood of Noah's day.

But even Noah, who had been so good before the flood, fell into error afterwards. Like Adam, he kept a garden, and he also grew vines, from which he made wine. Foolishly and ignorantly he drank too much of the wine and committed the folly of drunkenness.

Noah plants the first vineyard

Noah's son Ham saw him in a helpless state in a drunken sleep, and made fun of him; and for this Noah, when he awoke, placed a curse upon Ham and upon Ham's son Canaan. Noah blessed his sons Shem and Japheth but said the others should be the servants of their brothers.

This was because Shem and Japheth had not mocked their father, when they found him asleep after drinking too much wine. Instead, they had carefully put a robe over his naked body, keeping their eyes turned away, so that they need not embarrass him by looking upon him as he lay unclothed.

"Cursed be Canaan!" he declared when he awakened and learned what

"The rainbow in the clouds," said the Lord, "will be a witness of this promise forever."—Never will the world again be destroyed by flood.

had occurred during his sleep. "The meanest of slaves shall he be to his brothers."

When Noah said "Cursed be Canaan," he was not condemning Canaan as a person. By "Canaan" he meant all the descendants of Ham. It was about the same thing that might happen today when a father disinherits one of his sons and leaves all his property to his other sons. Under the

Noah curses Ham (shown with bowed head) and Canaan, Ham's eldest son.

system followed in Noah's day, the head of the family, tribe, or nation owned all the land and property; he was the patriarch and everyone else, even his brothers, had to obey him, so in effect they were his slaves. Noah was so angry at Ham that he made his other sons and their descendants rulers of his lands.

5

The story of the Tower of Babel

When Noah and his family left the ark, they scattered and went in different directions. This God had told them to do, so that the population of the earth might be replenished over a large area as soon as possible.

During the three hundred and fifty years that Noah lived after the flood, he had many children and his sons, Shem, Ham, and Japheth, also had many children each.

The descendants of Shem became the Semitic race, and all the Hebrews and most of the Arabs were descended from him.

The descendants of Ham became the Hamitic race, and the people of many parts of Africa and other nations of that part of the world were descended from him.

Some of the descendants of Japheth became the Ethiopians and Egyptians, and others moved northward into Europe and eastward into Asia.

Within a few hundred years after the flood, there were again millions of people on the earth. Even at the end of a hundred years the sons of Noah had thousands of descendants.

As the people were traveling about, undecided as to where they would remain permanently, a large group came upon a great plain that looked pleasant to them. They decided to stop there for a while.

"This is a good land," one man said. "Why do we not build a city here?"

"Yes," said another. "This is a fine place for a city. And why do we not do something that will impress all the world? Let us build a great tower here, and everyone will come to see it and to enter it."

"The top of our tower shall reach up to the sky itself!" exclaimed another man. "All the world will want to climb our tower and enter into heaven from the top!"

The Tower of Babel; about 600 feet high, was probably square at its base.

The people in those days had no idea of the great spaces beyond the earth's atmosphere. They believed that the blue sky they saw above them was a solid ceiling or canopy, on the other side of which lived God and all the heavenly host.

Some of the people, however, had a different thought about the tower that they planned to build. Some people by this time had begun to slip away from the worship of God, and were perhaps willing to give their adoration to the sun or moon and stars as gods. This tower to them would be a means of drawing nearer to the heavenly bodies they wished to consider their gods, though actually these were only bodies like the earth and sun and moon and stars, which God had made.

There were still others, among this group that settled on the plain, who wanted to keep the peoples of the earth together, instead of allowing them to live in all parts of the world, as God intended.

They continued with their plans for the tower, and started to build it.

"Let us make many bricks of good clay—bricks that will support the great weight of our tower," they said.

"And let us not pause for a moment in our work until the city and the tower are built," others said.

God saw what these people were doing, and it did not suit His plan for the world. He wanted people in every place on the globe. He could see that if they continued with the building of the tower they would remain in that one section, and the rest of His beautiful world would be uninhabited.

God could not allow this, and He determined to stop the building of the tower and the city. He chose a very remarkable way of making the people stop.

At that time, all the people of the world spoke just one language, and no matter where they lived, they all understood one another.

God decided to change that. He made the men who were building the tower speak in many different languages, so that one man could not make out what another was saying.

The confusion of languages

If you were to go to France you could not understand the talk of French people, unless you had been taught it, nor can French people understand English, unless they have been taught it. People who do not speak the same language can seldom work well together, so very soon these people stopped working on the tower.

They called the place Babel, which means "confusion." Then they separated into groups. Those that spoke alike kept together. These groups went away and settled in different parts of the earth, just as God had wished them to do.

That is how there came to be people in all parts of the earth, speaking different languages.

6

The story of Abram and Lot

SHEM, THE ELDEST SON OF NOAH, was not one of those who were driven out of the land after the Tower of Babel had been built. Shem had children and grandchildren, and many years afterwards there was one of his descendants living near where the Tower of Babel had been begun. This descendant of Shem's was named Terah. He had three sons, named Abram, Nahor and Haran. Haran died young, and left one son, Lot. The other brothers lived on. Abram married a woman named Sarai and Nahor married a woman named Milcah.

Abram was the ancestor of all the Hebrew people. (Later his name was changed by God to "Abraham," and it is by this name that he is best known.)

Abram's father, Terah, had lived for many years in the city of Ur, in the country of the Chaldees, a people who occupied a land about one hundred miles southeast of Babel. Ur was a very large city and an important city. It was part of a great civilization more than four thousand years ago.

The people of Ur worshiped idols, for the most part, but there were some who realized that there was but one true God. Among those who worshiped God were Terah, who was Abram's father; Abram himself and his wife Sarai (whose name God later changed to "Sarah"); Abram's brother Nahor and his family; and Abram's nephew Lot. The Bible does not say so, but some students of Biblical history have suggested that Terah decided to leave Ur because of the idol worship of the people who lived there. Terah feared that God would destroy the city because of the people's wickedness; and, in fact, the city was destroyed, though this happened long after.

Abram and Lot had no children and were not settled in Ur; so Terah

God appears to Abram (bowing, at the left) and promises him a new land.

took Abram and his wife Sarai, and Lot, the grandson of Terah and nephew of Abram, away from the land of Ur, where they had lived so long.

Terah intended to go into the land of Canaan, which perhaps he had heard of as being a very fine and fruitful country where his flocks and herds could find plenty of food; for in those days many people did not live in houses and towns, but in tents, and moved about from place to place. But Terah and his party did not get farther than the city of Haran (which, perhaps, Terah founded and named after his dead son). There Terah stayed until he died, many years afterward.

God had other plans for Abram. One day he spoke to Abram, saying:

God speaks to Abram

"Leave your land, your relatives, and your father's home, and go to the land that I will show you; and I will make a great nation of your descendants. I will bless you and make your name great, and through you all the nations of the earth can find a blessing."

Abram was a good man and obeyed God's command. He did not then know where God wished him to live, but when Abram was told to leave

Haran he did so, taking with him his wife Sarai, his nephew Lot, his servants, and all of his riches. Abram was an exceedingly rich man, with many hundreds of cattle and sheep, riches in jewels and gold, and hundreds of servants as well.

Abram passed through the land as far as the Plain of Sichem and Moreh, and was told by the Lord that all that fair land would be his. God showed Himself to Abram, who built an altar on that spot and another on a mountain near Bethel, where he lived in a large tent.

But although Abram was rich, and had been promised that all the land would be his, he was not without trouble. The people of the country, the Canaanites, were fierce and unfriendly. Then there came a famine, so that Abram could not get enough food for himself and those who were with him. He knew that Egypt was a rich and fertile country, and he made up his mind to go there and take with him his wife and family.

On the way, he spoke to his wife Sarai, and said:

Abram goes to Egypt

"You are a very fine-looking woman, and I fear that the Pharaoh (king) of this country, Egypt, may want to take you from me. He might even kill me so that you will be a widow and he can marry you. When we meet any of Pharaoh's people, tell them that you are my sister, instead of my wife."

Sarai understood this request, which sounds like a strange thing for a man to ask his wife. The reason was clear to her, however.

At that time, it was considered very wicked to take a man's wife from him. It was even more wicked than it was to kill a man, although this too was sinful, of course. By killing Abram and making Sarai a widow—if they knew that Abram and Sarai were married—Pharaoh would be committing only the lesser sin. Abram and Sarai both knew this, and they agreed that it would be better to say they were brother and sister. Then, if Sarai were taken, Abram would still be alive to pray to God for help, and so get Sarai back.

"I will tell them that you are my brother," Sarai promised.

And so she did, for it happened just as Abram feared it might.

Pharaoh, the king of Egypt, saw Sarai and took her into his house. For her sake he treated Abram (whom he thought was her brother) very well.

But the Lord was angry with Abram for telling a falsehood and with Pharaoh for taking Sarai away. He sent plagues (diseases) into the house

Abram and his family go to Egypt to escape the famine in Canaan.

of the king, who at length came to know the truth, and he was glad to give Sarai back to Abram. Pharaoh then scolded Abram.

"Why did you do such a thing?" he demanded. "You very nearly caused me to commit the sin of taking another man's lawful wife, and making her my wife."

Pharaoh did not take any of Abram's wealth, cattle, silver, and gold, but let him and all that were with him go. Abram and his wife, and Lot, with his own servants and cattle, then went back to Bethel, where Abram had built an altar. There they prayed to the Lord and gave thanks for their escape from the anger of Pharaoh.

Lot was almost as rich as Abram. He had flocks and herds, and many tents for his servants to live in. But he and Abram found that they could not live in the same place. There was not food enough at that place for all their servants and cattle; and the men who took care of the flocks and herds quarreled and fought among themselves. Abram was greatly pained at this strife, for he loved Lot, his brother's son; but he told Lot they had better part. Abram said that Lot might stay there if he chose and Abram would go away; or, if Lot would like better to go, Abram would remain.

"For we must not quarrel," said Abram to Lot. "You are my nephew—part of my own family. It is wrong for members of the same family to quarrel among themselves—or even for the servants of relatives to quarrel. Your herdsmen and my herdsmen are constantly fighting, and this is wrong. Choose which land you wish, and I will take the other."

Lot knew what a fine land there was to the east, in the valley of the Jordan River, a land like a garden, and he told Abram he would go and live there. There were two cities there, on the border of a large lake, in the midst of a beautiful country. The names of the cities were Sodom and Gomorrah.

The two men had parted in the friendliest of fashions, for neither was angry at the other, and Abram had shown his just nature and generosity by letting Lot choose the land he preferred. Abram would have been willing to take either section. Now he remained in the land of Canaan, where he had built an altar to the Lord.

When Lot had removed all his possessions to the plain of the Jordan, God told Abram to lift up his eyes and look about, in every direction, for as far as he could see the land would belong to him, or to his descendants, forever. God told Abram even more.

"I am going to make your descendants as numerous as the dust of the earth," he said, "so that it will be as possible to count the dust of the earth as to count your descendants. Go and travel the length and breadth of the land, for I am giving it to you."

7

The story of how Abram rescued Lot

When Lot moved to the plain of Jordan, he made his home in the city called Sodom. There he prospered, until a king named Chedorlaomer, king of Elam, with three other kings as his allies, attacked Sodom and captured the city. Not content with the victory, they sacked the place, taking away everything of value, and they carried off a great many Sodomites, whom they intended should serve them as slaves.

One of the men, however, escaped, and reached the place where Abram lived.

"Lot has been taken away, and is a captive," the man gasped. "There has been a great battle and the kings of Sodom and Gomorrah have been defeated by King Chedorlaomer and his allies. All the people of your nephew's household are held prisoner by Chedorlaomer. I escaped, and came to tell you the news."

Immediately Abram called together three hundred and eighteen of the men who served him. He armed them well and went in pursuit of the four kings. He came up with their armies in the country of Dan.

Dividing his forces, so that he could make attacks at the same time in different quarters, Abram approached during the night. He slaughtered many and put the rest to flight. He followed after the fleeing army as far as Damascus. At that point, in order to insure their own safety, the defeated kings gave up all their captives and all the wealth and property that the soldiers had taken. The kings of Sodom and Gomorrah recovered everything that had been stolen from them.

Abram guarded the released captives on the way back to Sodom, where he was met by the king of that place and by the pious Melchizedek, king of Salem. Melchizedek was a "priest of the most high God," as the Bible expresses it.

Melchizedek blessed Abram, and brought forth bread and wine, which were used (as they are today) as a means of worship—for Melchizedek was a priest as well as a king. Then Melchizedek gave Abram his blessing, in words such as these:

"Blessed be Abram by the Most High God,
"The Creator of the heavens and the earth!
"And blessed be the Most High God,
"Who delivered your foes into your power!"

The king of Sodom wished Abram to take, as a reward, all the wealth he had brought back; but Abram refused, saying that he had vowed to God he would accept nothing for what he had done, so that the king might not be able to boast that he had made him rich; but Abram allowed the men who went with him to have a portion of the rewards the king had offered.

Battle between Chedorlaomer's armies and the four rebelling kings.

The warrior Melchizedek thanks Abram (the bearded man at the right).

Abram himself did not wish to make profit from warfare. He had gone into battle only to save his nephew, Lot, and this had been accomplished. He wanted nothing further.

God was pleased that Abram had been so just and generous, and came to him in a vision.

"Do not be afraid, Abram," God said. "I am your shield (protection); your reward shall be very great."

For, with all his riches and power, Abram was not happy. He had no children, and he thought that when he died his steward, or chief servant, whose name was Eliezer, would take his place. But the Lord spoke to Abram in a vision and reminded him how He had before taken care of him and given him all things that were good for him.

Abram wondered how he could be rewarded. He already had great worldly wealth; all he wanted was a son who could take his place when he died.

"Since You have given me no son, my household slave will be my heir," said Abram.

The Lord told Abram that this would not happen. Abram would have a son to be his heir.

Still Abram was puzzled. He and his wife Sarai were old, and it did not seem to him that they would ever have any children, since they had not had children during their younger years.

But God spoke again.

"Now look at the sky, and count the stars if you can," He said. "It will be just as hard to count your descendants, there will be so many of them."

When the evening came, Abram fell into a deep sleep, during which the Lord appeared to him and told him many more wonderful things that were in store for him.

God promised Abram that he would have a son, and again said that his race would be as numerous as the stars in heaven, which no man can count.

God also told Abram that he would possess all the land; that his descendants would be for four hundred years captives and slaves in a strange land, but that they would return with great riches. To Abram himself it was promised that he would live to a good old age and die peacefully.

Abram made a sacrifice to the Lord and saw by strange signs that the vision he had had was real. The land that God promised to Abram and his children reached from the river of Egypt (the Nile) to the Euphrates River, a vast country.

8

The story of God's promise to Abraham

ABRAM WAS NEARLY A HUNDRED years old when God repeated His promise that Abram would be the father of a great nation.

Now in all this time Sarai had been just as troubled as Abram about the fact that they had no children. She was herself more than seventy years old and had given up hope. One day she spoke to her husband and told him of a thought she had.

"Take my handmaid, Hagar, as another wife," she said. "Perhaps in that way you may have children. She may provide you with an heir, which I have been unable to do."

Hagar was a young Egyptian woman whom Abram and Sarai had brought back from that country, when they went there during the time of famine in Canaan, to be a servant to Sarai.

In that time, many men had more than one wife. It was not considered wrong to do so, or Sarai would not have suggested such a thing to her husband, for she was a very good and righteous woman.

Abram listened to his wife and agreed that this was a good thought. He accordingly made Hagar his second wife, and soon he knew that Hagar was to bear a child to him.

Unfortunately, when Hagar realized this she became very proud. She was scornful of Sarai, who had not been able to do as much in all the years of her marriage.

Sarai was angry when she found that her handmaid looked down upon her for having been unable to bear Abram a child, and Sarai spoke to Abram.

"My handmaid, Hagar, is scornful of me," she said. "I do not wish to have her around me, because she feels that she is now better than I am."

"She is your handmaid," said Abram. "Do with her as you wish."

Sarai then treated Hagar so unkindly that the younger woman could not endure it. At length, Hagar fled from the tent of Abram and Sarai and started out across the desert, or wilderness (which word was often used to mean the same thing as "desert" in the English language many years ago).

When Hagar had walked many miles she sat down beside a spring of water in the desert. There an angel of the Lord spoke to her.

"Hagar, handmaid of Sarai, where have you come from, and why are you here?" the angel asked.

"I am running away from my mistress. She is cruel to me and hates me," said Hagar.

"You must go back," said the angel. "Go back, and do as she tells you. You are going to have a child, and because the Lord has heard your troubled cries, that child will be a boy. You are to call him 'Ishmael,' which means, 'The Lord heard.' "

Hagar hesitated, but the angel reassured her.

"Your son's descendants shall be a great nation," the angel said. "There will be many and many of them, and you can be proud to have been the mother of the man who will found that great nation."

So Hagar returned to the tent of Abram and Sarai, and in due time her son was born. As the angel of the Lord had commanded, he was named Ishmael. Abram was eighty-six years old when Hagar bore him this son.

Thirteen years after Ishmael was born, the Lord again appeared to Abram. At this time, Abram was ninety-nine years old, and Sarai, his wife, was eighty-nine.

God now told Abram to change his name to Abraham, which means "father of a great multitude," for, said God, "I have made you a father of many nations." Sarai's name, too, was changed to Sarah, which means "mistress," a title of honor; for God said, "I will bless her and she shall be a mother of nations."

The covenant and Abram's new name

And God made a covenant (agreement) with Abraham. He told Abraham that all of Abraham's descendants—and they would be very many—should worship Him, the one true God.

Not only should they worship the one true God, but there were other things that they must do.

"Every one of your males must be circumcised," was God's command. "At the age of eight days, every male baby among you, from generation to generation, must be circumcised."

This meant that the law would apply to boy babies born in the dim and distant future, as well as to those that had already been born, or would be born within a short while.

Then God told Abraham that to fail in this would be a violation of the covenant, and anyone who did not abide by this ruling would be cut off from the people of God.

There was more. God told Abraham that Sarah would bear him a son, and that her son would become the founder of a great nation of people, with many kings as his descendants.

At this, Abraham (who was kneeling before God) put his face down and laughed.

"Shall I, who am a hundred years old, be father to a child? And shall Sarai, who is ninety, become a mother for the first time?" he asked himself. He thought God must have meant that his son Ishmael would be the one to father the great nation God had mentioned. He asked God if this was what He had intended.

But God said,

"No, it is a fact. Your wife Sarah is to bear you a son, and you are to call his name Isaac (which means 'laughter'). I will establish my covenant with him, for himself and his descendants after him. With reference to Ishmael, I have heard your prayer and I will bless him. He will be the ancestor of twelve princes; I will make a great nation of his descendants." God promised that Sarah would become the mother of Isaac at the same time (the springtime) one year later.

On the very same day that God appeared to Abraham and told him all these things, every male in the household of Abraham was circumcised. Abraham himself circumcised all of his servants, and his slaves, and all their children down to the age of eight days.

Abraham himself was circumcised, in obedience to God's command, and his son, Ishmael, the son of Hagar, who was thirteen years old at that time, was circumcised.

9

The story of Abraham and the angels

AT FIRST ABRAHAM DID NOT HAVE FAITH enough to believe the promise God had made to him. It seemed too strange to him that Sarah and he would have any children now that they were so old. But the promise was exactly kept, and God even sent His angels to make the promise again.

One fine summer day Abraham was sitting at the door of his tent, on the plain of Mamre, resting perhaps after labor, when he saw three men standing near him. In those times weary travelers could always make sure of having food and rest offered them when they reached a tent.

In that hot dusty country washing the feet after a journey was very pleasant and refreshing. Water for that purpose was always offered as well as food; and Abraham, as soon as he saw the men, went quickly to them, and, bowing low, invited them to rest in the shadow of the trees, eat some food, and wash their feet.

While they rested, Sarah busied herself making a cake, and Abraham had a young calf killed, so that he might offer a good meal to the strangers. When the cake and meat were ready they were set before the strangers, who ate. Abraham, following the custom of his times, waited upon his guests.

Abraham was very kind and hospitable, but in those times it was the custom for everyone to entertain any travelers who came by. If travelers had not been welcomed in that way by those who lived in the desert lands, they mght have died from hunger and thirst. But it happens in this case that Abraham recognized the three strangers as messengers of God, or angels; and that he recognized one of them, the chief of the three strangers, as speaking with the voice of God himself.

Abraham welcomes the three angels. Actually his home was a large tent.

Then, when the strangers asked for Sarah, and when they repeated the promise that she would have a son, Abraham knew that he was in the presence of the Lord's angels. Sarah did not know this. When, hidden in the tent (for it was not the custom of Eastern women to show themselves much to strangers), she heard that before another year was over she would have a child, she laughed. The chief of the three angels promptly reproved her; and no doubt she was sorry, afterwards, that she had so little faith in the Lord.

When they left the tent the strangers told Abraham that they were going to Sodom, and Abraham offered to lead them on the way. As they were journeying, Abraham learned from the chief of the angels that the Lord had determined to destroy the cities of Sodom and Gomorrah because of the terrible wickedness of the people.

Abraham prays for the city of Sodom

The two other angels left Abraham and went on toward Sodom. Abraham, who knew that his nephew Lot and Lot's family

Abraham treats the men to washing of the feet, to drink and food in the shadow of the trees. As in the picture on the preceding page (an engraving by Hans Holbein) Sarah is shown hiding in the tent.

lived in the wicked city, prayed to the Lord, through the chief angel who remained with him, to spare Sodom and Gomorrah for the sake of the righteous men who lived there.

"If," was the Lord's answer, "I find in Sodom fifty righteous men within the city, I will spare all the place for their sake."

Abraham still prayed for the good men who might be there, even if there were not so many as fifty. Eventually Abraham received God's promise that even if only ten good men were there, the whole city would be spared.

Abraham had to be content with that. He hoped, no doubt, that good men enough would be found in Sodom to save it. He did not know how very wicked the people were. Not even ten good men could be found in it.

10

The story of Sodom and Gomorrah

HE OTHER TWO ANGELS WHO HAD VISITED ABRAHAM went on, when they left him, and completed the journey to the city of Sodom, where Lot lived. They arrived at the house of Lot when night was falling.

Lot was very polite to the strangers. He did not know, of course, that they were angels, but he invited them into his house and offered them food and water to wash their feet.

The angels did not want to accept Lot's hospitality. They said to him, "No, we will sleep on the ground, outside."

They knew, of course, that when morning came they would destroy the entire city of Sodom, and that Lot might be destroyed with it. In the meantime Abraham was praying to God, Who would later save Lot from death, but the angels did not yet know this. It was simply a matter of courtesy for them to refuse Lot's invitation.

But Lot insisted that the strangers (the angels) should come into his house; and the angels did go in, and were fed meat and bread and given a place to sleep.

The people of Sodom were wicked. Unlike Lot, they had no hospitality to offer strangers. Before the angels, disguised as simple travelers, were asleep in Lot's house the men and boys of Sodom assembled at the house and called to Lot.

"Bring out to us the foreigners who came to your house tonight!" they shouted. "We will make them entertain us."

Lot tried to keep the crowd from disturbing his guests. "My daughters will entertain you, if you wish," he said. "Let my guests sleep." But the crowd shouted louder than ever that they wanted the strangers. They tried to attack Lot because he would not do as they wished.

The angels protected Lot and themselves at the same time. They caused all the men and boys who surrounded the house to become blind. Then the crowd could not find the door of Lot's house and soon they went away.

After this, the angels let Lot know who they were; and they said to him,

"When morning comes we will destroy this city. If you want to save any member of your family, call him to you and take him out of the city before morning."

Lot tried to save his intended sons-in-law, the men who were going to marry his daughters, but they would not believe him when he said that angels of the Lord were about to destroy the city. But two of Lot's daughters believed him, and his wife believed him, and before morning came Lot, his wife, and his two daughters had left the city. Even so, the angels had to take these four persons by the hand and lead them out of the city, because it was so hard for anyone to believe that God was really going to destroy an entire city and everyone in it.

The angels warned Lot and the women with him,

"Do not look behind you!"

As Lot and his two daughters fled from the city they obeyed the instructions of the angels and did not look behind them. They did not see the Lord send a rain of fire and sulfur (which in olden times was called "brimstone") to burn up the cities of Sodom and Gomorrah so that no house or building and no living person remained in either of them.

Lot's wife is turned to salt

But Lot's wife, unfortunately, was curious. As she was running from Sodom she paused and looked back to see what was happening. At once she was dead, turned into salt! (The Bible calls her a pillar, or statue, of salt.)

Lot and his daughters, without looking back, ran until they came to a cave in the hills nearby. There they lived for a while. The Bible does not tell what happened to Lot afterward, but it is likely that his herds and flocks, which were in the country outside of Sodom, were not destroyed when the city was destroyed, and that Lot regained them and became rich again; for we know that Lot could always have gone back to live with his uncle Abraham, who loved him and had saved him more than once.

Lot's descendants were two great nations, or tribes, the Moabites and the Ammonites, who were descended from him through his two daughters.

11

The story of Abraham and Abimelech

AFTER THE DESTRUCTION of Sodom and Gomorrah, Abraham looked out and saw the devastation of the land. Not a living thing was in sight, where once had been houses surrounded by fertile fields full of grazing cattle and sheep. Abraham was very sad, but he knew that God's will had been done and that only the wicked had been punished.

Shortly thereafter, Abraham and his wife, Sarah, set out for the area of Negeb, which lay between Egypt and the land of Canaan. This was in the country of a king named Abimelech.

Once again Abraham and Sarah agreed that they would pretend to be only brother and sister, rather than husband and wife. The reason was the same as when they had done so in Egypt, the land of Pharaoh. Abraham feared that Abimelech would want to add Sarah to his household as another wife. In that case some of Abimelech's servants might kill Abraham so that Sarah would be a widow and it would be lawful for Abimelech to marry her.

And, once again, just as had happened in Egypt, the king Abimelech did indeed want to make Sarah his wife. He took her into that part of his house which was reserved for women. But as he was making preparations for the marriage, a terrible trouble came to his land. Suddenly, no women could have babies there, and no one knew what had happened to cause this.

It was a great disaster. In those times people tried to have as many children as possible. They knew that the world needed a much larger population, and every couple felt that the more babies the wife had, the better for the country and for the world as a whole.

Therefore, when no women could have children in the land of Abime-

Abimelech (in crown) restores Sarah to Abraham (shown bowing, at left).

lech, the cries of the people were loud in protest. They wanted to know what was wrong.

"Our wives cannot bear our children!" the men wailed. "We have kept faith with God, but still we produce no young! What is wrong?"

No one could answer them.

After a time, however, God appeared to Abimelech in a dream. God told Abimelech that Sarah was really the wife of Abraham, and that Abraham was a great prophet. God commanded Abimelech to return this woman to her husband immediately; then God told Abimelech he might pray to God that the trouble of the lands might be cured.

Abimelech was a good man and he quickly summoned Abraham.

"Why have you done this thing?" he asked sorrowfully. "You have caused me almost to commit a wicked sin. Why did you lie to me, and tell me that this woman was your sister, when she is truly your wife?"

"She is my wife, it is true," said Abraham, "but I did not lie to you, for she is also my sister. Her father and my father were the same, although we had different mothers."

(When the world was young, it was not unusual for a man to marry his half-sister. It was even necessary, if there were to be enough wives for all the men, and husbands for all the women. Otherwise there could never have been such a great increase in the world's population in a comparatively short time.)

When Abimelech had heard Abraham's explanation, he returned Sarah to Abraham and he gave Abraham many valuable gifts. There were oxen, and donkeys, and great quantities of silver. Then Abimelech spoke kindly to Abraham.

"You are most welcome to settle anywhere in my country that pleases you," he said. "Take whatever part of the land you like best."

After this had happened, God lifted the plague that had kept the women of the country from bearing children. Once again there were babies in the land of Abimelech, and the people were happy.

12

The story of God's test of Abraham

SPRINGTIME CAME AGAIN, and according to the promise, Isaac was born. His mother was full of joy, and said, referring to the name that had been given to her baby, "God has made me to laugh, so that all that hear will laugh with me." Isaac grew up a good child, and we may be sure was a great joy to his parents.

So tenderly, indeed, does Isaac seem to have been loved by his father that the Lord made him a means of trying Abraham's faith and obedience. God commanded the old father to take his little son Isaac to a mountain in the land of Moriah, and there to offer him as a sacrifice. To do this, Abraham would have to kill Isaac, his only son, the son he had waited for a hundred years. How many fathers could have done this, even when God commanded it?

Abraham must have felt bitterly how hard it was to obey such a command, but he had faith in God and knew that the Lord's will must be done. Early in the morning he took Isaac and two of his servants, with wood for the burnt offering and a pot of burning coals to light the fire, and asses to help them bear it, and to ride on.

For three days the party traveled, the father very sad, and the boy, not knowing why they were going so long a distance, enjoying the ride and talking innocently.

At length they reached the mountain. Then Abraham told his young men to remain behind, while he and Isaac went to make the offering.

"But where is the lamb for the sacrifice, father?" asked Isaac, looking about as they drew near the mountain top.

And Abraham answered him sadly.

"The Lord will provide a lamb for the burnt offering, my son," he said. "We must trust in Him."

Perhaps he hoped that the Lord was only trying his obedience, but yet he knew that he must obey; and when they reached the place Abraham built the altar, and then, binding his boy to it, took the knife and was about to kill him, when he heard his name called out of heaven.

"Abraham! Abraham!" called the voice.

"I am here," he answered.

"Do not lay hands on the boy," said the voice, and now Abraham knew that it was the voice of God, speaking to him through an angel. "Do nothing of the sort to him; for I know now that you trust and obey God, in that you have not withheld even your son, your only son, from Me."

Isaac is saved by an angel

Amazed and thankful, Abraham looked around and saw a ram, a male sheep, caught by its horns in a thicket. He took the ram, unbound Isaac, and made of the ram a burnt offering to the Lord. The place where the altar was built was long remembered as "the mount of the Lord," where the Lord had watched over Abraham and his son Isaac.

Again the voice of God was heard, repeating His promise of the greatness of the people of which Abraham would be the ancestor. They would be as many as the stars in heaven and the sand that is upon the seashore. Through them all the nations of the earth would be blessed.

Abraham, we may be sure, went down from the mountain a happier man than when he started on his journey. His dear child was with him, not led as a victim to be offered up but with a promise of life and happiness and future greatness.

AAC BLESSING JACOB (detail)

13

The story of Hagar and the angel

YOU KNOW THAT ABRAHAM HAD ANOTHER SON, Ishmael, the son of Hagar. Yet the Lord had described Isaac as "the only son" when the sacrifice was offered on the mountain. This was because Hagar and her son Ishmael had been banished from Abraham's house.

This had happened when Abraham held a great feast in celebration of the weaning of Isaac—the time when he no longer had to live only on his mother's milk.

At the feast, Sarah saw Ishmael laughing at the little boy Isaac and making fun of him. Now, it is not unusual for a boy to tease his little brother, but Sarah became very angry.

"This woman and her child must not live here any longer," she declared. "Send them away!"

Abraham did not wish to do such an unkind thing, but the Lord spoke to him and told him that it would be quite all right. God promised that He would take care of Hagar and Ishmael, and through Ishmael Abraham would become the founder of another great nation.

Abraham knew that he had been promised the same thing through Isaac, and this meant that both of his sons would found nations. Abraham would have many millions of descendants altogether.

"I will send them away," Abraham said to Sarah, after he had heard the words of the Lord.

Hagar was given food by Abraham, and a large water bag made of animal skin, which was the usual manner of carrying water in those days. She and Ishmael wandered across the desert, in the wilderness of Beersheba, until their food and water ran out.

Abraham sends Hagar and Ishmael into the desert: An engraving by Gustave Doré. Sarah and the infant Isaac are shown in the background. The tent is perhaps a shelter for the sheep shown; it is much too small to be Abraham's tent.

Hagar and Ishmael in the Desert.

Ishmael became so thirsty that he seemed near death. Hagar did not know of anything she could do for him. At length she laid him down under a shrub and turned away. She could not bear to watch him die of thirst, as she felt sure he must.

While she was weeping an angel of the Lord spoke to her. He showed her a well, from which she got water, and he told her that her son would live and be the father of a great nation.

So Ishmael grew up to be a great man. He was a great archer, or huntsman with the bow and arrow, and many of his children were famous men. Twelve of them were princes, or leaders of nations. The descendants of Ishmael, called Ishmaelites, became the people we know now as Arabs. They grew to be far more numerous than the descendants of Abraham's son Isaac, the people who were known as Hebrews, Israelites, or Jews.

14

The story of Isaac and Rebekah

SARAH DIED AT A PLACE that afterwards was named Hebron, in Canaan. She was a hundred and twenty-seven years old and Abraham greatly mourned her loss. He bought the field of Machpelah, in which there was a cave, for a burying-place, and there he laid the body of Sarah.

When the Hittites, who lived in that part of Canaan, learned of Sarah's death, they offered to let Abraham bury her body in any of their sepulchres.

"You are a mighty prince," they said. "Any one of us would be glad to allow you to use one of our family burying places for your dead."

"No," said Abraham. "I understand your kindness and generosity toward me in my grief, but I must buy my own burying ground."

Abraham spoke to a man named Ephron, who owned the field of Machpelah, and asked him if he would sell this field as a burying place for Sarah's body.

"Sir," said Ephron, "I would be proud to *give* you this field. Accept it as a gift, and one I am glad to give you in your grief. Use it as a burying ground, I beg you."

"I cannot do that," said Abraham. "I must buy it from you. It would not be right to accept your land without payment."

"Between us, there should be no such small thing as payment for a field worth at most only four hundred shekels," said Ephron.

When Abraham heard the price that Ephron had set on his field, he immediately paid him the four hundred silver shekels, in the presence of the Hittites who were standing near. These men were witness to the fact that Abraham owned the land, which would thenceforth be his family field for burying of their dead.

Sarah is entombed in the cave of Machpelah: An engraving by Gustave Doré.

Abraham was at this time very old, for he was ten years older than Sarah had been, and he was no longer able to rule over his household. Abraham felt that death was near. The Lord had blessed him in all things, and he wished that his son Isaac might be as happy in the future as he had been.

Abraham had a trusted servant, Eliezer. He ordered Eliezer not to let Isaac marry a woman from among the Canaanites in whose country Abraham then lived, but said that Eliezer should go into the country from which Abraham had come and there find a wife for Isaac.

Eliezer knew that this was a great responsibility. He asked,

"Suppose the woman I find does not wish to come here, even to become the wife of Isaac? What shall I do then? Should I take Isaac to her in that land?"

"No, under no circumstances take him back to that land," said Abraham. "God led me here and God has told me that Isaac and his descendants will inherit this land. If Isaac is to inherit this land he must live here. An angel of the Lord will doubtless lead you to the right woman to be Isaac's wife. Only if she refuses absolutely to come back with you are you released from this responsibility, and from the oath that you will now swear to me."

Abraham then made Eliezer swear that he would do as Abraham had directed: that is, seek a wife for Isaac in the land from which Abraham had come.

Eliezer obeyed. He took a party of men, riding on ten camels, and went to the land of Nahor, Abraham's brother, in Mesopotamia, the country we now call Iran. When Eliezer reached that place he made the camels kneel down outside the city, beside a well to which the women of the place came to draw water.

The servant had been trained by Abraham to fear God. He prayed and asked to be directed in the choice he was to make. He prayed that if he asked one of the young women to give him water from her pitcher, and she did so, and she gave his camels drink also, that she might be the one to be the wife of Isaac.

Eliezer meets the beautiful Rebekah

Eliezer had scarcely made the prayer before it was answered, for there came to the well a beautiful girl, Rebekah, the granddaughter of Abraham's brother Nahor. She carried her pitcher on her shoulder and she went down to the well and filled it.

"Would you give me some water to drink from your pitcher?" Eliezer asked the young woman. He did not then know her name, nor who she was.

"Most surely," Rebekah exclaimed. She let down her pitcher till it rested on her hand, and when he had drunk from it she saw that the camels were thirsty and ran down to the well again, bringing up enough water for all.

"Your camels, too, need water. I will draw enough so that they may all drink," she said.

Then Eliezer knew that this must indeed be the wife that he was to take back for Isaac, for she had done precisely as he had asked God in his prayers that she might do, to serve as a sign to him that this was the right young woman.

Immediately Eliezer gave to Rebekah many valuable gifts, including golden earrings and a golden bracelet.

Then Eliezer asked the young woman her name, and of what family she came.

When Rebekah told him that her father's name was Bethuel, and that he was the son of Abraham's brother Nahor, the servant gave thanks to God that his master had again known God's mercy and truth, and that he, the servant, who had been trusted so much, had been led to the house of his master's relations.

Rebekah made haste home and told her mother what had happened at the well, and her brother Laban went out to meet Abraham's servant.

"Come into our house," said Laban. "You are most welcome. There is plenty of room for you, and a place for your camels as well."

The camels were fed, but Eliezer would eat nothing until he had related the reason why he had come. He told them how his master, Abraham, had been blessed and had become powerful and rich; how he, Eliezer, had been sent into that country to seek a wife for Isaac; and how the Lord God had guided him in the way to meet with Rebekah, who was the child of Abraham's brother's son.

Bethuel, Rebekah's father, and Laban, her brother, saw that it was the Lord's will, and consented to let Rebekah go if she were willing.

"I will go," said Rebekah.

Rebekah returns with Eliezer

Eliezer then brought forth splendid presents, raiment, and jewels of gold and silver, and gave them to her, making also handsome presents to her mother and brother. He and his men were well feasted, and in the morning he started to return to Abraham. With him went Rebekah and her maidens, or servants. Her relations blessed her as she went.

The party bringing Rebekah reaches Abraham's country and is met by Isaac (shown with arm raised, at the right): A Doré engraving. The stone structure shown should probably be a tent. This scene is described on the next page.

"May you have many children, so that your descendants will number high into the thousands," they said. "And may these, your descendants, always be victorious in any battle in which they may engage."

Isaac was walking in the fields in the evening when he saw in the distance the camels, with Rebekah and her attendants riding on them. Rebekah had seen him also.

"Who is that man walking in this direction, from the other side of that field?" she asked Eliezer.

"That," the servant replied, "is my master Isaac, son of Abraham."

When told that it was Isaac, whose wife she was to be, Rebekah got off the camel and covered her face with a veil.

The faithful servant told his young master where he had been, and that he had brought Rebekah to be a wife for him. Isaac had greatly mourned the loss of his mother, who had been dead about three years. He now received Rebekah tenderly and loved her. He took her to the tent that had been Sarah's and made her his wife.

Isaac and Rebekah marry

After the death of Sarah, Abraham had another wife, Keturah, and six other sons; but as they grew up he gave them presents and sent them away into the east country, so that they would not trouble Isaac, to whom he gave all his wealth. At the age of one hundred and seventy-five Abraham died. He was buried by the side of his wife Sarah in the cave of Machpelah. God had greatly blessed him in his lifetime, and He continued His blessing to Isaac, and made him prosperous.

15

The story of Jacob and Esau

Isaac and Rebekah were living happily together, near Abraham's tents. But they had one great trouble—they had no child. They had been married a great many years, but still Rebekah bore no children. Isaac knew he must have descendants to inherit the land as the Lord had promised Abraham, and so he prayed very earnestly to God about it.

God answered Isaac's prayer. He said Rebekah would have two sons and that they would become afterwards—in many years—the heads of two nations. But God said that one of these nations would be stronger than the other and that the nation headed by the younger son would be greater than the nation headed by the older son.

Not long after this two little baby boys were born. They were twins, which means they were born almost at the same time. The one who was just a few seconds older was covered with red hair, and they called him Esau. The other, who was smooth and just like any other little baby, they called Jacob. But these names have meanings. Esau means "hairy," or "rough" (and later, Esau was called also Edom, meaning red, just as we might give the nickname "Red" to a red-haired boy). Jacob means "a supplanter"—that is, one who takes the place of another.

When the boys were about fifteen years old their old grandfather Abraham died. All his life he had led an upright, holy and prayerful life, believing and loving God with all his heart; and he died at last in a good old age, being a hundred and seventy-five years old.

Six of the sons of Abraham became the founders of a large nation of nomads, or wanderers. Later they were called the Keturah Arabs, because the name of their mother, Abraham's last wife, was Keturah. They wandered the deserts and wildernesses of the great lands to the east of Canaan. Their descendants are wanderers or nomads in the eastern lands to this day. They are called Bedouins.

Isaac, the son of Sarah, and Ishmael, the son of Hagar, shared in the sad task of preparing their father's body for burial. They placed his body in the cave of Machpelah, which he had bought for the burial of Sarah, his wife.

Death and burial of Abraham

After the death of Abraham, God blessed Isaac, Abraham's son. Isaac and Rebekah took their two boys and went to live by "Hagar's well," the place where the angel had appeared to Hagar.

Ishmael went away after his father's death. He spent the rest of his life as a wanderer, like the Keturah Arabs. His twelve sons all became great princes, but they spent their lives as nomads and warriors.

Ishmael lived fifty years after the death of Abraham, and was one hundred and thirty-seven years old when he died. The Bible does not say where Ishmael was buried. But the promise of the Lord to Hagar was fulfilled, and she did indeed become the mother of a man who was destined to found a great nation. The Arabs of today are in a large measure descendants of Ishmael, and, through him, of Hagar and Abraham.

Isaac's two sons Esau and Jacob grew up. They were quite different. Esau became a clever and successful hunter. He often went out into the fields with his bow and arrows, to shoot birds and wild beasts. He shot wild deer also and took it home to have it roasted and made into a tasty stew for his father, Isaac. The flesh of deer is called venison. Isaac liked venison very much.

Jacob did not care for hunting. He was a plain man, with simple tastes and habits. He lived quietly in a tent and took care of sheep and goats and cattle, and managed the farms on which grain and vegetables were grown. Jacob loved God. Though he was sometimes tempted to be sly, untruthful, and selfish, God knew all that was in his heart and He saw that Jacob was humble and really did try to walk uprightly; so God loved him.

But God did not love Esau, for Esau was wicked and had no wish to serve God. Esau never tried to please God. Yet Esau was the favorite son of his good father, Isaac, because he was the firstborn son.

Jacob feeds Esau (kneeling) in return for Esau's giving up his birthright.

Rebekah, however, loved her younger son better.

One day Esau had been out in the fields hunting, and he came back very tired, and quite faint for want of food. Jacob had just made some pottage, or soup, of lentils, which are a small kind of bean; and when Esau saw it he longed for it.

Esau sells his birthright to Jacob

"I am so hungry I am dying," said Esau. "Please, I beg you, let me have some of that pottage you have made."

"If I do, will you give up all your rights as the firstborn son, and let me have them instead?" asked Jacob, holding the soup away from his brother.

"If I die of starvation, what good will it do me to have any rights as the firstborn?" cried Esau. "And I feel now that I will die this minute unless I have something to eat!"

Still Jacob withheld the soup.

"First you must promise me faithfully that I may have your birthright," he demanded. "Then I will give you the pottage."

In his desperation, Esau promised. He gave up his birthright and ate the soup that Jacob had prepared, along with some bread that Jacob gave him.

This is the incident in the Bible that is often used to illustrate the exchange of something valuable for something nearly worthless. It explains what is meant when someone says, "He sold his birthright for a mess of pottage."

God's prophecy—that the younger would be greater than the elder—was fulfilled by what Esau had done. As eldest son, Esau was supposed to be his father's heir. Special blessings and privileges were to be the portion of the firstborn. All the land of Canaan was promised to Abraham's children, and it would naturally come to be the inheritance of the firstborn. But it would seem that Esau did not care for blessings that were in the future and that he could not see; the reason, perhaps, being that he did not believe in them.

Jacob had faith, and believed all God's promises. Since his father Isaac was the one of Abraham's children most blessed by God, so Jacob wished that God's special blessing should come to himself and not to his elder brother.

16

The story of Isaac and Abimelech

NOT LONG AFTER ESAU HAD SOLD HIS BIRTHRIGHT to his twin brother Jacob, there was a famine in the land of Canaan. Because of the famine, Isaac left the place where he was living and went to a nearby place called Gerar. The king of that country was Abimelech, whom Isaac's father had known well.

Isaac must have had some thought of continuing toward the land of Egypt, for one day the Lord spoke to him and told him he should remain where he was.

Isaac obeyed, and soon thereafter he observed that the men of Gerar greatly admired the beauty of his wife, Rebekah. As his father Abraham had done many years before when men admired Sarah, Isaac pretended that Rebekah was his sister instead of his wife.

"We must do this," he explained to her. "If they think you are my wife, one of them may kill me in order to marry you."

This was the land of the Philistines, ruled by King Abimelech. One day Abimelech saw Isaac with Rebekah and thought that the fond embrace he witnessed was of the kind that a husband would give his wife, rather than that which a man might give his sister. He approached Isaac, and accused him of having told an untruth.

"This woman must be your wife," declared Abimelech. "Why did you tell us she was your sister?"

"I feared that your men might kill me so that one of them might marry my wife," Isaac explained.

"This was a very wicked thing to do," said Abimelech. "If one of my men had taken your wife, thinking she was your sister, and married her, we would have been guilty of a wicked sin against the Lord. You know this very well."

And with that Abimelech gave an order to all of his kingdom:

"Let no one lay a hand on this man or his wife. Anyone who does so shall be put to death."

So Isaac stayed in Gerar. He sowed wheat in that land; and God prospered him as He had promised, and gave him a wonderful harvest. While his neighbors scarcely reaped at all, Isaac had an abundance of wheat. And he went on prospering in all that he did, so that he became very great and rich; for he had large flocks of cattle and sheep and a very great number of servants. The people of Gerar were jealous, and envied him.

Then they began to show their angry feelings by doing spiteful things. They stopped up all the wells that Abraham's servants had made, and filled them with earth. This was doing much mischief, and a great unkindness, for now the cattle were in danger of dying of thirst. But Isaac's servants dug the wells again and called them by the same names that Abraham had given them.

Still the men of Gerar were constantly quarreling with Isaac's men about the wells, and the king at last begged Isaac to go away.

"Please take your family and possessions and move a little distance from here," he said. "You are so prosperous and so powerful that my people are filled with fear."

So Isaac moved into another valley, not far from where he had been living but far enough so that he thought the Philistines would no longer be troubled.

Even after they moved, Isaac's men continued to have trouble with the Philistines about the matter of wells, for the shepherds of the Philistines wandered many miles with their flocks and often quarreled over wells that supplied the animals with water.

Each time, Isaac made his servants dig other wells, because he did not wish to have trouble. The third well they made seemed to be in a place where the Philistines did not go with their flocks, for there were no disputes over this third well. Isaac called it Rehoboth, which means "space" or "room," because this time, he said, there was plenty of room for his men and no one tried to drive them away.

The Lord appears to Isaac

After a time, Isaac took his wife and his two sons, Esau and Jacob, and returned with them to Beersheba, which was the place where he was born, where he grew up, and where he lived so long near his parents' tents.

In Beersheba, the Lord appeared to Isaac.

"I am the God of your father Abraham; do not be afraid," said the Lord. "I will bless you and make your descendants numerous, for the sake of Abraham."

There Isaac built an altar, that he might worship God.

Soon Abimelech visited this place, with two of his trusted ministers, and Isaac was astonished to see them.

"Why did you come here to see me?" he asked. "You seemed to hate me when I lived in your land, and you made me leave it."

"We have come because we can see that the Lord is with you, and we wish to have peace between us," they answered.

So they all swore a solemn oath to be friends from that day on, and never to fight each other.

Then Isaac gave a great feast for everyone, and the next day Abimelech and his men returned to their homes.

17

The story of Isaac's blessing

ESAU WAS THE FAVORITE SON of his father Isaac, while the mother, Rebekah, had made Jacob her favorite.

One thing that set Rebekah against Esau seems to have been his marriages. When Esau married he did not choose a wife from among his own people. He married two women (as was permitted in those times) from among the Canaanites, the people who had been living in the land before Abraham went there.

The people of Canaan were cursed by the Lord, and to marry into them was to lose all chance of God's blessing on the marriage, but Esau did not care. He was not a God-fearing man. This was a sore trouble and a grief of mind to Isaac and Rebekah.

Yet still Isaac loved his godless son the best and wished to give him the blessing—the blessing of the firstborn. This meant that Isaac wished to make Esau his heir, to leave to Esau most of his riches and to pass on to Esau all those glorious promises of spiritual blessings of which Esau was quite unworthy, and for which he did not care.

Some years had passed and Isaac had become a very old man. He was a hundred and thirty-five years of age (at that time each of his sons was seventy-five years old). Isaac's eyes had become dim, so that he could not see.

One day he called to his older son.

"Esau, come to me," he said.

"I am here, father," said Esau.

Then Isaac told him why he had called.

"I am a very old man," said Isaac. "I do not know when I may die. I want to give you my blessing before that happens. Please take your bow and arrows and go kill a deer, so that I may have some venison prepared as I like it so well. Bring me this, and then I will bless you."

Esau went to the field to hunt for venison. But Rebekah had heard what Isaac said to their son Esau, and she began to think how she might get the best blessing for her own favorite, Jacob. She thought this might be done by deceiving her husband, who was blind and old; and she was so anxious that the younger son should get the blessing intended for Esau, that she made up her mind to steal it for him if she could.

She told Jacob what she had planned.

"I have heard your father talking to Esau," she said. "He told Esau to go out and kill a deer for venison, and to bring him that meat prepared as he likes it so well. He said that he would first enjoy his meat, and then he would give Esau his blessing, in case he might die soon."

Jacob did not understand yet what his mother had in mind, but she continued to explain.

"Now, this is what you must do," she said. "Go out and select two of the best kids in the flock, and bring them to me. I will fix the meat to taste like the venison he likes so much, and you can take it in to him. He will then give you his blessing, as he now intends to give it to Esau."

"But Esau is hairy, and I am not," protested Jacob. "Suppose my father should touch me, and notice that he touches a smooth skin. Then he will know that I was trying to deceive him, and I shall bring a curse on myself—not a blessing!"

"Let me be the one who bears the curse, if there is one," said Rebekah. "Now go and do as I have told you!"

Jacob went and did as his mother said. He killed two kids and she prepared them to taste like the deliciously flavored venison that Isaac liked so much. Then Rebekah took some fine garments that belonged to Esau and put them on Jacob, her younger son. She covered Jacob's hands and his neck with the hairy skins of the kids of the goats, so that his hands and neck might feel hairy like those of his brother Esau.

Rebekah disguises Jacob

When all this was done, Rebekah put into Jacob's hand the savory meat and the bread she had prepared.

Jacob took the food to his father, and Isaac, when he heard someone in the room with him, spoke.

"Which of my sons has come to me?" he asked.

Jacob answered with a lie.

"I am Esau, your firstborn," he said. "I have done as you told me to do. Here is the venison you asked for. Eat it, I beg you, so that you may bless me, as you said you would do."

But Isaac was puzzled.

"How did you manage to get the venison so quickly?" he asked.

"Because the Lord helped me, I was able to find the deer without delay," lied Jacob.

Although Isaac could not see, his hearing was good and it seemed to him that this was not the voice of Esau. He felt a trifle doubtful, and he spoke again.

"Come close to me, my son," he said. "I should like to feel your skin and make sure that you are indeed my son Esau."

Jacob went near his father; and Isaac felt him and said, "The voice is Jacob's voice, but the hands are the hands of Esau."

Thus Isaac did not find out who it was, because Jacob's hands seemed as hairy as his brother Esau's hands. But once more Isaac asked, "Are you truly Esau?"

And again Jacob lied to his father and said, "I am."

Then Isaac said, "Bring the meat to me, my son. I will eat it and then I will give you my blessing."

Jacob took the meat to his father and he ate. Jacob took wine to his father and he drank. Then Isaac said, "Come near now, and kiss me, my son."

Jacob came near and kissed him. Isaac was finally convinced when he smelled the smell of Jacob's clothing (for Jacob was wearing Esau's garments, and most likely they were perfumed, as was often the case then).

The blessing of Isaac to Jacob

Isaac then gave his blessing to Jacob, thinking him Esau. Isaac said, "See, the smell of my son is as the smell of a field which the Lord has blessed; therefore may God give you of the dew of heaven, so that the earth may bring forth abundantly for you, and that you may have plenty of corn and wine. Let people serve you, and nations bow down to you; be lord over your brothers, and let your mother's sons bow down to you. May God punish everyone who injures you, and may He bless all those who do you good." This was the blessing.

Jacob receives the blessing of his aged father Isaac.

Isaac had forgotten that God had said, "The elder shall serve the younger." Such words as these, "Be lord over your brothers, and let your mother's sons bow down to you," should never have been spoken to Esau, for it was against God's command. Therefore God's will was served by Isaac's mistake.

Isaac had barely concluded his blessing of Jacob, and Jacob had been gone only for a moment, when Esau came in from hunting. He also prepared meat in the fashion that he knew his father liked, and he took it in to Isaac. He spoke to his father.

"Let my father get up," Esau said, "and eat the venison that his son has brought. Then may I be blessed, as you said."

Isaac was confused, and attempted to straighten out his confusion.

"Who are you?" he asked.

Esau answered, telling his father who he was. He stated only the truth—that he was Esau, the firstborn son of Isaac and Rebekah.

"But I was given venison by someone who said he was Esau, and I believed him!" cried Isaac. "Not only have I eaten the meat he gave me, but I have also given him my blessing! And that blessing I cannot withdraw. It is given."

At that Esau cried out, in anger and bitterness.

"Give me a blessing, too," he begged. "Please, my father!"

And Isaac said, sadly, "Your brother came, with deceit in his heart, and took away your blessing, which should not have gone to him."

Then Esau's anger burst forth.

"He was indeed well-named Jacob, meaning one who steps into another's place—for he has done this twice already! First he took my birthright, and now he has stolen my blessing!"

It was Isaac's sad task to tell Esau what he had said in his blessing to Jacob.

"I have made him your lord, and I have told him that all his brothers shall bow down to him and be his servants. I have also assured him that he will have plentiful corn and wine. What is there left that I can give you as a blessing, my son?"

Esau said to his father, "Have you but one blessing, my father? Bless me, bless me also, O my father!" And Esau lifted up his voice and wept.

Then Isaac did give a blessing to Esau, though it could not be as good as the blessing given to Jacob. "You shall have a home where the soil is fertile and the rainfall plentiful," said Isaac. "You shall have an abundance of the good things of this world, and you shall live by your sword, and shall serve your brother; but some day, when you shall have the power, you shall set yourself free from him again."

Isaac blesses Esau

Esau was not fully satisfied, and he was still angry. He said to himself that after his father died he would kill his brother Jacob, who had stolen so much from him. Rebekah suspected what was in the mind of Esau, and she sent for Jacob.

"Your brother Esau is planning to kill you some day," she said. "Now you must do as I tell you, for your own safety's sake. Go quickly and secretly to my brother, Laban, who lives in Haran, and stay with him for a while—until your brother's anger turns away from you and he forgets what you have done to him. Then I will call you home again."

Rebekah did not tell Isaac about the murder Esau was planning; perhaps she thought it would distress the old man too much. She gave Isaac another reason for wanting to send Jacob away to her own country. She said to her husband,

"I am weary of my life because of Esau's wives, the daughters of Canaan. If Jacob should take a wife of the daughters of the land, as Esau has done, it will distress me all my life long."

Isaac felt that Rebekah was right in what she said. He called Jacob and blessed him, and gave him a solemn charge, or order, and said to him,

"You shall not take a wife of the maidens of Canaan; but go to Haran, to the house of your mother's father, and take one of the daughters of Laban, your mother's brother, to be your wife. And God Almighty bless you, and make you prosperous, and increase you, that you may be the father of a great number of people; and give you the blessing of Abraham, to you and to your children also, that you may inherit the land which God gave to Abraham."

Then Isaac and Rebekah sent away Jacob; and Jacob went out from Beersheba, and took the way toward Haran. Jacob was then seventy-five years old, but he had never had a wife.

While Jacob was on his way, one night when he lay down to sleep, in the first part of his journey to Haran, he had a dream he was never to forget.

18

The story of Jacob's two wives

While Jacob slept, he dreamed that he saw a ladder set up on the earth. The top of the ladder reached to heaven, and angels were going up and down on it. The Lord stood above it. The Lord spoke to Jacob; He told Jacob that he would give the land of Canaan to Jacob and to Jacob's descendants, and that Jacob's descendants would be a great multitude of people. The Lord said he would be with Jacob to take care of him wherever he went and would bring him back to Canaan again.

Jacob awoke and was afraid, because the Lord had been there and had spoken to him in his dream. He rose early in the morning and worshiped the Lord.

"Surely the Lord is here!" Jacob exclaimed. "I will call this place Bethel, which means that it is the house of the Lord."

Jacob promised that if the Lord would take care of him, and give him bread to eat and clothes to wear, and keep him from harm so that he might come back safely to his father's house again, then he would obey the Lord; and of all the silver and gold, the flocks and the herds, which God might give him, he would give one-tenth (which is often called a *tithe*) to the Lord in the form of offerings.

Actually, these offerings (of food and other possessions) went often to build altars and feed the poor and support the worship of God, just as offerings do today.

Jacob continued on his journey until he came near the city of Haran, where Laban lived. There he saw a well in a field, with three flocks of sheep lying down by it, and there were shepherds with their flocks. A great stone was rolled over the mouth of the well, to cover it. When the flocks

Jacob's Ladder: The Doré interpretation, showing God at the head.

came in from feeding, the shepherds would roll the stone away and draw up water for the sheep. After the sheep had finished drinking, the stone would be rolled back again over the mouth of the well.

Jacob uncovers the well for Rachel. The artist made the scene and costumes like those of his own country and time.

Jacob asked the shepherds where they lived.

"At Haran," they answered.

Then Jacob asked yet another question.

"Do you know Laban?" he said.

"Indeed we do know him," the shepherds replied.

"Is Laban in good health, and doing well?" asked Jacob.

"He is well," they told him. "But look, here comes his daughter, Rachel, with her father's sheep. She tends them for him."

The meeting of Jacob and Rachel

When Rachel approached the well with her father's flock the shepherds would not help her, but Jacob rolled away the stone and watered the flock for her. He then told her that he was the son of Rebekah, and therefore her cousin. He kissed her, greeting her as a relative, and Rachel immediately ran to tell her father of Jacob's arrival.

When Laban heard that his sister Rebekah's son had come, he ran out to meet Jacob and put his arms around him and kissed him and took him to his house. Laban spoke kindly to Jacob, and Jacob stayed at his house for a month.

Laban had another daughter beside Rachel. Her name was Leah. But Rachel was more beautiful than Leah. Jacob loved Rachel, and he told Laban he would stay and serve him for seven years if, after they were ended, Rachel would be given to him as his wife. Laban said he would give Jacob Rachel as his wife, so Jacob served Laban seven years for her, and they seemed like only a few days to him, because his love for her.

Jacob works seven years and is cheated

But when Jacob had served the seven years Laban would not give him Rachel, because she was the younger sister. Instead, Laban gave Leah to Jacob as his wife.

"It is not right that the younger should be married before the elder," said Laban, when Jacob protested that he had been promised Rachel, not Leah.

"If you wish to marry Rachel also, you must serve me for seven more years," Laban added.

"Very well, I will remain another seven years tending your flocks, if I may have Rachel for my wife now, before that time is up," Jacob agreed.

Laban agreed to this, so Jacob married both sisters. Then Jacob stayed and served Laban seven years longer, and he had both Leah and Rachel for his wives, and God gave sons to him.

Jacob stayed and worked for Laban nearly seven years more, twenty years in all. After this Jacob asked permission of Laban to take his wives and his children and go back to the land of Canaan. He wanted to see his father and mother if they were still alive; and Jacob thought, perhaps, that after so long a time Esau would forgive the unkindness Jacob had done him (when Jacob took away Esau's blessing).

But Laban was not willing to let Jacob go.

"The Lord has blessed me because of you. If you leave, I shall lose the great good fortune that has been mine since you came here," said Laban. "What wages must I give you, to make you willing to remain here and care for my flocks?"

"Only give me some of your cattle for my own," said Jacob. "If you will do this, I will remain and continue to tend your flocks, but I shall have a small flock of my own and perhaps it will increase."

Leah (right) and Jacob in the field. Leah is attended by her maids and children.

Laban gave Jacob some of his cattle, and Jacob stayed and took care of Laban's flock. Jacob also had sheep and goats of his own, which he kept separate from Laban's in a different place. It took three days to go from Laban's flock to the place where Jacob kept his flock. Jacob's flock grew to be a great many; after a while he was rich and had herds of cattle, and his sons took care of them. Jacob had menservants and maidservants, and camels and asses.

One day Jacob heard Laban's sons speaking unkindly of him.

"Look at the riches of this man!" they said. "He has taken away our father's cattle and has grown rich on them. He is becoming richer than our father!"

Jacob saw that Laban did not look on him as kindly as he used to do. Laban's face was changed and he looked displeased.

The Lord speaks to Jacob

The Lord then spoke to Jacob in a dream. He commanded Jacob to go back to the land of his fathers; that meant that Jacob was to return to the land of Canaan, where Abraham, his grandfather, had lived when he was alive, and where

Jacob prepares to leave the country of Laban and return to the land of Canaan.

Isaac, his father, was still living. The Lord said He would be with Jacob, to take care of him and keep him from harm.

Jacob sent for Rachel and Leah to come to him while he was out in the field with his flock. He wanted to talk with them there where Laban could not hear what he said.

"Your father, Laban, is displeased with me," said Jacob to his wives. "He is angry because the cattle that he gave me as payment for staying here have grown fat and healthy, and my flocks have increased greatly. He is no longer friendly toward me."

Leah and Rachel agreed that their father was unfriendly, even to them.

"The Lord has told me to return to Canaan, and I must do as the Lord commands," he said. "I will take you, my wives, and all our children and return to the land of my father."

Rachel and Leah told Jacob he should do as the Lord commanded. Jacob made ready to go. He set his wives and his children upon camels, and took all his cattle and everything that belonged to him, and started on his journey to the land of Canaan.

Laban had gone away from his home to shear his sheep, and he did not know when Jacob left because Jacob had kept it a secret from him. On the third day after Jacob had gone, someone told Laban about it. Laban took men with him and followed after Jacob. No doubt he was angry and wanted to do Jacob harm; but in the night, in a dream, God spoke to Laban and told him not to harm Jacob or to speak unkindly to him.

Laban did not overtake Jacob until he had been following him seven days, for Jacob had gone a long way, across a river and through a wide lonely country, to a mountain called Gilead. There Laban came up with him.

Jacob had set up his tent at Mount Gilead, and when Laban came there he set up his tent at Mount Gilead also.

"Why did you leave my land secretly, taking my daughters and my grandchildren with you?" Laban asked. "Why did you not let me know you were leaving, so that I might at least have been able to kiss my grandchildren and my daughters before you took them away from me!"

Jacob answered that he had gone away secretly because he was afraid Laban would take Rachel and Leah away from him if Laban knew he was leaving. Jacob was angry at Laban for coming after him.

"Why have you followed me?" he asked. "I have served you well for twenty years, taking care of your sheep and goats for you. I have given them good care. If God had not been with me to help me, you would have sent me away without giving me anything for all the work I have done!"

Laban spoke kindly to Jacob:

"Your wives and children are the same to me as if they were my very own," said Laban. "I would not do them any harm. As for you and me, we should be friends and promise never to do each other harm. Let us make a covenant, or agreement, as to this."

Mizpah, or the watch-tower

So Laban and Jacob piled up stones and made a heap of them, and promised they would do each other no harm. The heap of stones, which they called Mizpah, or a watch-tower, was always to stay there to remind them of the covenant they had made. If ever they were angry and wanted to harm each other, the heap of stones would remind them of their promise never to harm each other.

Jacob built an altar and offered a sacrifice on Mount Gilead, and he and

Laban, and the men who were with them, ate bread together. They stayed all night on the mountain. Early in the morning Laban arose, kissed Rachel and Leah and their children and blessed them, and then returned to his own home.

JACOB IN PRAYER

Jacob prays, on his way from Laban's country to the home of his father.

Jacob wrestling with the angel.

19

The story of Jacob's fight with the angel

JACOB LEFT MOUNT GILEAD and continued on his journey toward Canaan. As he went some angels met him. Jacob called them God's host, or army. Perhaps God had sent them to take care of him on his way.

When Jacob came near to the place where his brother Esau was, he sent messengers ahead to tell Esau that he had been living with Laban until that time. Jacob sent word that he was rich, owning many oxen and asses and flocks, and menservants and maidservants. He sent the messengers to tell Esau about it, he said, so that Esau might not be angry with him. Jacob was afraid of Esau, for although it had been twenty years since he had deceived his father and taken away Esau's blessing, Jacob remembered his sin and it made him afraid.

Soon his messengers returned.

"Your brother Esau is coming to meet you," they told him. "He is bringing a company of four hundred men with him."

When he heard this, Jacob was in great fear. He took his flocks, and his herds, and his camels, and made two companies of them instead of one large company; and some of Jacob's men went with one company and some with the other.

"If my brother Esau attempts to hurt or kill one company," said Jacob, "then the other company must make great haste to get away. In that way I shall not lose all of my people and flocks, even if some of them are destroyed by Esau and his army of four hundred men."

Jacob prayed that God would save him from Esau, for he was afraid that Esau would kill him and his wives and his children. In praying, Jacob admitted that the Lord had been very kind to him, and that he did not deserve the good things the Lord had given him. When Jacob had left Canaan, twenty years before, he had only the staff that he carried in his hand. Now, on his return, he had two companies, or bands, of men, with flocks and herds and camels. Then he had been very poor, but now God had made him rich.

Jacob stayed in that place all night. He took some of his cattle and sent them as a present to Esau. He sent two hundred and twenty goats, two hundred and twenty sheep, thirty camels with their colts, forty cows and ten bulls, and twenty asses with ten little ones. He did not send all of these together; he made different droves, or flocks, of them, and sent each flock by itself. Then when Esau met the first flock, and asked the man who was driving it whose cattle they were and where they were going, the man was to say,

"They belong to your servant Jacob; it is a present he has sent to lord Esau."

When Esau met the next drove and asked the same question, the man driving it was to answer as the first had done. And so they all were to answer, until Esau had seen every drove.

Jacob sent the flocks to make Esau feel kindly toward him, so that Esau might not hurt him or his wives or his children, or take his flocks or his herds from him.

Jacob got up in the night and sent his two wives and his eleven sons over the stream of water that was nearby, and he was left alone.

During the night, while Jacob was sleeping, there came a man and wrestled with him, putting his arms around him and trying to throw him down, and Jacob put his arms around the man. They wrestled together until the light of the morning shone a little in the sky. (See the picture at page 86.)

How Jacob wrestled with an angel

When the man saw that Jacob did not fall, but was strong and still wrestled, he touched Jacob's thigh; and just by this touch Jacob's thigh was put out of joint and he was lame.

Then the man said,

"Let us stop wrestling, for the day is breaking."

But Jacob would not let him go.

"I will not release you unless you first give me your blessing," he said.

"What is your name?" the man asked.

"Jacob," was the answer.

Then the man spoke again, and suddenly Jacob knew it was an angel of the Lord speaking to him.

"Your name shall no longer be Jacob, but Israel, which means Prince of God," said the Lord's angel.

The reason the angel changed Jacob's name was that Jacob had wrestled with him so long to get his blessing. For this angel was the same as the one who had talked with Abraham and had told Abraham that God would destroy Sodom and Gomorrah. This man was an angel of the Lord.

"Tell me, I pray, your name," said Jacob.

The angel answered, "Why do you ask my name?"

And the angel blessed Jacob there.

Then Jacob said, in reverent awe, "I have seen God."

For that was as it seemed to him, when the angel spoke to him.

Jacob named the place Peniel, or Phanuel, which means "the face of God." For Jacob said, "I have seen God face to face."

As Jacob crossed the stream, the sun rose, and he was lame in his thigh where the angel of the Lord had touched him. He limped as he went on to rejoin his company.

20

The story of Jacob and Esau as friends

Jacob looked up and saw Esau coming, and four hundred men with him. Jacob took his eleven sons, and put some of them with the two handmaids and the others with Rachel and Leah, so that they might bring them to Esau when he came near. But Jacob went on ahead by himself to greet his brother, and as he went he bowed down to the ground seven times before him.

When Esau saw this he ran to meet Jacob and put his arms around him and kissed him, and they both wept.

When God commanded Jacob to leave Laban's house and go back to Canaan, He promised to be with Jacob and keep him from harm. God kept His promise, as He always does. He would not let Laban hurt Jacob or even speak unkindly to Jacob. Now He made Esau, the angry brother who had wanted to kill Jacob, feel so kindly toward him that when they met, Esau ran to Jacob and kissed him and wept.

When Esau saw the women and children, he asked who they were, and Jacob answered him.

"These are the children that God has sent to me and my wives," Jacob said.

Then the handmaids and Leah and Rachel came near, bringing the children with them, and they bowed down before Esau.

"And all the cattle that I met on the way here," said Esau. "You sent them on ahead of you, but I do not understand why you did so."

"These are a gift for you, my brother," Jacob answered. "I wanted to please you, and I thought that a present of some fine cattle might be acceptable to you."

But Esau did not want to take Jacob's cattle.

"I have flocks and herds of my own," said Esau. "You must keep what you have for yourself, my brother, for I already have ample for my needs."

But Jacob kept urging Esau to accept the gift of cattle, until at length the elder brother agreed to take them.

Then Esau wanted Jacob to go on his journey and wait no longer at that place; if Jacob would do this, Esau said, he would go with him. But Jacob told Esau that his children were young and weak and might easily be made sick. His flocks and herds had to be driven very carefully, because if they were made to go too far or too fast, for only one day, many of them would die. Jacob begged Esau to go on first by himself, and Jacob said he would come after him more slowly, as the children and cattle were able to bear it.

"At least let me leave some of my men with you," Esau then said. "They can help to drive your cattle, if you wish. Or, if robbers should attack you along the way, they could protect and defend you, so that no harm will come to your family."

"Thank you, my brother," said Jacob. "But truly, I do not need them."

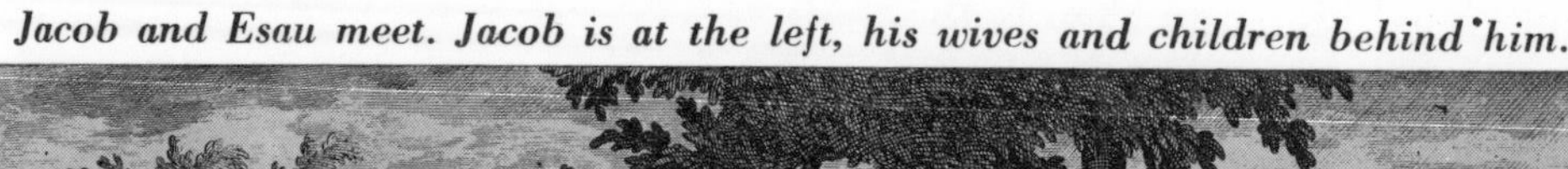

Jacob and Esau meet. Jacob is at the left, his wives and children behind him.

Esau and Jacob part

So Esau left Jacob and went away to his own home. After he had gone, Jacob went on his journey until he came to a place called Succoth; there he stopped and made sheds for the cattle to rest in. These were shelters, in former times called also *booths,* made out of the branches of trees. When his cattle had rested, Jacob left Succoth and came into the land of Canaan, to a place called Shechem.

The Story of Dinah and Shechem

At the time that Jacob reached the city of Shechem, his daughter Dinah—the daughter of Jacob and his wife Leah—was not quite sixteen years old. One day Dinah decided to go for a walk, so that she might make the acquaintance of some other young women in that part of the land.

As Dinah was walking alone, the son of Hamor, who was the king of the country, saw her—and he thought her most attractive. The young man's name was Shechem, and the city of Shechem was named for him. His people were one of the heathen tribes that inhabited Canaan at that time.

Dinah had been taught that she must not marry any man who did not worship God, so she did not want to meet Shechem, but he forced his attentions on her, and she was unable to defend herself against his superior strength. Shechem wanted very much to make Dinah his wife, and he spoke to his father, Hamor.

"Please arrange a marriage between me and this girl, Dinah," Shechem asked his father. "She is the daughter of Jacob."

Jacob had already learned of the treatment his daughter had suffered at the hands of Shechem. He told his sons, Dinah's brothers, when they returned from the field, where they were working.

When the sons of Jacob heard that their sister had been ill-treated by Shechem they were wildly angry and plotted to avenge Dinah's injury.

At about that time Hamor, Shechem's father, went to see Jacob. He pleaded with Jacob to allow Dinah to marry his son.

"My son loves her," he said. "Let them be married, and let our two nations be friends. Your young men can marry the daughters of our people, and our young men the daughters of your people. We will be one family. You can have our land for your own, and you will prosper."

Shechem added his plea to that of his father.

"Any dowry or marriage settlement you wish me to make, no matter how great, will be made, if only you will allow me to marry Dinah, whom I love dearly."

The sons of Jacob then did a very wicked thing. They pretended that they objected only to the fact that Shechem and his father were heathens, and did not worship the one true God.

"If you will accept our God, then we will allow our sister to marry Shechem," they said. "If not, then we will not allow the marriage."

Shechem and Hamor were quite satisfied with this arrangement. They and all the people of Shechem accepted Jacob's religion and worshiped Jacob's God. Yet one night a few days later, Dinah's brothers Simeon and Levi, with an army of Jacob's followers, attacked the city of Shechem and brutally killed every man and boy in the city. They killed both Hamor and his son Shechem. Then they took Dinah back to her father's tent.

Jacob was ashamed at the faithless behavior of his sons. He told them that they had made his name a thing of shame in all the land.

"The people of this land are far greater in number than my people,"

Dinah's brothers kill the Shechemites. The city was not nearly so elaborate.

said Jacob. "Surely they will destroy us all, as vengeance for this evil thing you have done."

"Should we let them go unpunished for treating our sister as Shechem did?" his sons asked him—and they did not repent of their sin.

Then God spoke to Jacob. God told Jacob to go up to Bethel and build an altar there. Bethel was the place where Jacob had his dream and saw the ladder reaching to heaven, with the angels going up and down on it. God had promised in that dream that He would be with Jacob wherever he went and would bring him back to Canaan; and now God had brought him back.

Jacob spoke to his wives, Rachel and Leah, and to his sons.

"Let us go up to Bethel, so that I may build an altar there to God," he said. "Many years ago, the Lord appeared to me there and promised to care for me wherever I might go. At that time I was fleeing from the anger of my brother, Esau, whom I had wronged. And the Lord has indeed cared well for me ever since."

Then Jacob, and his wives, and his sons, journeyed toward Bethel. There

After returning home, Jacob made the people surrender all their idols.

were cities in the land they passed through, but God made the people who lived in them afraid, so that they did not come out to do Jacob any harm. When they came to Bethel, Jacob and all his company, Jacob built an altar there and offered up a sacrifice to the Lord.

Rebekah, Jacob's mother, had a nurse named Deborah. Perhaps she was the same nurse that Rebekah had brought with her when she came into Canaan with Abraham's servant, to be Isaac's wife. Deborah, Rebekah's nurse, died, and they buried her under an oak at Bethel.

And God spoke to Jacob, and blessed him, and said again,

"Thy name shall not be called Jacob any more, but Israel shall be thy name." After this, the Bible sometimes speaks of Jacob as Israel.

God makes a promise to Jacob

God told Jacob also that He would give the land of Canaan to him, and to his descendants after he died, and that his descendants would be so many there would be whole nations of them, and that some of them would be kings. After He had talked to Jacob, God went up toward heaven. Jacob set up a pillar of stone at Bethel, so that it might always be remembered as the place where God had spoken to him.

Then Jacob left Bethel, and came near to Bethlehem, and there God gave him another son, whom Jacob named Benjamin. But Rachel, the little boy's mother, died before they came to Bethlehem, and they buried her on the way there. Jacob set up a pillar upon Rachel's grave to show where she was buried, and that pillar stood there for hundreds of years.

After these things Jacob came to Hebron, where his father lived; for Isaac, Jacob's father, was still alive. Though it had been so long a time since Isaac had become old and blind, and since he had sent Esau for the venison, that he might bless him, because he thought he was going to die, yet God had kept Isaac alive until Jacob came again. But after Jacob had come, and when Isaac was a hundred and eighty years old, he died; and Jacob and Esau buried him in the cave where Abraham and Sarah were buried.

Death of Isaac

Although Isaac had lived until the return of his son Jacob, Jacob's mother Rebekah had not lived. She had deceived her husband so many years before for the sake of Jacob, her favorite son, but she never saw Jacob again after she had sent him away for fear Esau would kill him.

After Isaac had died, Esau took his wives, and his sons, and his daughters, and his cattle, and all that he had in the land of Canaan, and went away to live in another country called Edom. For he and Jacob had so many cattle that there was not enough food for them all in the land where they both had lived.

The descendants of Esau were called Edomites, because they lived in Edom, the land of Esau. The descendants of Jacob were called Israelites, because of the new name Israel that the angel had given to Jacob after they wrestled.

21

The story of Joseph the dreamer

JACOB HAD TWELVE SONS. Benjamin, who was born near Bethlehem after Jacob came back to Canaan, was the youngest of them all. Joseph was next to the youngest. Benjamin and Joseph were the two sons of Rachel, the wife whom Jacob had loved so very dearly and for so many years. They were the only two sons she had before her death, on the journey to Canaan, when Benjamin was born.

When Joseph was seventeen years old, one day he went out in the field with his ten older brothers to feed his father's flocks. When Joseph came home, he told his father of some wicked things that his brothers had done. It was right for Joseph to tell his father about these things, so that his father might speak to Joseph's brothers and command them to do so no more.

Now Jacob loved Joseph more than all his other children. This was partly because God had given Joseph to him when he was an old man; but it was not only because of this that Jacob loved Joseph the most. It was also because Joseph was more obedient and kind than Jacob's other children. The Bible says that Jacob made Joseph a coat of many colors. We cannot be sure what kind of a coat this was, except that it was different from the coats Joseph's brothers wore and was more beautiful than theirs.

When Joseph's brothers saw how much their father loved him, they hated him and could not speak peaceably to him.

Then Joseph dreamed a dream and told it to his brothers (see the picture at page 87). It made them hate him even more.

"Let me tell you of a dream I have had," Joseph said to his older brothers. "I dreamed that we were all binding grain into sheaves, and my sheaf stood up straight. Then your sheaves bowed down before my sheaf."

Joseph's brothers were angry, because if their sheaves bowed down to Joseph's sheaf it seemed to mean that they were to bow down to Joseph.

"Does this mean that you are going to rule over us?" they demanded.

Joseph then dreamed another dream and told it to his brothers.

The dreams of Joseph

"I have had another dream," he said. "I dreamed that the sun, the moon, and eleven of the stars in heaven all bowed down to me."

Now there were just eleven of Joseph's brothers, so they thought the eleven stars meant them, and the sun and moon meant their father and their father's wife. They were displeased with Joseph, because he seemed to be boasting that some day he would be greater than they. Joseph told this same dream to his father and his father also found fault with him.

"My son," he said, "do you really believe that some day my wife and I, and all of your brothers, will be forced to bow down before you? This is not fitting."

Joseph's brothers went to feed their father's flock at Shechem, a city and surrounding land that were a long way from Hebron, where Jacob lived.

"Your brothers are tending the flocks in Shechem," said Jacob to Joseph. "Please go there and see if everything is all right with your brothers and with the flocks. Then come back and tell me what you have learned."

So Joseph left his home at Hebron and went to Shechem, where his brothers were supposed to be tending the flocks.

When Joseph came to Shechem, his brothers were not there. As he was wandering in the field, a man saw him.

"What are you seeking?" the man asked.

"I am looking for my brothers," Joseph answered. "Do you know where they have gone to feed their flocks?"

"They have left here," the man answered. "I heard them say they were going to Dothan."

Dothan was still farther off than Shechem, so Joseph went after his brothers and soon found them near Dothan. His brothers saw him coming, even while he was yet a good way off, and they began to talk with each other about killing him.

"Behold, this dreamer cometh"

"Look! the dreamer is coming," said one of the brothers. "Why do we not kill him and throw his body into a pit? Then we can say that a wild beast has killed and eaten him. After that, we shall see what becomes of all of his fine dreams!"

Joseph (shown in the center, held by two of his brothers) is cast into the pit.

When Reuben, Joseph's oldest brother, heard what the other brothers said, he wanted to save Joseph from them; so he persuaded them to put him into the pit without harming him.

"Place him in this pit, out here in the wilderness," Reuben said, "but do not hurt him."

Reuben thought that afterward he would come back, after the others had gone, and take Joseph out of the pit and take him home to their father.

The brothers agreed to do as Reuben said. When Joseph came to them, they stripped off his coat of many colors and took him and put him into the pit. There is often water at the bottom of deep pits in the ground, but this pit was dry; there was no water in it.

Then the brothers sat down to eat their food. But looking up, they saw some men, of the people called Ishmaelites, or Arabs, coming that way with their camels. These Ishmaelites were merchantmen who carried things to sell, and they were going to Egypt. When Judah, one of Joseph's brothers, saw them, he asked what good there would be in killing Joseph.

"Instead of killing him, which could make us no profit, why do we not

The Ishmaelites pay the twenty pieces of silver to Joseph's brothers.

sell him to the Ishmaelites?" Judah asked. Such men often bought human beings to sell as slaves, or servants, to rich people in Egypt.

The idea seemed good to Joseph's other brothers (except Reuben, who was not there) and they agreed to do it.

Then the Ishmaelites with their camels came by, and Joseph's brothers lifted him out of the pit and sold him to the Ishmaelites for twenty pieces of silver; and the Ishmaelites took Joseph and carried him into Egypt.

Reuben finds Joseph gone

Reuben, the brother who had wanted to take Joseph back to his father, was not there when his brothers sold him. Afterward Reuben went to the pit to find Joseph, and when he could not find him he was greatly distressed. He tore his clothes to show his grief.

"Joseph is gone," Reuben wailed. "Where can I go to look for him?"

The brothers had already planned how to fool their father Jacob. They took Joseph's coat, and killed a kid (a young goat), and dipped the coat in the kid's blood. They took the coat to their father and told him they had found it; he could tell, they said, whether it was Joseph's coat or not.

Jacob of course recognized Joseph's coat.

"It is indeed my son's coat," he cried. "It is evident that a wild beast has killed him and has torn him in pieces!"

Then Jacob tore his clothes. The men of that country dressed in clothes different from ours. A man wore a long coat, or sack, made of linen. It reached from the neck down below the knees and was fastened around the waist with a belt, or girdle. Over this coat a man wore a loose garment like a shawl or blanket. When in great distress a man sometimes took hold of his linen coat and tore it from the neck down to the girdle.

Jacob tore his clothes, because he thought Joseph was torn in pieces. Jacob put on sackcloth, too. Sackcloth was a dark, coarse kind of cloth that persons wore to show they were unhappy. Jacob was very unhappy for many days, and no one could persuade him to stop mourning. He said that he would mourn until he could go down into the grave to join Joseph; he meant until he himself should die.

Jacob faints when he sees the bloody robe of Joseph.

22

The story of Joseph as a slave

THE ISHMAELITES HAD TAKEN JOSEPH into Egypt. The king of that country was called Pharaoh, and the chief officer in Pharaoh's army was a man named Potiphar. Potiphar bought Joseph from the Ishmaelites, and Joseph became Potiphar's servant and lived in his house. The Lord helped Joseph to serve his master well, and Potiphar was very pleased with Joseph and set him over his other servants. Joseph had the care of Potiphar's house and of everything in it, for Potiphar trusted Joseph with all he had. And the Lord blessed Potiphar, and made Potiphar richer than ever before, because Joseph was with him.

Now, Potiphar had a wife who thought Joseph was a very handsome and likable young man. She was not a good woman. She forgot her duty to her husband and she had no respect for Joseph's sense of duty and honor toward her husband, who was Joseph's master.

"Come, Joseph," she often urged him. "Your master, Potiphar, is often away from the house. Why do you not pay some attention to me, while he is gone?"

"My master trusts me," Joseph would always reply. "I could not betray his trust."

"Come now," Potiphar's wife would persist. "Am I not attractive?"

"Indeed, my master's wife is most attractive," Joseph always said. "But she is my master's wife. This to me means that she must not be attractive to me."

Potiphar's wife grasps Joseph's robe as he runs from her.

Finally, one day when Joseph refused to accept her advances, the woman became very angry and seized the edge of Joseph's coat. As he pulled away from her, and fled from the house, the coat tore, so that she was holding most of it in her hand.

Joseph, falsely accused by Potiphar's wife, is arrested and imprisoned.

At this point she screamed, and called for help, pretending that Joseph had been rough with her and had attacked her.

Unfortunately for Joseph, Potiphar believed his wife. He thought that Joseph had been disloyal to the master who had treated him so kindly. Joseph was put into prison, and there he remained for a long time.

But the Lord was kind to Joseph and made the keeper of the prison his friend, so that the keeper set Joseph over the other prisoners just as Potiphar had set him over his other servants. The keeper gave the care of all the men in the prison to Joseph and did not watch over them any longer himself; he let Joseph do it for him. The Lord helped Joseph to do all things well.

Joseph in prison

At about this time, two of Pharaoh's servants had offended him. One was his chief baker, who attended to the cooking of his food, and the other was his chief butler, who carried his wine cup to him when he wanted to drink. Pharaoh was displeased with them both and he put them into the prison where Joseph was. Joseph had the care of them there.

Each of these servants of Pharaoh dreamed a dream the same night, and when Joseph came in to them in the morning, he saw that they looked sad.

"Why do you both look so sad this day?" Joseph asked.

"Each of us had a dream last night," they answered. "We do not know what our dreams meant, and there is no interpreter to tell us."

"Cannot God interpret all things?" Joseph rebuked them. "Perhaps if you tell me your dreams, God will give me the meaning, that I may tell you."

So the chief butler told his dream to Joseph. He said that he thought he saw a vine, and on the vine were three branches. While he was looking, buds came out on the branches, and very soon these buds changed into bunches of ripe grapes. The butler thought he was holding Pharaoh's wine cup in his hand, so he took the grapes and pressed the juice out of them into the cup, and gave the cup to Pharaoh, so that Pharaoh might drink. This was the chief butler's dream.

The butler's dream

Then Joseph interpreted the dream for the chief butler, for God showed Joseph what the dream meant. Joseph told the butler that the three branches the butler saw on the vine meant three days; for within three days, Pharaoh would send for his butler and take him out of prison and put him into the king's house again. There the butler would wait on the king and give the cup to him, as he used to do when he was butler before.

Then Joseph asked the chief butler to remember him when he had returned to the king's house, and to speak to Pharaoh about him, so that he might be taken out of prison. Joseph told the chief butler that he had been stolen away from the land of the Hebrews, that is, the land of Canaan; and since he had been in Egypt he had not done anything that they should have put him in prison for doing.

The baker's dream

When the chief baker saw that the butler's dream meant something good, he told Joseph his dream. He said that he thought he was carrying three baskets on his head, one above the other. In the highest basket were all kinds of cooked meats for Pharaoh, and the birds flew down and ate the meats out of the basket.

Then Joseph told the baker the interpretation of his dream, for again God had showed him what the dream meant.

The three baskets meant three days.

"Within three days," Joseph said, "Pharaoh will command that you be hanged, and your body will be devoured by birds of the air, who will eat your flesh after you are dead."

All came true as Joseph said. Three days later the king celebrated his birthday and made a feast for all his servants. He sent for the chief butler and brought him back to the palace again, and once more the butler gave the wine cup into Pharaoh's hand, as he had done when he was butler before. But Pharaoh hanged the chief baker, as Joseph had said he would.

The chief butler, when he had been taken back to the king's house, did not remember Joseph and speak to Pharaoh about him. The chief butler forgot all the kindness that Joseph had shown to him in prison.

Joseph, in prison, tells Pharaoh's butler and baker the meaning of their dreams.

23

The story of Pharaoh's dream

AFTER JOSEPH HAD BEEN IN PRISON two whole years, Pharaoh dreamed a dream. He dreamt that he stood by the river in Egypt (the Nile) and he saw seven cows come up out of the water. They were fat and healthy-looking, and they went into a meadow and ate the grass there. After them came up seven other cows, but these were thin and starved-looking. The thin and starved-looking cows ate up those that were fat and healthy-looking. Then Pharaoh awoke.

Then Pharaoh slept and dreamed again. He dreamt that he saw seven ears of corn grow up on one stalk. They were all good ears, filled with grain. After them came up seven bad ears that were spoiled and had no good grain in them. The seven bad ears ate up the seven good ears. Again Pharaoh awoke and found that it was a dream.

In the morning Pharaoh was troubled. He sent for all the wise men of Egypt and told them his dreams; but they could not tell him what his dreams meant.

Then the chief butler spoke.

"I remember, at the time when you were angry with me and the chief baker, and had put us in prison, there was a young man in prison who interpreted our dreams for us. We had both dreamed on the same night, and those things that the young man told us all came true, most completely."

So Pharaoh sent for Joseph; and Pharaoh's soldiers brought Joseph quickly out of prison, and Joseph shaved himself, and put on clean clothes, and came to Pharaoh.

"I have dreamed a dream," said Pharaoh to Joseph. "No one here can interpret it, and I have heard that you know well how to interpret dreams."

"It is not I, but the Lord, Who gives the meanings of dreams," Joseph answered him. "The Lord has sometimes allowed me to see what He means by dreams, but it is always God Who interprets."

Then Pharaoh told Joseph his dreams: the one in which he thought he stood by the bank of the river, and saw the seven bad cows eat up the seven good ones; and after they had eaten them, no person could have told they had eaten anything, for they were as thin and starved-looking as before. Pharaoh also told Joseph his dream about the ears of corn.

Joseph said that the king's two dreams both meant the same thing, and that God had shown Pharaoh in these dreams what He was going to do.

"The seven good cows and the seven good ears of corn," said Joseph, "mean seven years. The seven bad cows and seven bad ears of corn mean seven other years."

Joseph explains Pharaoh's dream.

The meaning of Pharaoh's dreams

First there would come seven good years in Egypt, when the grain would grow well and there would be plenty for the people to eat. But after those seven good years would come seven bad years, when the people would not have enough bread, because there would be a famine in all the land.

Then Joseph told Pharaoh to look for some wise man who could attend to saving up the grain for him in the seven good years. Then, when the bad years should come, the people would have bread to eat and would not starve.

"I shall do as you have said," Pharaoh told Joseph. "But since it was you who interpreted the dreams, and told of all the things that are to happen, surely there can be no wiser man than you, nor one better suited to attend to this matter. You shall take charge of saving up the grain for the people of my land."

Joseph is made great in Egypt

So Pharaoh did not send Joseph back to prison, but instead Pharaoh made Joseph a great man. Pharaoh took off the ring from his hand and put it on Joseph's hand; and Pharaoh dressed Joseph in rich clothing and put a gold chain around his neck. Pharaoh made Joseph ride in a chariot that was almost as fine as Pharaoh's chariot; and as Joseph rode along, the people had to cry out, "Bow the knee." So Pharaoh made Joseph ruler over all the land of Egypt.

Pharaoh said that every man in Egypt must do as Joseph commanded him. Also, Pharaoh gave Joseph a wife named Asenath, the daughter of a priest. Joseph was thirty years old when he interpreted Pharaoh's dreams.

Joseph went out over all the land and attended to saving up the grain for Pharaoh. In the seven good years it grew well. When it was ripe and cut down, the people had much more than they could eat. Joseph took a part of all the grain that had grown and had it carried into the cities that were nearest the fields where it grew. He put the grain away in buildings called storehouses, so that it might be kept safe until the seven years of famine came. Joseph saved up very much grain in this way until he stopped counting how much, for there was more of it than anyone could count.

During this time, God gave Joseph and his wife two sons. One of the sons Joseph named Manasseh, the other Ephraim.

Joseph as governor requires the Egyptians to bring in their grain for storage.

Then the seven good years ended, and the seven bad years began. The famine was not only in the land of Egypt, it was in other lands besides; but in Egypt there was enough food, because Joseph had saved up the grain before the famine came.

The famine begins

When the people had nothing to eat, they cried to Pharaoh for bread.

"Go and see Joseph," said Pharaoh. "He is in charge of all the grain of Egypt. Whatever he tells you, you must do. If Joseph says you may have grain, you may have it."

Joseph opened all the storehouses where the grain was kept, and he sold the grain to the Egyptians. People came from other countries also to buy grain, because the famine was in the countries where they lived.

24

The story of Joseph and his brothers

NOW JOSEPH'S BROTHERS WERE STILL LIVING in the land of Canaan. It had been many years since they had sold Joseph to the Ishmaelites, and they did not know what had become of him, but they thought he was dead.

When the famine reached Canaan, Joseph's brothers wanted bread for their father Jacob and for their little children to eat. They looked at one another as if they did not know where they could get it, or what they should do.

"Why do you merely stand there, looking at each other?" Jacob asked his sons. "I have heard that there is plenty of grain in Egypt. Go there and buy grain for us, so that we may have bread and not starve."

Ten of Joseph's brothers set out from Canaan to buy grain in Egypt. Only Benjamin, Joseph's youngest brother, remained with his father, for Jacob was afraid that some harm might befall him if the boy went to that distant land.

Joseph's brothers arrived in Egypt at the same time as many other persons who had gone there to buy grain, for the famine was in all the countries around Egypt.

Joseph was now governor over Egypt. It was he who sold the grain to the people. When his brothers arrived in Egypt they went and bowed down before Joseph with their faces to the earth. Joseph saw them and recognized them, but pretended that he did not.

"What land do you come from?" he asked them.

"From the land of Canaan, to buy food," they answered.

Though Joseph knew his brothers, they did not know him; nor could they have imagined that it was their brother, whom they had sold to the Ishmaelites so many years before to be a lowly slave, who was now the master of all Egypt.

Joseph spoke roughly to them.

"You are enemies, and spies!" he exclaimed. "You have come to find out if Egypt is weak because of the famine, and if it would be easy for a conqueror to capture the country at this time."

"Oh, no," they replied, aghast that they should be so accused. "We are not spies. It is just as we said. We have come only to buy food, so that our families will not starve. We are all the sons of one man, in the land of Canaan."

Joseph pretended not to believe them. He insisted again that they were spies. But it was not because he was angry that he spoke roughly to them. He wanted to make sure that they would not know him. He was soon going to be very kind to them, for Joseph was a good man and willing to forgive his brothers for their unkindness to him.

Then they told Joseph that they were all brothers, and that their father had had twelve sons. One of them, they said, was with their father, in the land of Canaan—that was Benjamin—and one, they said, "was not." They meant that he was dead. The one that they told Joseph was dead was Joseph himself.

Yet Joseph still pretended not to believe them. He said he would find out whether they spoke the truth or not, and this was the way he would do it: One of them would have to go home to Canaan and bring their youngest brother to Egypt. All the rest must stay until that one came back. Joseph then put his brothers in prison for three days.

Joseph's cruelty to his brothers

On the third day, Joseph had his brothers brought to him and spoke to them again. This time Joseph said that only one of the brothers need stay. The rest might go home to take grain for their families to eat. Yet they must leave one brother in Egypt, a prisoner, so that Joseph might be sure that the others would come back and bring their youngest brother with them.

When Joseph's brothers heard him say this, and saw that he was in earnest and meant to do as he said, they were in great distress. They did not know it was their brother Joseph who spoke to them and had put them

Joseph's brothers appear before him to plead for food, not knowing who he is.

in prison. They thought that God was punishing them for their sin in selling their brother Joseph to the Ishmaelites so long ago. They talked with each other about it and confessed how wicked they had been.

One of Joseph's brothers, the oldest, was named Reuben. It was Reuben who had intended to take Joseph out of the pit and save his life, so many years before, and who had found Joseph gone when he returned. Now Reuben spoke sorrowfully to his brothers.

"Did I not tell you, when you treated Joseph cruelly so long ago, that you were committing a wicked sin for which you would be punished? You would not listen to me then, and now trouble has come upon all of us. It is because of the wickedness you committed against Joseph then."

Joseph heard them talking together. They talked freely in his presence, for they thought he could not understand what they said. They thought Joseph could not understand their Hebrew language, but could understand only Egyptian, for he had talked with them only in the Egyptian language and when he did so he had an interpreter to explain what he said.

Of course, Joseph understood every word that they spoke. In fact, he had to go away from them so that they might not see the effect that their words had on him, for what they said made him weep. Afterward he came back and talked to them again.

Still Joseph pretended to think his brothers were spies. He took Simeon, one of his brothers, and put him in prison, and all the rest saw him do it. Simeon was to stay in Egypt while the others went home to get Benjamin and bring him back to Joseph.

Then Joseph commanded his servants to fill his brothers' sacks with grain, and to put the money that each one had paid back again into his sack. He did not tell his brothers of this, and they did not know that their money had been put back; but Joseph would not accept money for feeding his own family.

When their asses were loaded, all of the brothers except Simeon started on the journey to their home in Canaan. On the way, they came to an inn on the road, where travelers could stop to rest. Here, as one of the brothers opened his sack to give his ass some food out of it, he saw his money.

"Look," he said. "My money is in my sack—the money with which we paid for the grain!"

Then all the brothers were afraid, for they did not know who had put the money there.

The brothers continued on their journey. Finally they came to Jacob, their father, in the land of Canaan. They told Jacob of the things that had happened to them while they were gone.

"Pharaoh's chief lord thought we were spies," they told their father. "He spoke roughly to us and thought us enemies.

"We told him we were not spies," they continued, "but that all of us were the sons of one man. We told him that we had one brother who was no longer living and another, younger, brother who had remained with our father in Canaan. Then he said he would test us, to find out whether we were indeed speaking the truth. He ordered us to take food for our families and then to bring back to him our younger brother. If we did this, he said he would give our brother Simeon, whom we left as hostage, back to us, and we would be permitted to buy more grain in the land of Egypt; but if we did not come back with Benjamin, our brother Simeon would die."

When they came to empty the grain out of their sacks, the brothers found that every man's bundle of money, which he had paid for the corn, had been put back into his sack. They and their father saw the bundles of money and were afraid. Jacob reproached his sons for taking his children from him; Joseph was gone, and Simeon was gone, and now they wanted to take Benjamin away.

Joseph's brother Reuben had two sons of his own. He offered his sons as hostage for Benjamin, if only Jacob would allow him to take the youngest brother to Egypt.

"Let me take Benjamin," he begged his father. "I promise to bring him back safely to you."

"Do not ask this of me," said Jacob. "My son Joseph is dead, and now Simeon is gone. Would you have me lose Benjamin as well? This would be greater trouble than I could bear."

So Joseph's brother Simeon remained a prisoner in Egypt, bound to die if the other brothers did not bring back Benjamin; but the old father, Jacob, would not let Benjamin go.

25

The story of Joseph and Benjamin

NOW THE FAMINE WAS VERY DREADFUL in the land of Canaan. When all the grain that had been brought out of Egypt was eaten, Jacob asked his sons to go again to Egypt and buy more food.

Judah told his father Jacob that they would go and buy food if Jacob would let Benjamin go with them; but if he would not let Benjamin go, the brothers would not go again to Egypt; for the man, the lord of the country, had said to them,

"You shall not be allowed to see my face again unless your brother is with you."

Then Jacob asked his sons why they were so unkind to him as to tell the man they had another brother. They explained how this had happened.

"When the man asked us if our father were still living, and if we had another brother at home, how could we dream that he would tell us we must bring that other brother to him also?"

Judah told Jacob, his father, to send Benjamin with him, under his care. Then, he said, the brothers would go, so that their people would not starve and so they would have food for their father and themselves and their children. Judah said he would watch over Benjamin and that no harm would happen to him. Jacob should trust Benjamin to him, Judah said, and if he did not bring Benjamin back safely, then he, Judah, would bear the blame forever.

Then their father, Jacob, told them that if it must be so, if they must take Benjamin, they must do so; and they had better take also a present to the lord in Egypt.

"Do this," he said. "Take some of the best fruits of the land, and take the lord a present, a little balm, and a little honey, spices and myrrh, nuts and almonds. Take more money with you, and take the money that was brought back in your sacks. Perhaps it was a mistake. Take also your brother, and go again to the man."

Jacob prayed for his sons, that God would make the man kind to them; for, he said, if his children were taken away from him, he would be left lonely and sorrowful indeed.

So the brothers took the present, and the money, and Benjamin, and went to Egypt and stood before Joseph again. When Joseph saw Benjamin with them, he said to his steward who took care of his house,

"Bring these men to my house and make ready, for they shall eat dinner with me at noon."

The servant did as Joseph commanded; but the brothers were afraid when they came to Joseph's house. They said to one another that it was because they had carried the money home in their sacks the first time they were brought there, and that now Joseph was going to blame them for it, so that he might make them his slaves.

The brothers approached Joseph's steward, and talked with him at the door of the house. They wanted very much to make him understand.

"The first time we came here," they explained, "it was only to buy food, for our families were starving in Canaan. We were quite astonished when we found the money in our sacks. We have brought all that money back, and more money as well, to buy grain. But still we do not know who put the money in our sacks. We know only that we found it when we reached home."

Joseph's steward told them not to fear. He brought Simeon out of prison to them; this was the brother who had been left in prison in Egypt while the other brothers went home to Canaan. The steward gave the brothers water to wash their feet, and he gave food to the asses on which they had ridden. The brothers made ready the present they had brought for Joseph, to give it to him when he came home at noon, for they had heard that they were to stay and eat dinner there.

When Joseph came back to his house, they brought his present to him and bowed themselves down to the earth.

Joseph spoke kindly to them and said,

"Is your father well, the old man of whom you spoke? Is he still alive?"

"Thy servant, our father, is in good health, he is still alive," they answered.

And the brothers bowed down to him again.

Then Joseph saw his brother Benjamin, and said,

"Is this your younger brother of whom you spoke? May God be good to thee, my son."

Then Joseph made haste to find a place where he might go and weep, and he went into his chamber and wept there, because he was so full of joy at seeing his young brother. (Benjamin was his only full brother, the only other son of his mother Rachel.) Afterward he washed his face, and came out, and kept back the tears, so that his brothers could not tell he had been weeping.

Joseph gives a feast for his brothers

Joseph told his servants to set food on the table, and they put food for Joseph in one place, to eat by himself; and for his brothers in another place, to eat by themselves (for the Egyptian and Hebrew religions did not permit them to eat the same food). Joseph wanted now to pretend that he was an Egyptian. When his brothers came to take their seats, they found that the oldest one had the first seat, and the next oldest the next seat, and so they were all placed according to their ages. Then they wondered how Joseph could have known their ages, so as to place their seats in that way.

Joseph sent food to his brothers from his own table, but to Benjamin he sent five times as much as to any of the others. He loved Benjamin more than the others because Joseph and Benjamin had the same mother. All of the brothers had the same father, Jacob, but they had different mothers; and Joseph and Benjamin were the only ones who had Rachel for their mother. Rachel had died long before, and Jacob had buried her on the journey to Bethlehem.

Joseph's brothers ate and drank with him in his house, but they did not know it was Joseph.

Then Joseph commanded the steward of his house to fill the men's sacks with food, as much as they could carry, and to put every man's money back in his sack, as had been done when they had come to Egypt before.

"And put my cup, the silver cup," he said, "in the sack of the youngest."

The steward did as Joseph commanded. In the morning, as soon as it was light, the brothers started on their journey back to Canaan. When they had left the city, but were not far off, Joseph told his steward to follow them and ask why they had taken his silver cup. So the steward followed, and when he came up to them he asked as Joseph had told him.

Benjamin is accused of stealing

The brothers were very much surprised. They wondered why the steward spoke such words to them.

"God forbid," they said, "that we should do such a thing as to steal your master's cup. We brought back the money that we found in our sacks when we went home to Canaan the first time. We could have kept it if we had chosen to do so, but we brought it back of our own accord. Having done this, would we now take from your master's house silver or gold that does not belong to us? If one of us has taken the cup, you may put that one to death, and the rest of us will be your slaves."

"The one who has taken the cup shall be my servant," the steward answered, "but the rest shall not be blamed."

Joseph's cup is found in the sack of his brother Benjamin.

Each of the brothers then quickly took down his sack from the back of the ass, and rested it on the ground; every man opened his sack so that the steward could look into it. The steward looked, beginning with the sack of the oldest, and continuing until he reached the sack of the youngest; there he found the cup in Benjamin's sack. The brothers tore their clothes with grief, but they would not abandon their young brother Benjamin. All eleven of them loaded their asses and returned with the steward to the city.

Probably Joseph was simply testing his older brothers, to see if they would be as cruel to their young brother Benjamin as once they had been to him.

26

The story of how Joseph revealed himself

WHEN THE BROTHERS CAME TO JOSEPH'S HOUSE, Joseph was still there. They all fell down and bowed to him, with their heads touching the ground.

Joseph pretended to think they had really stolen his cup. He asked if they did not know he would find it out.

Then Judah spoke to Joseph, saying,

"What can we say? What shall we do that we may not be punished? God has found out our wickedness; we are all your servants."

Joseph answered, "Only the one who had the cup shall be my slave. As for the rest, you may go home to your father."

Then Judah asked Joseph to let him speak, and Joseph listened.

Judah said that when the brothers came into Egypt the first time Joseph had asked if they had a father and a brother at home in the country where they lived. (Of course, he did not use the name Joseph; he did not yet know that this Egyptian lord was actually his brother Joseph.) The brothers had told him they had a father, an old man, and also a brother who was only a boy, and that their father loved the boy, for the boy's mother was dead and his only brother was dead. And Joseph had told them to bring that younger brother down to Egypt so that he might see him. Then they had answered that the boy could not leave his father, for if he did so the father would die of grief. Joseph had told them that if they did not bring their brother, they would never see his face again. So when they went home to their father, they told him what Joseph had said. After a while their father wanted them to go to Egypt again to buy a little more food. But they had said to him,

"We cannot go unless our youngest brother goes with us, for we may not see the man unless Benjamin is with us."

Then their father had told them that if they took Benjamin, and any harm should happen to him while they were gone, he would die of sorrow. All this Judah explained.

Now, Judah said, if he went home without Benjamin, when their father saw that Benjamin was not with them, he would die. Judah had promised to bring Benjamin back safely to his father, and had told his father that if he did not bring him back he would bear the blame forever. Then Judah begged Joseph to let him stay and be a slave in Benjamin's place and to let Benjamin go home to his father.

Joseph is overcome and weeps

Then Joseph could hide himself from them no longer, and he commanded all his servants to go out of the room, so that no one was left there but Joseph and his brothers. Joseph wept out loud, and his brothers heard him and saw him weeping. And Joseph said to them,

"I am Joseph; does my father still live?"

But they were afraid and could not answer him. And Joseph said,

"Come near to me, I pray you."

They came near; and Joseph said,

"I am Joseph, your brother, whom you sold into Egypt."

Then he told them not to be troubled, nor angry with themselves, because they had sold him. It had been God's plan. God had sent him into Egypt to save the people and to keep them from starving in the famine.

Joseph did not mean that his brothers did right when they sold him. He meant that God had made good to come out of the evil that they had done. Joseph told his brothers this so that they might not be unhappy and afraid, for he loved them and had forgiven their unkindness to him. He did not want them to be unhappy now, when he was so glad to see them once more.

Joseph told them that the famine had been in Egypt two years, and would be there five years longer. In those years there would be no harvest or planting of seed in the ground, for God had said the famine would last that long. Joseph told his brothers that God had sent him into Egypt before them to keep them from starving. Then he said,

"Make haste to go back to our father Jacob in Canaan and tell him that God has made me ruler over all Egypt. Tell him to come down to me, and he shall live in the best part of the land, and be near to me; he and his children, his flocks and his herds, and all that he has. I will take care of him."

Joseph reveals himself to his brothers.

Joseph also said to his brothers,

"You shall tell my father of all my greatness in Egypt, and of all that you have seen, and you shall make haste and bring my father here."

Joseph embraced his brother Benjamin and wept, for he was more glad to see him than he could tell; and Benjamin wept also. Then Joseph kissed all his brothers and wept, and afterward they talked with him.

When Pharaoh heard that Joseph's brothers had come, it pleased him. He told Joseph to tell them they should load their beasts and go back to the land of Canaan, and get their father, their wives, and their children, and bring them to him. They should take wagons for their wives and children to ride in, and they should bring their families and come; but they need bring nothing else, Pharaoh said, for it was the same as if all the good things in the land of Egypt belonged to them.

Pharaoh invites the Israelites

JACOB IS TOLD OF JOSEPH

The brothers soon set out for the land of Canaan. Joseph gave them wagons, as Pharaoh had commanded, and food to eat while they were gone. To all of them he gave fine clothing, and to Benjamin he gave more than to any of the others and also three hundred pieces of silver. To his father he sent twenty asses loaded with bread and meat and other good things from the country of Egypt. Then Joseph sent his brothers to their own home, and told them not to quarrel with one another on the way.

So the brothers went up out of Egypt. When they came to their father in Canaan they said to him,

"Joseph is still alive, and is governor over all the land of Egypt."

This seemed too wonderful to be true, and Jacob did not believe them; yet when he heard all the kind words that Joseph had spoken, and saw the wagons that Pharaoh had sent to carry him, Jacob believed what his sons told him; and he said,

"It is enough. Joseph, my son, is still alive; I will go and see him before I die."

Jacob is told by Joseph's brothers that he is alive in Egypt.

Jacob sets off for Egypt: The interpretation of Gustave Doré. It is probably not wholly accurate, since it shows Jacob on a camel and does not show the carts Pharaoh had sent so that Jacob and his sons' wives could ride in comfort.

Jacob, meeting his son Joseph, was so glad to see him alive, that he felt as though there was nothing else he need stay for in this world; he felt willing to die.

27

The story of Jacob in the land of Pharaoh

JACOB LEFT HIS HOME IN CANAAN and went on the journey to the land of Egypt. When he came to Beersheba, where his father, Isaac, had built an altar many years before, Jacob stopped and offered up sacrifices to God. God spoke to him in the night, calling,

"Jacob, Jacob!"

Jacob answered, "Here I am."

God said, "Do not fear to go down into Egypt, for I will there make of your people a great nation."

By a nation was meant, in those days, a great many people who were descended from one man and who lived together in the same country. God said He would make Jacob's descendants so many, while they were in Egypt, that they would be a great nation there. He told Jacob He would go down with him to take care of him, and that when the time came for him to die, Joseph would be at his side.

So Jacob left Beersheba. His sons took him, and their wives and their children, in the wagons that Pharaoh had sent to carry them. They took their cattle and all that belonged to them in Canaan, and went into Egypt—Jacob and all his children with him, his sons and their sons and daughters; they did not leave one behind. Sixty-six of Jacob's descendants, that is, of his children and his grandchildren, were with him. Joseph and his sons made three more—that was sixty-nine; and Jacob himself made seventy, altogether, of the family of Israel that left their former home and settled in Egypt.

Jacob sent Judah, his son, to go on before him and tell Joseph that his father was coming. When Joseph heard it he got into his chariot and rode

Joseph introduces his father and five of his brothers to Pharaoh.

out to meet his father. And when Joseph met Jacob, Joseph went to him, and embraced him, and wept with joy.

Jacob said to Joseph,

"Now I am willing to die, since I have seen your face and know you are still alive."

Jacob was so glad to see Joseph, and to know he was still alive, that he felt as though there was nothing else he need stay for in this world; he felt willing to die. But he lived happily for seventeen years more.

Now Joseph told his brothers that he would go and tell Pharaoh they had come and had brought their flocks and their herds with them. He said that when Pharaoh called them to him, and asked what kind of work they had been used to, they should tell him that they had always taken care of sheep and cattle, and that their fathers also had taken care of sheep and cattle. Joseph told them to say this because it was the truth, and because he wanted Pharaoh to let them live in Goshen, which was the best part of the land of Egypt for feeding cattle.

The land of Goshen is given

Joseph went to Pharaoh and said,

"My father and my brothers, and their flocks and herds, and all that they have, have come out of the land of Canaan, and they are in the land of Goshen."

Joseph took five of his brothers and introduced them to Pharaoh. When Pharaoh asked them what kind of work they were used to, they answered him as Joseph had told them. They said that they had come to stay for a while in Egypt, because there was no food for their flocks in the land of Canaan, the famine was so dreadful there. They begged Pharaoh to let them live in Goshen.

Pharaoh spoke to Joseph, and said that his father and his brothers might live in the best part of the land of Egypt, which was Goshen. Pharaoh also told Joseph that if any of his brothers were especially industrious men he would let them take care of his own cattle; for Pharaoh had many cattle of his own.

After this Joseph brought Jacob, his father, to Pharaoh, and Jacob blessed Pharaoh. Pharaoh asked Jacob how old he was, and Jacob said he was a hundred and thirty years old. Jacob called these hundred and thirty years the "years of his pilgrimage." A pilgrim is a person going on a journey to a holy place. Jacob had been going on a journey all those hundred and thirty years, a journey through life to heaven.

So Joseph gave his father and his brothers a place in which to live, in the land of Goshen, as Pharaoh had commanded him. Joseph was very kind to them and made sure they and their children had as much food as they needed.

28

The story of the famine in Egypt

STILL THE FAMINE WAS VERY DREADFUL in Egypt and in Canaan, and the people had no bread to eat. They came to Joseph to buy grain until they had given him all their money, and he gave the money to Pharaoh. After they had given all their money, the Egyptians still came and asked Joseph for bread. They could not pay, they said, for they had no more money; he had already taken it all for Pharaoh.

Joseph told them to bring their cattle, and they did so. For their cattle he gave them bread—enough to last them through that year.

When the year was ended the people came to Joseph again. They told him their money was spent and they had given him all their cattle; so they had nothing left to give but their lands and themselves. They said they would give their lands to Pharaoh, and they would become Pharaoh's slaves, if Joseph would let them have bread. Joseph gave them more bread, and in this way he bought all the land of Egypt for Pharaoh and made slaves of all the people of Egypt except the priests. Then he sent the people to the different cities to be fed, for the grain was stored in those cities.

At last the seven years of famine were ended and Joseph gave the people seed to plant in the ground, because he knew now the grain would grow again. He told the people that as they had sold all their land to Pharaoh, it was not their own any longer; yet Pharaoh was willing to let them keep it if, when the grain grew, they would give a fifth part of it to him. The people answered that Joseph was the one who had saved them from starving, and therefore they were willing to do as he said.

So the famine was over in Egypt, but Joseph's brothers still lived in the land of Goshen; and they and their children came to be a good many people. Jacob, their father, lived with them for seventeen years; then the time came near for him to die. He called Joseph and told him that he did not wish to be buried in Egypt, but in Canaan; and he made Joseph promise that he would carry his dead body up to that land and bury him there.

29

The story of Jacob's blessing and death

SOON AFTER THIS, someone came to Joseph and said, "Your father is dying." Joseph took his two sons, Manasseh and Ephraim, and went to the house where his father was.

When Jacob heard that Joseph had come, he made ready to see him, and sat up on his bed. Jacob talked with Joseph. He told Joseph how God had spoken to him and blessed him many years before, when he had his dream in the land of Canaan. Then Jacob told Joseph that Ephraim and Manasseh were like his own sons to him; that is, Jacob took Joseph's sons to be his sons. When Jacob knew that the boys were there, he asked Joseph to bring them to him that he might bless them.

Jacob was very old, and his eyes were dim. When Joseph brought his sons, Jacob could not see them but he put his arms around them and kissed them. He said that he used to think he would never see Joseph again, but now God had let him see not only Joseph but Joseph's children too.

Joseph bowed down with his face to the earth before his father, and he took his two sons and brought them to his father. Jacob stretched out his hands and laid his right hand on Ephraim's head and his left hand on Manasseh's head, to bless them. Jacob blessed both the sons of Joseph, and he also blessed Joseph. Then he called all his other sons, and blessed each one of them, and told them he was going to die but that God would be with them and would at last bring them back to the land of Canaan.

Jacob called all his sons and blessed each one of them.

Jacob commanded his sons to bury him in the land of Canaan, in the cave in the field that Abraham had bought from Ephron the Hittite.

"There," said Jacob, "they buried Abraham and Sarah, his wife; there they buried Isaac and Rebekah, his wife; and there I buried Leah."

After Jacob had finished speaking to his sons, he lifted his feet up into the bed and died.

Joseph put his face down to his father's face and wept over him and kissed him. He commanded the physicians to embalm his father. To embalm a dead person was to put spices and various chemicals into his body, to keep it from decaying and going to dust too rapidly. Joseph's servants embalmed Jacob. The Israelites and even the Egyptians mourned for him seventy days.

Joseph sent word to Pharaoh that his father, before he died, had made him promise not to bury him in Egypt, but in his own sepulchre in the land of Canaan, and he asked permission of Pharaoh to go and bury him there; afterward, Joseph said, he would come back to Egypt. Pharaoh told him to do as he had promised.

The great funeral of Jacob

So Joseph went up to bury Jacob, and with him went all Pharaoh's chief officials and many other great men from the land of Egypt. Joseph's brothers also went; only their children and their flocks and their herds stayed behind. There were hundreds of people in Jacob's funeral procession. Some went in chariots and there were many men riding on horses. Jacob's sons did as he had commanded them, for they carried him into Canaan and buried him in the cave that Abraham had bought from Ephron the Hittite. Afterward Joseph went back into Egypt, with all those who had gone to Canaan with him.

After their father was dead, Joseph's brothers began to fear him again. They said, among themselves, that now Joseph would surely punish them for the evil they had done to him so long before. They sent a messenger to Joseph, to tell him that his father left word, before he died, asking Joseph to forgive them.

Joseph's brothers fear him

When Joseph heard his brothers' words he wept, for he knew they had sent that message because they were afraid of him. The brothers came and bowed before Joseph, saying,

"We are your servants."

But Joseph told them not to be afraid, for though they had intended to do him harm, God meant to do good by sending him into Egypt, that he

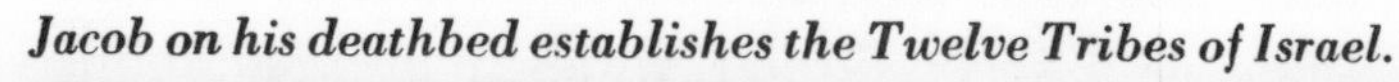

Jacob on his deathbed establishes the Twelve Tribes of Israel.

Burial of Jacob in the cave at Machpelah. His body, mummified in accordance with Egyptian custom, had been bound in about three hundred yards of cloth.

might save many people from starving in the famine. And Joseph said to his brothers,

"I will take care of you and of your children."

And he spoke kindly to them and comforted them.

Joseph and his brothers stayed in Egypt, and Joseph lived until Ephraim's sons and Manasseh's sons were grown up and had children of their own, so Joseph was a great-grandfather. But after many years, Joseph told his brothers that he was soon going to die. Some day, Joseph said, God would certainly come to the children of Israel (that is, to all of Jacob's descendants), and would lead them out of Egypt into that land which He had promised Abraham, and Isaac, and Jacob, that He would give them. Joseph meant the land of Canaan. Joseph made the children of Israel promise that when God took them there they would take his dead body with them and bury him with his ancestors.

Joseph died when he was a hundred and ten years old, and they embalmed him and put him in a coffin in Egypt.

30

The story of the Israelites as slaves

HUNDREDS OF YEARS PASSED AWAY. Joseph was long dead, and all his brothers. A new generation of Israelites now lived in Egypt. There were very many, and the country was full of them. There may have been as many as three million Israelites in Egypt.

A new king ruled over Egypt. His name was Pharaoh, like the one who had been so kind to Joseph: but this Pharaoh had never known Joseph. And when he saw how many there were of the people of Israel, he was afraid of them. He feared that some day, if enemies should come and make war against Egypt, the people of Israel might help them, and afterward would rise up and go out of his land. He did not want them to do this. He wanted them to stay and work for him.

This wicked king persuaded the people of Egypt to treat the people of Israel very cruelly. They set harsh taskmasters over them, and made their lives unhappy by forcing them to labor as slaves, building houses and cities and doing all kinds of work in the field (see picture at page 150).

The more cruelly the Israelites were treated, the more there came to be of them, for God had promised Jacob, when he was coming down into Egypt, to make his descendants a great nation there; and now God was doing as He had promised. He was making them so many that they would be a great nation.

God had told Abraham that his people would be prisoners in a foreign land for four hundred years, and this was the time of the captivity. God knew how much of that time had passed, however, and soon the four hundred years would be over. Then the Israelites would be able to live in the land God had promised them, through Abraham—the land of Canaan.

Pharaoh soon saw that hard labor and his cruel taskmasters had not the least effect on the numbers of the Israelites. They still had many children.

Pharaoh determined to reduce those numbers, and he struck on a very wicked plan.

Pharaoh told the midwives, the women who took care of the Israelites' newborn babies, to kill all the boy babies as soon as they were born. The girls he was willing to let live, because they would never be able to fight against him.

But the Egyptian midwives feared God and would not obey the king. They let the little boys live also, and God blessed them for doing it.

When his plan failed to succeed, and the Israelites continued to increase, Pharaoh decided upon another plan, just as wicked as the first. Pharaoh told his people to take the little boys of the people of Israel and throw them into the river, to drown them. The little girls, he said, they might allow to live.

No people were ever unhappier than the Israelites when this cruel order was given. The Israelites hid and guarded their little sons in every way imaginable. Nevertheless thousands of babies were drowned in the Nile every year. But there was one who was saved, and this was God's will be-

The Hebrews, or Israelites, in captivity in Egypt, driven by Egyptians with whips.

cause God had chosen this Israelite boy not only to be saved himself but to save all the people of Israel.

The name of this Israelite boy was Moses. All the five first books of the Bible are called the Books of Moses, because they were either told by Moses while he was alive or were told about Moses after his death. The second of these books is called *Exodus,* which means "the going out"—that is, the time when the Israelites, led by Moses, went out from the land of Egypt toward the Promised Land, the land of Canaan. We are now telling the story of the Exodus, and in the next story you will read about Moses, the little Israelite boy who was born into captivity, or slavery, in Egypt.

The Israelites as slaves; in background, the killing of their sons.

31

The story of Moses, the babe in the bulrushes

THERE WAS A MAN AMONG THE ISRAELITES named Amram. His wife's name was Jochebed, and God gave them a son. They already had an older son, named Aaron, and a daughter, named Miriam. Their second son, however, was born during the time when Pharaoh had ordered all male children of the Israelites to be drowned in the Nile River.

This child was very beautiful, and his mother loved him, but she feared that some of Pharaoh's servants would come and take him from her, to kill him. Therefore she hid him for three months after he was born, but then found she could hide him no longer.

Trying to save her baby, Jochebed made a basket in the form of a little boat. She made the basket out of the reeds, or tall grasses, that grew at the edges of the river; in former times the English called these bulrushes, which means "big reeds." She filled in all the chinks and cracks with pitch, so that the little boat would be waterproof and float. The inside she padded carefully, to make it soft, and she placed her baby in it.

This baby was Moses—and although his mother had no idea of it at the time, God had very wonderful plans for Moses in his life.

With Miriam, her daughter, Jochebed carried the basket with the baby in it to the edge of the river and set it in the shallow water. Then Jochebed went home to pray, and Miriam stayed to watch the ark and see what happened.

Soon an Egyptian princess, the daughter of Pharaoh, came down to bathe in the river, and she and her maids walked along by the river's side. When the princess saw the basket in the river she sent one of her maids to bring it to her. The maid brought it, and as Pharaoh's daughter looked into it the little boy wept. She pitied him, for he was a very beautiful baby.

"This must be one of the Hebrew babies," said Pharaoh's daughter. "I will take him and bring him up as my own child."

At this Miriam stepped forward. She had been watching from behind some bushes near the water's edge, and when she heard Pharaoh's daughter say this she dared speak.

"May I not go and call one of the Hebrew women to nurse this child for you?" she asked.

Pharaoh's daughter agreed immediately.

"Go," she said. "Bring the woman here to me."

With that Miriam ran swiftly to her mother and told her the news. Jochebed immediately went back to the river, to where Pharaoh's daughter and her maids were standing beside the baby in his basket.

"Take this child and nurse him for me," said Pharaoh's daughter to Jochebed. "I will pay you fair wages for your work."

Joyfully, Jochebed took her baby back to her house and lovingly nursed him until he no longer needed her care.

After a while Pharaoh's daughter sent for the child, and Jochebed took

The baby Moses in his basket, guarded by angels.

The daughter of Pharaoh takes the infant Moses from the river.

him to her. Pharaoh's daughter took him into her house to be as her own son, and she called him Moses, which means, "drawn out," because, she said, "I drew him out of the water."

Yet when Moses was grown to be a man he knew that he was not the son of Pharaoh's daughter, but was one of the children of Israel. Although he might have been rich and great if he had stayed with her, he chose rather to go and live with his own people.

32

The story of how Moses killed the Egyptian

MOSES WENT OUT ONE DAY to the place where the Israelites worked for the Egyptians. There he saw a cruel Egyptian kill a Hebrew. Then Moses looked this way and that, and, when he saw no one near, he killed the Egyptian and hid his body in the sand. Moses may have believed that God had sent him to help set the children of Israel free, and perhaps he supposed God would understand this act of revenge.

Soon afterward, Moses again went out among his own people. This time he saw two of the children of Israel quarreling together. He spoke to the one who did wrong, and asked him why he struck the other. "You belong to the same people and should not fight each other," Moses said.

The man answered him angrily.

"Who has made you a judge or a ruler over us?" he asked. "Perhaps you would like to kill us both, as you killed the Egyptian!"

This frightened Moses, for he felt that if even one other person knew about his act of violence, probably many others did also. Soon everyone would know, and the news would reach Pharaoh. And Moses was quite correct in this, for the news did at last reach Pharaoh, and the king was very angry and bitter at Moses for killing one of the Egyptian people. He sent soldiers to arrest Moses and put him to death.

But Pharaoh was not able to kill Moses. Moses fled out of Egypt to the land of Midian, where Pharaoh could not find him. He sat down by a well in that land, and rested.

While Moses was sitting there, some women came to draw water. There were seven of them, and they were sisters. They had come to draw water for their father's flock, but some shepherds drove them away.

Moses fought the shepherds and beat them. Then he helped the sisters and gave their flock water. When the sisters went home to their father, a Midianite priest whose name was Jethro, he asked them,

"How is it that you are come so soon today?"

They answered,

"An Egyptian saved us from the shepherds, and also drew water for the flock." (They called Moses an Egyptian because he had come from Egypt.) Then Jethro asked where the man was, and why they had left him. He told his daughters to go and call Moses, to bring him home and give him something to eat.

So Moses went to Jethro's house, and he lived there many years. He worked for Jethro and he took one of Jethro's daughters for his wife. Her name was Zipporah.

While Moses was living in the land of Midian, Pharaoh, the king of Egypt, died. But the people of Egypt were just as cruel as ever to the children of Israel, and the children (the people) of Israel cried to the Lord because of their sufferings.

The Lord heard them and looked down from heaven and pitied the children of Israel. He decided that the time had come to free them.

Killing of the Israelite by an Egyptian; then Moses (right) kills the Egyptian.

33

The story of Moses and the burning bush

MOSES TOOK CARE OF JETHRO'S FLOCK, and one day he led it out far into the wilderness, to find pasture, till he came to a mountain called Horeb.

On this mountain, an angel of the Lord spoke to Moses. Suddenly a bush in front of Moses seemed to burst into flames. As Moses watched, he noticed that the flames did not seem to burn the stems or leaves of the bush, but still the fire was there.

"I must watch this wonderful sight," said Moses, "and find out why these flames do not consume the bush."

Then it was that an angel of the Lord spoke to Moses from out of the burning bush. The angel called Moses by name, and Moses answered.

Moses was told not to come any closer, and to remove his shoes, because this was holy ground and should not be soiled. Moses was not to come nearer because God was there.

Then, through his angel, God spoke to Moses from the bush again.

"I am the God of your fathers, the God of Abraham, the God of Isaac, and the God of Jacob."

Moses hid his face, for he was afraid to look upon God. Then God told him that He had seen the affliction of the people of Israel, and had heard their cries, and had come down to set them free from the Egyptians.

The king who ruled at this time in Egypt was called Pharaoh, like those who had lived before him, because the Egyptians called all their kings Pharaoh.

The Lord told Moses He would send Moses to Pharaoh, so that Moses might tell Pharaoh to let the children of Israel go. The Lord said that Moses was to lead the Israelites out of Egypt and bring them to the mountain of Horeb, where God was then talking with him.

God speaks to Moses from the burning bush.

Moses was afraid to go. He said, "Who am I that I should go to Pharaoh and bring the children of Israel out of Egypt?"

But God said that He would always be with Moses, to help him.

Then God commanded Moses to go and tell the people of Israel that the Lord God of their fathers, the God of Abraham, the God of Isaac, and the God of Jacob, had chosen Moses to lead them out of Egypt to a good land, where they would have milk to drink and honey to eat. After telling his people this, Moses was to speak to Pharaoh and ask him to let them go.

Moses answered the Lord again. He said, "If I go to Egypt and tell the people of Israel these things, I am sure they will not listen to me or believe that the Lord has spoken to me."

The miracles God showed to Moses

Now, Moses was holding a staff, the kind of long stick or rod that the Israelites, being shepherds, customarily carried. The angel of the Lord said to him,

"What is that in your hand?"

"My staff," Moses replied.

The angel said,

"Cast it on the ground."

Moses cast his staff on the ground and God made it change into a snake, so that Moses was afraid of it and fled away before it. But the Lord said,

"Put out your hand and take it by the tail."

Moses obeyed, and at once the snake was changed back into a staff in his hand.

Next the Lord said to Moses,

"Now put your hand into your bosom."

Moses put his hand into his bosom, and when he took it out it was white as snow; for it was covered with a disease called leprosy, which made it look white.

And the Lord said,

"Put your hand into your bosom again."

Moses did so, and when he took his hand out again it was healed and was just the same as his other hand.

God gave Moses power to do these two wonderful works, or miracles, so that when the people of Israel saw them they would believe that God had sent him. If they would still not believe after Moses had done both, then, God said, Moses should take some water out of the river Nile and

Moses, with his wife and sons, meets his brother Aaron (left) on the road to Egypt.

pour it on the dry ground. The water would be changed into blood on the ground where Moses had poured it.

Still Moses did not want to go; he was afraid. He began to make excuses for not going. He was not eloquent, he said; he could not speak well before the people. The Lord commanded him again to go, promising to teach him what to say. Yet Moses begged the Lord to send someone else. Then the Lord was angry, because Moses was still unwilling to go.

Aaron named to speak for Moses

Moses had a brother named Aaron. God reminded Moses that Aaron could speak well, and God commanded that Aaron should go with Moses into Egypt. Moses would tell Aaron what to say, but Aaron would tell it to the people. God said he would teach them both what they should do; and he told Moses to take his staff in his hand, for with it he would be able to do wonderful things.

All this time, while God was talking with Moses, Moses was on Mount Horeb by the bush that burned with fire. He had gone there with Jethro's flock. When the Lord was done talking with him, Moses went to Jethro's house again and asked permission to go into Egypt, so that he might see his people, the children of Israel. Jethro willingly gave him permission to go.

The Lord had commanded Aaron, Moses' brother, to leave Egypt and meet Moses at Mount Horeb. Aaron went there and met Moses, and Aaron was happy to see his brother again after so many years, and kissed him.

Moses told Aaron of all the words that God had spoken. Then Moses and Aaron went into Egypt to speak to the people of Israel.

34

The story of Moses and Aaron in Egypt

Moses and Aaron could not speak to all of the Israelites at once, for there were too many to hear; so they sent for the chief men among them, called elders. Moses and Aaron told the elders and the elders told the people. Moses showed many of the people the miracles that God had given him power to do. When the people of Israel saw these, they believed that God had sent Moses and Aaron, and that they would be taken out of Egypt, as God had promised.

After they had spoken with the elders, Moses and Aaron went to Pharaoh.

"The Lord, God of Israel, asks you to let his people go, so that they may hold a feast to the Lord in the desert," they said to Pharaoh.

"And why should I obey this Lord of yours?" Pharaoh demanded. "I do not know your God. What is more, I will not let the Israelites go!"

Then Moses and Aaron told Pharaoh that God Himself had spoken to them and commanded them. They begged Pharaoh to let the Israelites go.

"If you do not," they said, "God may punish us for disobedience."

Pharaoh became angry when they said this to him. He scolded Moses and Aaron for keeping the Israelites from their work, by telling them they would soon be allowed to go out of Egypt. Pharaoh told Moses and Aaron to go and work themselves, like the rest of their people.

At that time the Israelites were digging clay out of the ground and making bricks with it, for that was the work Pharaoh made them do. These bricks were not burned in the fire, as ours are, to harden them; they were only baked in the sun. To make the bricks tough and strong, the clay they were made of was mixed with pieces of straw. This straw was gathered out in the fields by Egyptians, who carried it to the Israelites.

Moses and Aaron appear before Pharaoh to plead for their people.

Pharaoh had become so angry with the people of Israel, for wanting to go out of Egypt, that he said they must go and gather the straw themselves; and yet that they must make as many bricks as they used to make when the straw was gathered for them. For they were idle, Pharaoh said, and that was the reason they cried,

"Let us go and worship the Lord."

The taskmasters told the Israelites what Pharaoh had said.

"We will give you no more straw," the taskmasters said. "Go and get straw yourselves, wherever you can find it!"

So the poor Israelites went into the fields, after the grain had been reaped, and gathered up the straw that was left, and carried it away to make bricks with. But though they worked very hard, they could not make as many bricks as they had made when the straw was brought to them, and many of them were beaten because they did not.

Straw for the bricks

The Israelite elders went to Pharaoh and told him it was not the fault of their people. But Pharaoh answered, "You are idle, you are idle! That is the reason you say, 'Let us go and sacrifice to the Lord.'" Pharaoh told them to go and work, for no straw would be given them.

The people of Israel were in great distress. Some went to Moses and Aaron, to reproach them.

"You have done us harm and not good," the Israelites said. "You have made Pharaoh hate us and treat us more cruelly than he treated us before."

Moses went and prayed to the Lord. He asked why he had been sent to speak with Pharaoh; for, Moses said, since he had spoken to him, Pharaoh had not set them free.

Moses prays for God's help

The Lord answered that Moses would soon see what He, the Lord, would do to Pharaoh to make him let the people of Israel go. The Lord commanded Moses to tell the Israelites that God would bring them out of Egypt and would take them to be His people. He would lead them to the land He had promised to their fathers, Abraham, Isaac, and Jacob.

Moses went and told the people of Israel what God had said, but they would no longer listen to Moses. Then the Lord sent Moses and Aaron to speak with Pharaoh again. Moses was now eighty years old, and Aaron was eighty-three. The Lord said that when Pharaoh asked them to do a miracle for him to see, Aaron should take his staff and throw it on the ground, and it would be changed into a serpent.

So Moses and Aaron went to Pharaoh, and Aaron threw down his staff and it was changed into a serpent. Pharaoh called for the magicians, or priests, of Egypt. They came with staffs like Aaron's in their hands, and when they had thrown them down, their staffs also were changed into serpents, because the Lord let the magicians do as Aaron had done. But Aaron's staff swallowed up all the other staffs, proving God's power. Because such staffs were usually called "rods" in England many years ago, there are some flowers that we still call "Aaron's rod"; they are named for Aaron's staff to which God had given magical powers.

Still Pharaoh would not let the people of Israel go. The Lord next told Moses to stand, in the morning, by the river's side. Pharaoh would come there, and Moses should speak with him.

Moses was to say, "The God of the Hebrews (that is, of the people of Israel) has sent me to say, 'Let my people go, so that they may offer up a sacrifice to God in the desert.'"

Aaron throws down his rod before Pharaoh and it turns into a snake.

Moses did as the Lord said. He went to the river, and when Pharaoh came there Moses told him the words that the Lord had spoken. But Pharaoh still would not let the people go.

35

The story of the plagues of Egypt

THE LORD HAD CHOSEN HIS WAY of dealing with Pharaoh, the cruel king of Egypt who had made the Israelites his slaves. The entire land of Egypt would be afflicted with plagues, or great troubles and hardships that make the people unhappy and threaten them with death. There would be one plague after another, until Pharaoh let the people of Israel leave his land and go to another land where they would not be slaves. But the Lord would not let the plagues hurt the people of Israel, even though they too lived in Egypt, for they were the people He had chosen to protect.

There were nine plagues that God "visited on" or brought to Egypt before Pharaoh would let his Israelite slaves go; and finally there was a tenth plague that made Pharaoh obey the Lord. The plagues were:

THE PLAGUES OF EGYPT

1. The plague of BLOOD.
2. The plague of FROGS.
3. The plague of insects such as LICE or GNATS.
4. The plague of insects such as FLIES.
5. The plague of MURRAIN, a PESTILENCE or disease of cattle.
6. The plague of BOILS.
7. The plague of HAIL.
8. The plague of LOCUSTS.
9. The plague of DARKNESS.

and finally

10. The plague of the DEATH OF THE FIRSTBORN.

God could have made Pharaoh release the Israelites with the very first plague—or without any plague, for that matter, because God can do anything. But He wanted His own people, the Israelites, to know His power.

So He "hardened Pharaoh's heart"—He made Pharaoh refuse, after each plague, to let God's people go.

In the following pages you will read about each of the plagues that the Lord visited on Egypt.

The First Plague: The waters of the Nile become blood.

The first plague

THE LORD COMMANDED AARON TO TAKE HIS STAFF and strike the waters with it, that they might be changed into blood. Aaron took the staff in his hand and struck the waters of the Nile, and Pharaoh and his ministers saw Aaron do it.

All the water in the river was immediately changed into blood. All the streams, and ponds of water, all over the land of Egypt, were changed at the same instant into blood. The fish that were in the river died, and the Egyptians could not drink the water.

Pharaoh's priests, or magicians, came, and they, too, proved that they could turn water into blood, because the Lord again let them do as Aaron had done. So Pharaoh, whose heart was hardened by the Lord, went home to his house and would not let the people go.

Then all the Egyptians dug in the ground about the river, to find water that they could drink. The blood stayed in the river seven days.

The Second Plague: Frogs infest the land of Egypt.

The second plague

NEXT THE LORD COMMANDED MOSES to tell Pharaoh that if he would not let the people go, frogs would come over all the land. Pharaoh would not let them go, so God told Aaron to hold out his rod over the waters of Egypt. When Aaron held out his rod, millions of frogs came up out of the waters, so many of them that they covered the land. They went into the houses of the Egyptians, into their ovens and into their kneading troughs where they made the bread; they went into Pharaoh's house, and up into his bedchamber, and on his bed. But Pharaoh's magicians also brought up frogs, for God allowed them once more to do as Aaron had done.

Still, Pharaoh and the people of Egypt were in great trouble because of the frogs. Pharaoh called for Moses and Aaron, and asked them to pray to God that He would take the frogs away. Then, Pharaoh said, he would let the people go to worship in the desert.

Moses said, "When shall I pray for you?"

Pharaoh answered, "Tomorrow." And Moses and Aaron went out from the place where Pharaoh was.

The next day Moses prayed to the Lord, and the Lord did as Moses asked; the frogs that were in the houses, the villages, and the fields died, and the people gathered them in heaps, and the smell of their decaying bodies was all over the land.

But when Pharaoh saw that the frogs were dead, he would not let the children of Israel go.

The Third Plague: The dust of Egypt becomes insects.

The third plague

THEN THE LORD COMMANDED AARON to strike the dust on the ground with his staff.

When Aaron did so, every grain of dust was changed into a small insect. There were billions of lice and gnats on the people and on the cattle.

Pharaoh's magicians tried to bring up insects but they could not, because God would no longer let them do as Aaron had done. Then they told Pharaoh that it was God who did these things for Moses and Aaron, and they would have been glad to let the Israelites go and escape the further wrath of God.

But Pharaoh's heart was wicked and he would not listen to them, nor would he let the people go.

The Fourth Plague: Flying insects infest all Egypt.

The fourth plague

THE LORD TOLD MOSES to rise up early in the morning and stand where he would see Pharaoh when he came out to the water. There, the Lord said, Moses should command Pharaoh again to let the people go. If Pharaoh refused, Moses should tell him that the Lord would send swarms of flies over all Egypt.

Moses did as the Lord commanded, and Pharaoh would not let the people go. Then the Lord sent swarms of flies and gnats, and they were over all the land. They crept on Pharaoh, and on his officials, and on the people; they went into their houses, so that the houses of the Egyptians were full of swarms of flies and the ground was covered with them. But in the land of Goshen, where the people of Israel lived, there were no flies, for the Lord did not send them there.

Pharaoh was as troubled because of the flies as he had been because of the frogs. He called Moses and Aaron to him and told them they might go to worship and offer sacrifices to God, but they must not go into the desert to do it; they must do it in Egypt. But Moses warned him that the Egyptians would be offended if the children of Israel offered sacrifices to God in Egypt; for the Egyptians worshiped idols that were formed like oxen and calves, and if they saw the children of Israel killing those animals and burning them on an altar, they might be angry and try to kill the Israelites. Moses suggested to Pharaoh that the Israelites go a three days' journey into the desert, where no one could harm them, and there they would offer sacrifices to the Lord.

Pharaoh finally agreed. He said he would let the Israelites go, only they must not go very far. Also he asked Moses to pray for him, that the flies might be taken from the land. Moses said he would pray that they might be taken away the next day, but he told Pharaoh not to deceive him any more by refusing to let the people go.

So Moses went and prayed to the Lord, and the Lord took away the swarms of flies from Pharaoh, and from his servants, and from his people, so that there was not one left.

Pharaoh saw that the flies were taken away, but God made his heart wicked this time also, and Pharaoh would not let the people go.

The Fifth Plague: Cattle die throughout Egypt.

The fifth plague

NEXT THE LORD COMMANDED MOSES to tell Pharaoh that if he would not let the people of Israel go, the Lord would send, the next day, a great sickness or plague, of a kind that was formerly called murrain but that today we would probably call anthrax, to kill the cattle of Egypt, but that He would not send it among the cattle of the people of Israel; none of the Israelites' cattle would die. Moses told Pharaoh this, but Pharaoh would not let the people go.

The Lord sent that sickness; and the cows, the horses, the asses, the camels and the sheep died all over the land. But not one of the cattle of the children of Israel died. Pharaoh sent to see of any of their cattle were dead. He found they were not, yet his heart grew more wicked and he would not let the people go.

The Sixth Plague: Boils break out on Egyptian men.

The sixth plague

THE LORD TOLD MOSES AND AARON to take handfuls of ashes from a furnace, where fire had been burning, and to sprinkle them up in the air so that Pharaoh could see them doing it. Those ashes, the Lord said, would go like dust over all the land, and cause sore boils to come on Egyptian men and on the animals that were still left in Egypt.

So Moses took ashes and stood before Pharaoh, and sprinkled them up in the air; afterward boils broke out on men and on beasts over all the land.

As he had done so often before, Pharaoh called his own priests to come and prove that they could do what Moses and Aaron had done.

But the magicians could not come to try to do as Moses had done, for the boils were on them also.

But Pharaoh's heart was still wicked, and he would not let the people go.

The Seventh Plague: A great hailstorm falls on Egypt.

The seventh plague

THE LORD COMMANDED MOSES to rise up early in the morning, and stand before Pharaoh, and say that on the next day God would send a great storm of hail, such as had never before been in Egypt. Moses was to tell Pharaoh to bring into his barns all his cattle from the fields, for every man and beast that was out in the storm would be killed.

Moses did so; and those Egyptians who feared the Lord made their servants and their cattle come quickly into the houses and barns, where the hail could not hurt them. The others let them stay out in the field.

And the Lord told Moses to stretch out his hand toward heaven, after which the hail would come. Moses stretched out his hand, holding up his rod. The Lord sent thunder and hail, and there was fire, also, running along on the ground. So there was hail, and fire mixed with the hail, very dreadful, such as had never before been in the land. The hail came down on the fields, killing the men and the animals that were there. It broke the bushes and every tree that grew in the fields. All the grain that was grown up was broken and spoiled by the hail. (Some of it was not grown up above the ground; this was not spoiled.) Yet in the land of Goshen, where the children of Israel lived, no hail came.

Then Pharaoh sent for Moses and Aaron. He said to them,

"I have sinned; the Lord is good, and I and my people are wicked. Pray to the Lord to take away the mighty thunder and hail, and I will let your people go."

Moses answered that as soon as he left Pharaoh he would pray to the Lord, and the thunder would cease and there would be no more hail. But, he said, he knew that Pharaoh and his servants would not obey the Lord.

Moses went out from Pharaoh's palace into the terrible storm, but God kept the hail and fire from harming him. And when Moses had left the palace, he lifted up his hands and prayed to God, and the thunders ceased, and the hail stopped coming down.

Pharaoh saw that the thunder and hail had ceased, so he made his heart still more hard and obstinate, both he and his officials, and they would not let the people go.

The Eighth Plague: Locusts eat all the crops of Egypt.

The eighth plague

Moses and Aaron went to Pharaoh again. They said that if Pharaoh would not obey the Lord, on the next day locusts would come into Egypt.

Pharaoh's ministers were afraid to be punished any more. They remembered when the Nile was turned into blood, so that the people had no water to drink. They remembered the frogs, and the lice, and the flies; the sickness of the cattle, the boils, and the hail, all of which had been sent into Egypt already. Therefore they begged Pharaoh to let the children of Israel go, so that no more punishments might be sent by God.

Moses and Aaron were again brought before Pharaoh. He said to them, "You may go and worship God; but tell me which of your people will go."

Moses answered, "All the people of Israel will go—the young and the old, with their sons and their daughters, their flocks and their herds; for they must hold a feast to the Lord."

"No," said Pharaoh, "only the men may go—the women and children must stay in Egypt." And Moses and Aaron again were driven away from the place where they talked with Pharaoh.

So the Lord told Moses to stretch out his hand and make the locusts come. Moses took the staff and held it out; and the Lord made an east wind blow over Egypt all that day and all that night, and in the morning the wind brought the locusts. They went over all the land of Egypt and covered the ground so that it could not be seen. They filled Pharaoh's house, and the houses of his ministers, and the houses of all the Egyptians. They ate up whatever fruits the hail had left, and all the vegetables in the farms, and everything that was green, until there was not a leaf to be seen on the bushes or the trees throughout Egypt.

Then Pharaoh called Moses and Aaron, and said to them, "I have sinned against the Lord and against you." And he asked Moses to forgive him only this once, and to pray that God would take away the locusts.

Moses went out and prayed to the Lord, and the Lord sent a very strong west wind, which blew away the locusts and cast them into the Red Sea, where they were drowned, so that there was not one locust left in all Egypt. But when Pharaoh saw that the locusts were taken away, he would not let the people go.

The Ninth Plague: Darkness covers the land of Egypt.

The ninth plague

THE LORD COMMANDED MOSES to hold up his hand toward heaven. Moses held up his hand and there came a great darkness over all Egypt, so that the Egyptians could not see one another, nor move from the places they were in, for three days. But in the houses of the children of Israel there was light.

Then Pharaoh called for Moses, and said,

"Go and worship the Lord; only let your flocks and your herds stay."

But Moses told him that the flocks and herds of the Israelites must go also, so that they might have sacrifices and burnt offerings, for they did not know how many of these they would need in the desert. The Lord would tell them there what animals they must kill and offer up to him.

When Moses said this, Pharaoh would not let the people of Israel go; and he told Moses to leave him and come before him no more, for if he ever saw Moses' face again, Moses would be put to death.

The tenth and last plague

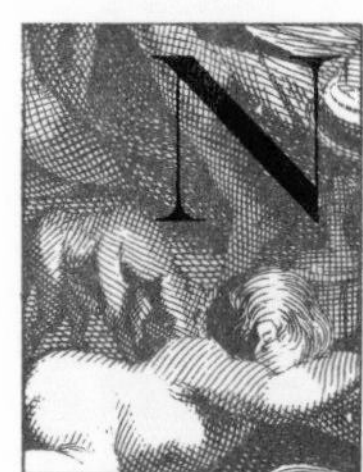

NOW NINE PLAGUES HAD BEEN VISITED BY GOD on Pharaoh and his fellow-countrymen, the Egyptians; and only one more was to come. But this tenth and last plague was so horrible that no man or nation on earth could have withstood it. Pharaoh, his heart hardened by God, had endured every one of the first nine plagues and still had refused to let the people of Israel leave his land and be slaves no more; but when the tenth and last plague came, Pharaoh had to give in.

For the tenth and last plague struck the Egyptians in a way that no father and mother throughout the world can bear to be struck—by striking at their children.

God Himself, represented by His angel, traveled through the land of Egypt and in every Egyptian house He caused the firstborn, or eldest son, to become dead. This punishment was visited on every Egyptian house whether the eldest son was a grown man or only a baby.

But the eldest sons of the Hebrews, or Israelites, were not struck dead by God; for the Lord told Moses how the Israelites could protect their sons.

Moses warned Pharaoh of the tenth and last plague, and he gave Pharaoh every chance to save the sons of all the Egyptians, including the eldest son of Pharaoh himself.

"The Lord is coming into Egypt," Moses told Pharaoh. "He will come in the middle of the night. He will cast His curse on every house in Egypt, and in every house of Egypt the eldest son will die: Your eldest son, Pharaoh, and the eldest son of every one of your ministers, and the eldest son of every one of your people."

The Tenth Plague: The angel of the Lord travels through Egypt and kills the oldest son of every Egyptian family (see page 165). Gustave Doré's interpretation.

But Pharaoh was not moved by this threat.

"There will be a great cry of trouble and grief such as has never before been known in Egypt, and will never be again," Moses continued. "After this last punishment of the Lord, you and all the people of Egypt will come and bow down to me, and beg me to lead the people of Israel out of your land. But to the houses of the Israelites no trouble will come; none of our sons will die; not even a dog will harm a child of Israel. Then you will know that it is you, and your people, that the Lord is punishing, and not the Israelites."

When Moses had told Pharaoh this, he left Pharaoh's presence angrily.

36

The story of the first Passover

GOD DID COME, AS HE HAD SAID HE WOULD, and killed the firstborn sons in all the houses of Egypt; but the houses of the Israelites He *passed over,* or spared, not stopping at those houses to kill the firstborn sons. For that reason, the Hebrews or Jews to this day celebrate each year the Feast of the Passover, or the time when God passed over the houses of their ancestors and let their sons live.

God had told Moses and Aaron everything the Israelites should do to show that they loved and worshiped God, and to mark their houses so that the avenging angel of God would pass over them when he came to kill the firstborn of the Egyptians.

Every man among the Israelites was to take a lamb from the flock and keep it four days. Then he was to kill it in the evening, and he was to take a bunch of leaves from the plant called hyssop, and dip this bunch in the blood of the lamb, and go to the door of his house, and strike the bunch of hyssop on each side of the door and over the door, so that there would be three marks of blood on the outside of every house in which a pious Israelite lived. When the man had done this he was to go inside his house and stay there. No one was to leave his house until morning.

The lamb that had been killed was to be roasted and eaten that same night by all the people living in the house. They were to eat it when they were fully clothed, with their shoes on, all prepared to leave Egypt and journey toward the Promised Land where they would be free.

God promised the Israelites that when He saw the marks of blood on a house, His angel would pass over that house and not stop there to kill the firstborn son.

That is why the "supper of the lamb," which the Israelites ate that night, was called the Lord's Passover. There was another command, too, that the Lord gave the Israelites for this supper. At this supper they were to eat only unleavened bread—that is, bread in which there was no yeast, or leavening, to make it rise; for the Israelites had to be prepared to leave Egypt so hastily that there would be no time to wait until their bread might be leavened. To this day, also, Jews celebrating the Feast of the Passover eat only unleavened bread, which they call *matzoth*.

"The supper of the lamb"

All came about, as it always does, just as the Lord had said. At midnight, the Lord visited His tenth plague on all the land of Egypt. In Israelite houses that were marked with the blood of the lamb, no one died. Into every Egyptian house the Lord's avenging angel went to kill the firstborn son. Pharaoh's eldest son died that night, and the eldest sons of all his ministers. And Pharaoh rose up in the night, and all his ministers and all his people, and there was a great cry of sorrow throughout the land, for there was not one house in which there was not one dead.

The angel of the Lord passes over an Israelite house marked with blood.

Pharaoh calls Moses to him and tells Moses to take the Israelites and leave Egypt: Gustave Doré's interpretation. Pharaoh is shown with arms outstretched; Moses is seen from the back, at Pharaoh's left. Dead Egyptian firstborn sons are shown.

Pharaoh frees the Israelites

Then Pharaoh was convinced that he could not resist the will of the Lord; and he called to him Moses and Aaron, and he said to them,

"Tell your people, all the Israelites, to take their wives and their children, and their flocks and their herds, and all their possessions, and go from our land!"

The Lord had told Moses, "Before My people go, let them ask the Egyptians for gold, and silver, and precious jewels, to take with them."

But the Israelites hardly needed to ask. The Egyptians were so anxious to see them gone that they offered the Israelites gold, and silver, and jewels, and fine clothing, just to see them gone.

Then the Israelites began their great "going out from Egypt," which is called the Exodus. They took their herds and their flocks, and the unbaked dough that the Lord had told them not to leaven with yeast, and the jewelry that the Egyptians had given them.

It was not only the Israelites who went. Great numbers of Egyptians, who worked for the Israelites and lived with them, went with them.

Between Egypt and the promised land of Canaan, to which the Israelites were going, lay more than a hundred miles of deadly desert. In this desert there was no food or water for the great horde of Israelites who left Egypt on that fateful night. It was to take forty years of wandering in the desert before the Israelites finally reached the Promised Land; without the help of God they could never have done it, as you will see. But God was with them and went before them, a shield against their enemies; and you will read in the next stories how the Israelites came through the desert.

37

The story of crossing the Red Sea

THE ISRAELITES HAD BEEN SLAVES IN EGYPT for hundreds of years, under the cruel Egyptian king, Pharaoh. Now at last the great Moses, chosen by God to be leader of the Israelites, had Pharaoh's permission to lead his people out of Egypt to a land where they would be slaves no longer.

The body of Israelites was a mighty group. There were 600,000 men, plus their wives and children—probably three million persons in all, the largest group that ever changed their homes all at one time. They could move only slowly, for with them they drove their millions of sheep, cattle, camels, and asses or donkeys.

The Israelites had known for some time that they might leave Egypt, but still they were not prepared to leave in such haste. They snatched up their possessions and began their journey at once. The women had mixed dough for bread, but they had not had time to leaven it—that is, put in yeast to make the dough rise—and they took along their unleavened dough, to be baked while they were on their journey. The Egyptians were so anxious to have the Israelites leave at once, before God brought any more plagues to Egypt, that they gave the Israelites much gold, silver and jewels to take along.

The destination of the Israelites was the land of Canaan, which God had promised to them as their future home. God sent signs to guide them, as you will learn.

The Lord did not lead them toward Canaan by the shortest way, which passed through the land of the Philistines. The Philistines might have made war against them and they might have become discouraged and turned back into Egypt. The Lord showed them another way, toward the Red Sea.

Moses took the bones of Joseph with him, because, as we have read, Joseph, before he died, made the children of Israel promise that they would carry his body up to Canaan when they went back there.

The people of Israel journeyed to a place called Etham on the edge of the desert, which the Bible calls the wilderness. There they set up their tents and made a camp.

As they journeyed, the Lord sent before them a cloud to show them the way.

The pillars of cloud and fire

The cloud was shaped like a pillar, reaching up toward heaven. They could see it all the time. In the day it was the color of a cloud, but at night it was the color of fire. It gave them light at night, so that they could journey both in the day and in the night when the Lord commanded. The Lord did not take away the pillar of cloud in the day, or the pillar of fire in the night. It was always before the people.

After the people of Israel had left Egypt, Pharaoh and his ministers were sorry they had let them go.

"Why have we let the people of Israel go? Now we have lost our slaves!" they said.

The Israelites leave Egypt. They are shown here assembling for their journey.

Then Pharaoh made ready his chariot, and took with him all the chariots in which his soldiers rode out to battle, and went after the Israelites. He came up to them while they were encamping by the Red Sea.

When Pharaoh came near, the Israelites looked back and saw the Egyptians marching after them. Then they were greatly afraid and cried out to the Lord. They blamed Moses also for bringing them away from Egypt.

"It would have been better for us," they said, "to stay and work for the Egyptians than to be slain here in the wilderness."

But Moses told the people not to fear. He said,

"Wait, and see how the Lord will save you; for the Egyptians you have seen today you will never see again. The Lord will fight for you and you need do nothing but have faith."

Pharaoh and his army followed after the people of Israel until they had almost come up with them. Then the cloud that had gone before the people of Israel changed its position, and went behind them. It stayed between Pharaoh's army and the children of Israel. That side of it which was turned

The pillar of cloud leads the Israelites, who are now divided into tribes and groups.

The waters of the Red Sea pour down on the Egyptians and drown them.

toward the Israelites was bright as fire and gave them light in their camp.

Then the Lord said to Moses,

"Speak to the people of Israel and tell them to go forward. And lift up your staff and stretch out your hand over the sea, and the people of Israel shall go on dry ground through the sea."

The waters of the sea draw back

Moses lifted up his staff, and stretched out his hand over the sea, and the Lord sent a great wind all that night, which blew the water away from that part of the sea, so that the bottom of the sea was left dry. The Israelites went down into it and walked on the bottom of the sea on dry ground. The waters were piled up high on each side of them like a wall; yet they did not come down to drown them, all the while they were walking through the sea.

And that is the way the children of Israel went out of Egypt. They walked through the Red Sea on dry ground till they all safely reached the other side. (See the picture at page 151.)

When Pharaoh saw they had gone, he and his chariots and his horsemen followed after them, for he thought that his army would be able to pass through the sea as the Israelites had done. In the morning the Lord looked out of the pillar of fire and cloud at the Egyptians as they were marching through the sea. He made the wheels of the Egyptian chariots come off, so that the Egyptians could drive only very slowly.

This troubled the Egyptians. They were afraid and said to each other, "Let us make haste back, for the Lord fights against us, and He fights for the children of Israel."

But before the Egyptians had time to go, the Lord told Moses again to stretch out his hand; and the waters came together again and covered the Egyptians in the bottom of the sea. All Pharaoh's horses and horsemen and all his army were drowned. Not one of them was left alive. The Israelites saw them lying dead upon the seashore where the waters washed them up.

But Moses and the Israelites were safe on the other side of the Red Sea. There they sang a song of praise to the Lord for saving them from Pharaoh.

Moses and the Israelites, seeing the Egyptians dead, give thanks to God.

Manna, fallen from heaven to feed the Israelites, is gathered by them.

38

The story of the manna in the desert

Moses led his people into the wilderness, or desert, and they journeyed for three days without finding water. Finally they came to a place called Marah. There they found water, but when they tasted it they could not drink it, for it was bitter. Then they complained against Moses, and said,

"What shall we drink?"

Moses prayed to the Lord, and the Lord showed him a tree which he took and threw into the water, and the water was made sweet so that the people could drink it.

Again they journeyed and came to Elim, where there were twelve wells and seventy palm trees. Later they journeyed until they came to the desert of Sin. Here the people, because they were hungry, spoke wickedly to Moses and Aaron. They said that while they were in Egypt they had plenty of bread and meat to eat. They wished that God had left them to die there, for Moses and Aaron had brought them out into the wilderness just to kill them with hunger.

The Lord told Moses he had heard the people's complainings and that in the evening they would have meat to eat, and in the morning as much bread as they wanted. Then they would know that the Lord was taking care of them.

The Lord did as He promised. In the evening, about the time the sun was going down, great numbers of quail came flying up to the camp, so that the people could catch them. In the morning, after the dew was dried, there was left, spread all over the ground, small, white, round things that looked like frost. When the Israelites saw it they did not know what it was. But Moses said to them,

"This is the food the Lord has given you to eat."

The Lord did as He promised. In the evening, about the time the sun was going down, great numbers of quail came flying up to the camp.

The Lord commanded the people to go out and gather it, each man as much as he and his family would need for one day. But the Lord said they must not gather any to keep till the next day, for by that time there would be more on the ground for them; and the Lord wanted them to trust Him, each day, for their daily bread.

Some of the people disobeyed the Lord and kept part of what they gathered until the next morning, but by that time it was spoiled and had worms in it.

After that the people went out every day and gathered the food the Lord sent for them. When they had gathered enough, and the sun had grown hot, all that was left on the ground melted away. But on the day before the Sabbath the men gathered twice as much as they did on other days, and what they saved of this was not spoiled by the next morning. The Lord sent none on the Sabbath because he did not want the people to go out and gather it or to do any work on that day. Therefore he sent them enough for two days on the day before the Sabbath.

Some of the people went out to gather food on the Sabbath, but they found none. The Lord was displeased because they went; so after that they rested on the Sabbath day, as the Lord had wanted them to do.

The people called this new food *manna*. It was small, and round, and white, like coriander seed, and it tasted like wafers made with honey. Moses told Aaron to take a pot and put into it as much as one man could eat in a day. That pot of manna, the Lord said, must always be kept, so that the Israelites who would live long afterward might see what kind of food the Lord had given the people of Israel, when He led them through the wilderness to the land of Canaan. The people ate manna throughout the years until they reached that land.

39

The story of how Moses got water from rock

AGAIN THE ISRAELITES JOURNEYED ON and reached a place called Rephidim, but they found no water there. Once more the people found fault with Moses.

"Give us water to drink!" they cried. "We must have water. Our children and our cattle will die of thirst. Why did you bring us to this place?"

Moses tried in vain to make them wait patiently for the Lord to provide, as He had always done.

"Why do you find fault with me?" Moses asked. "Can you not have a little faith, and trust the Lord?"

But the people still complained, and as they grew thirstier, they became angry. At length they were so angry they threatened to stone Moses.

Moses cried out to the Lord.

"What can I do with these people?" he prayed. "They are almost ready to stone me!"

By now they were near the mountain called Horeb, where Moses had seen the burning in the bush. The Lord had told him he should lead the people to Horeb. Now when Moses asked what he should do, to give the people water, the Lord commanded him to take his staff in his hand and go on before the people, until he came to a rock that the Lord would show him. The Lord said that Moses should strike that rock with his staff and then water would come out of it.

Moses obeyed the Lord. He took the staff in his hand and struck the rock, and water flowed out of it, so that the children of Israel had water to drink.

In the land about Rephidim, where the Israelites were encamped, there were warlike people called the Amalekites. These were descendants of Esau, and they considered the Israelites their enemies because the Israelites were descendants of Jacob, who had taken Esau's birthright.

Moses touches the rock with his rod and water gushes forth.

Now the Amalekites came to attack the people of Israel.

Among the Israelites was a brave young man named Joshua, and to him Moses spoke.

"Choose the bravest and strongest of the young men of Israel," said Moses, "and prepare to fight the Amalekites. Tomorrow you will attack, and I will go stand at the top of the hill, holding the rod of God in my hand, and God will give you His help, that you may defeat them."

Joshua did as Moses told him. He chose men and went out and fought with the Amalekites. Moses went up to the top of the hill, and Aaron and a man named Hur went with him.

Moses held up the rod, and as long as he held it up the soldiers of Israel were able to win over the Amalekites, but whenever he let it down the Amalekites beat the Israelites. Moses' arms grew tired, holding up the rod so long, and so Aaron and Hur got a stone on which Moses could sit down. Then they both held up Moses' arms, one standing on each side of him, until the sun went down. In this way God gave the Israelites the victory.

God was displeased with the Amalekites for making war against the Israelites, and He said that the time would come when those people would all be destroyed and no one would remember them.

After the defeat of the Amalekites, Jethro, Moses' father-in-law, visited the encampment of the Israelites to see him. Jethro was also called Reuel, and he was a priest of Midian. With Jethro were Moses' wife, Zipporah, and their two sons, Gershom and Eliezer.

Moses was happy to see his family, and greeted his father-in-law warmly.

Jethro listened while Moses described all the wonderful things the Lord had done for the people of Israel—how they had been sent food and water when it seemed they would die of hunger and thirst, and how the Lord had saved them from the armies of Pharaoh in crossing the Red Sea, and how the Israelites had been able to defeat all their enemies.

"The Lord is great," said Jethro. "There is no other god who could have done such wonders for you."

The Israelites make war against the Amalekites and defeat them.

Moses builds an altar to give thanks for the defeat of the Amalekites.

On the next day, Moses was very busy judging problems the people brought to him, and Jethro asked if he always sat in judgment over all questions.

"The people come to ask me the meaning of God's laws on many subjects," said Moses. "I explain those laws to them, because there is no other way for them to learn the word of God."

"This is far too much for one man," said Jethro. "You cannot spend so much of your time in such work. Why do you not choose other men to judge the smaller problems, and bring only the large ones to you? Then you can conserve your strength."

Moses thought that this was good advice, and did as Jethro had suggested. He appointed many men to answer the questions of the people in lesser matters, saving himself and his own time for the serious cases that occurred.

40

The story of the Ten Commandments

SAVED FROM SLAVERY IN EGYPT, led by Moses across the Red Sea and southward through the desert, the Israelites came to a mountain called Sinai and made their camp before it.

God had first spoken to Moses on Mount Horeb. At that time He had told Moses to lead the people of Israel back to that mountain. Now, in the third month after leaving Egypt, Moses had done as the Lord commanded, for Sinai and Horeb are neighboring mountains, only a few miles apart.

The Lord now spoke to Moses again. He said He would come down in a thick cloud and speak to Moses on Mount Sinai, so that the people could hear Him; when they heard God Himself speak to Moses, they would know they could trust Moses too. But, the Lord said, the people must wash their clothes and make themselves clean, and be very careful not to sin.

"They must make themselves ready for the third day from now," the Lord told Moses, "for on that day I am coming down before them all on

Mount Sinai." On that day, God said, none of the people were to be allowed to go up on the mountain; if anyone did, he would be put to death. When the people heard the great sound of a trumpet far up on the mountain, they should come and stand at the foot of the mountain.

After the Lord had spoken these things, Moses went down and told the people, and they washed their clothes and were careful not to sin.

On the third day, in the morning, there was thunder and lightning, and a thick cloud was seen on Mount Sinai. The trumpet, which, no doubt, an angel blew, sounded very loud, and all the people trembled in fright when they heard it.

Then Moses led the great hordes of Israelites out of the camp, and they stood near the foot of the mountain. All the mountain smoked, because the Lord had come down in fire upon it, and the smoke went up like the smoke from a furnace, and the mountain shook greatly. The trumpet sounded long, and grew louder and louder. God called Moses again to the top of the mountain, and there, on Mount Sinai, God spoke the words of

While the Israelites stood near the foot of the mountain, all the mountain smoked, because the Lord had come down in fire upon it.

Moses, descending with the tablets from Mount Sinai.

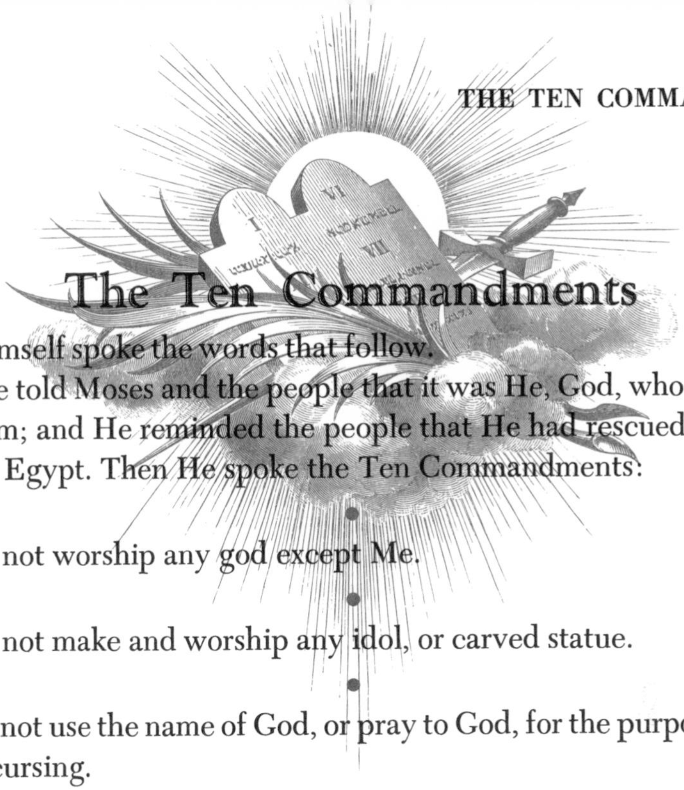

The Ten Commandments

God Himself spoke the words that follow.

First He told Moses and the people that it was He, God, who was speaking to them; and He reminded the people that He had rescued them from slavery in Egypt. Then He spoke the Ten Commandments:

•

You must not worship any god except Me.

•

You must not make and worship any idol, or carved statue.

•

You must not use the name of God, or pray to God, for the purpose of doing evil or of cursing.

•

Keep the seventh day holy as God's Sabbath, or day of rest; do all your work on the other six days.

•

Honor, or respect, your father and mother.

•

You must not commit murder.

•

You must not commit adultery; this is an act in which a husband is not faithful or true to his wife, or a wife to her husband.

•

You must not steal.

•

You must not tell a lie that will harm someone else.

•

You must not covet, or desire, another person's house, or his possessions of any kind.

•

You must not covet, or desire, another person's wife.

The Ten Commandments are called also the Decalogue, a word meaning "ten speeches." It was not God who divided the list of His commandments into ten parts. In the Bible, the commandments are not numbered; but the Bible does call the list "the ten commandments," though it does not tell which number applies to which commandment.

The list of commandments on the preceding page is divided into eleven parts, instead of ten. In the Catholic method of numbering the commandments, the first two sentences together are the First Commandment, and the remaining sentences are numbered consecutively from 2 to 10. Many Protestants also number the commandments in that way. Many other Protestants, and Jews, number the first nine sections as Commandments 1 to 9 and treat the last two sentences together as 10.

The people hear God's voice

When God gave the Ten Commandments to Moses, all the people heard the thunder and the sound of the trumpet, and they saw the lightning and the mountain smoking. They heard God's voice, also, and were afraid.

"Pray to God not to speak to us Himself," they begged Moses. "If you speak we can hear you and still live, but we are afraid that the voice of God speaking to us would kill us all."

Moses assured the Israelites that they had nothing to fear.

"The Lord is not coming to kill you," he said, "but only so that you will know Him, and ever after fear to sin against Him."

The people stood a good way off from the mountain, but Moses went up to the mountain, near the dark cloud where God was.

There God talked with him, and gave him many more laws for the children of Israel to obey. Afterward Moses came down from the mountain and wrote those laws in a book, and read them out to the people. When the people heard them, they promised to obey all the laws that the Lord had made.

41

The story of Moses and God on Sinai

THE LORD TOLD MOSES TO COME UP on Mount Sinai again. He said that He would give Moses tablets of stone with the Ten Commandments written upon them. Moses went up on the mountain and Joshua went with him; Joshua was acting as Moses' assistant, or minister.

There came a cloud that covered the mountain for six days. On the seventh day the Lord called to Moses out of the cloud, and Moses went up into the cloud. Moses stayed on the mountain for forty days and forty nights. The people of Israel saw the glory of the Lord on the top of the mountain, like a bright burning fire there.

While Moses was on the mountain God told him exactly how the Israelites were to worship Him. God said that Moses' brother Aaron should become the high priest, and that Aaron's sons and other descendants were also to be priests. The Levites—descendants of Levi, who was one of Jacob's twelve sons—were to assist the priests. The Israelites were to build a tabernacle, or church, where the priests would be in charge. The tabernacle was to be very beautiful, with objects of gold, silver, and brass, and with fine wood and cloth.

To be in charge of making the tabernacle, the Lord told Moses to appoint a man named Bezaleel, one of the Israelites, whom the Lord had taught to work in silver and gold, and in brass and precious stones, and to make all kinds of beautiful work. Another man, named Aholiab, was to help him. Many other workmen were to help those two.

When the Lord was done talking with Moses, He gave Moses the two tablets of stone with the Ten Commandments written upon them, which God had written there with His own hand.

A few days after Moses was gone, the people of Israel became restless.

The people of Israel were in their camp at the foot of the mountain all through the forty days and nights that Moses was on the mountain. After a few days they grew impatient and complained to Aaron.

"This man Moses, who led us out of Egypt, has not come back for many days," they said. "We have no idea what has become of him. Perhaps he will never come back! We need a god to worship, so that we may have a god to protect us! Make us a golden idol, that we may have a god!"

Aaron listened to them. He knew there is only one God, but he was afraid of the people and decided to do as they asked.

The Israelites set up the golden calf.

"Give me the golden earrings you and your wives wear, and the golden jewelry that you own. I will make an idol with the gold," said Aaron.

The Israelites did as Aaron had said, and he melted the gold and cast it in the shape of a calf. This made a golden calf, which was the kind of idol, or false god, that most people worshiped in those early times on earth.

Then the people said that the golden calf was their god, and that the golden calf, not God Himself, had brought them out of Egypt. Aaron built an altar before the golden calf and told the people that the next day they would hold a feast.

Early in the morning of the next day, the people offered burnt offerings to the golden calf, instead of to the Lord, and they had a feast and ate and drank before the idol.

While they were doing these things Moses was still on the mountain. He could not see them, but the Lord saw them and told Moses to go down, because his people had done wickedly. They have made a calf, the Lord told Moses, and have worshiped it and sacrificed to it and called it their god.

Moses turned and went down Mount Sinai, with the two tablets of stone in his hand, the ones on which the Ten Commandments were carved. Joshua was with him. As they came near the camp, they heard the noise of the people shouting, and Joshua said to Moses:

"There is a sound of war in the camp of our people," he said.

"It is not the sound of war that I hear," Moses answered, "but the sound of singing and celebration!"

Moses breaks the tablets of stone

When they came nearer Moses saw the golden calf and the people dancing before it. He was so angry that he threw the two tablets of stone out of his hands, and they were broken in pieces as they fell down the side of the mountain.

Moses took the golden calf away from the people. He melted it in the fire, then he ground it up into very small pieces, like powder or dust. Then he sprinkled the dust on water and made the children of Israel drink the water, so that they themselves would consume the idol they had made.

Moses asked Aaron why he had helped the people commit this great sin. Aaron tried to excuse himself, saying that the people were determined to do wickedly, and they asked him to make an idol for them. They gave him their gold, and when he put it into the fire, it came out in the shape of a calf. However, it could not have come out so unless Aaron had given it that shape. When the people asked him to make them an idol, he who was to be their high priest should have told them how wicked it would be, instead of helping them to do it.

Now it was the duty of Moses to punish the Israelites, as a sign of God's anger that they had disobeyed Him.

Moses stood at the gate of the camp, and said that all the men who were on the Lord's side should come to him. All the men who were the descend-

Moses asked all the men who were on the Lord's side to come to him.

ants of Levi, one of the sons of Jacob (or Israel), came to Moses.

Then Moses told these men, the Levites, that God commanded each one of them to take his sword and go through the camp, from one end of it to

Punishment of the idolaters

the other, and kill every man he met. In this way God would punish the people for their wickedness. The Levites did as Moses told them, and they killed that day about three thousand men. Only the wicked died, for God guided each sword to protect the innocent.

The next day Moses spoke to the people and said that although they had done a great sin, he would go and pray to the Lord for them, and perhaps their sin might be forgiven. He went and prayed to the Lord, saying,

"O Lord God, these people have sinned a great sin, and have made an idol of gold." But he begged that God would forgive them.

God answered that He would punish those who had sinned against Him, and that He would not go with them in the cloud, as He had done before, to show them the way to Canaan. But Moses again prayed very earnestly, and the Lord heard his prayer and promised that He would still go with the people of Israel.

God told Moses to make two tablets of stone like those he had broken. God said He would write on these new tablets the same words that were written on the first tablets. He commanded Moses to be ready in the morning and to come up to the top of the mountain. No man was to come with him, nor to be anywhere on the mountain.

Moses cut two tablets out of rock, like those he had broken, and he rose early in the morning and went up on Mount Sinai with the tablets in his hand. The Lord came down in the cloud and passed by before him, so that Moses could hear His voice. Then Moses bowed down to the earth and worshiped. He prayed again that the Lord would forgive the people of Israel and would keep them as His people. The Lord heard Moses' prayer and took the Israelites to be His people again.

The Lord told Moses that he must be careful, when he reached Canaan, not to make friends with those wicked nations. He must tear down the altars they had built to their idols, and break those idols in pieces, because the people of Israel were not to worship idols but only the Lord.

Moses stayed on Mount Sinai forty days and forty nights, as he had once before. In all the forty days and forty nights that he spent there, Moses neither ate nor drank.

The Lord wrote the Ten Commandments again, on the two tablets that Moses brought.

42

The story of the first tabernacle, or church

AFTER THE FORTY DAYS AND FORTY NIGHTS were ended, Moses came down with the tablets in his hand. The skin of his face was bright and shining, because he had been so near to the Lord, though Moses did not know that his face shone.

When Aaron and all the people of Israel saw Moses' face shine they were afraid to come near him, but he called them to him. Then they came, and he told them the words that the Lord had spoken. But while Moses was speaking he put a veil on his face, so that it would not dazzle them.

Moses called all the Israelites together and commanded them to bring gold and silver, and brass and wood, and whatever else was needed to build the tabernacle. The people brought whatever they chose to give—bracelets and earrings, ornaments of gold and silver, brass and fine linen, and wood. Some gave precious stones for the breastplate, or oil for the lamp. Both men and women brought offerings for all the different kinds of work that the Lord had commanded Moses to have done. They did this willingly; and even after enough had been brought, they still kept on bringing more every morning, until Moses sent word through the camp that they should stop bringing. He gave their offerings to Bezaleel, and Aholiab, and other men whom the Lord had taught to do the work.

Then these men made curtains of fine linen, of blue and purple and scarlet, for the tabernacle; and curtains of goats' hair, and of goats' skins dyed red, to be spread over the tabernacle for its roof. Also that beautiful curtain of blue and purple and scarlet, called the Veil, that was to be hung inside the tabernacle to make two rooms there; and the curtain that was to hang down in front to serve as a door. They made the boards also, covered with gold, which were to be set up and fastened together for the sides of the tabernacle.

The tabernacle: Above and right, *planning the building of the tabernacle.* Below, *the altar of burnt offerings; and, at its right, the laver in which the priests washed their hands.*

The tabernacle: Above, *Aaron in the garments of the high priest.* Left, *the weaving of the fine cloth.* Below, *the altar for incense at left and the candelabra, right.*

Bezaleel made the ark that God had commanded should be made. First he made it of wood and then he covered it, inside and outside, with gold. He also made the cover of the ark; this formed a seat, or throne, and was considered as the throne of God when His presence was in the tabernacle. There was no wood in this—it was all of pure gold. He then made two cherubim, or angels, of gold, one for each end. Their faces were turned toward each other and their wings spread out.

Bezaleel made the table for the inside of the tabernacle, the border, like a little fence or railing. He made dishes and bowls and spoons also for the table, all of gold. And he made the golden candlestick that seemed to have six branches growing out of its sides, three out of one side and three out of the other. On these branches almonds and flowers were carved. There were seven lamps belonging to the candlestick, to hold oil and to burn.

Then Bezaleel made the altar for incense, of wood covered with gold. He mixed the oil that was to be poured on Aaron's head when Aaron was anointed as high priest, and the sweet incense that was to be burned on the golden altar. He made the altar for a burnt offering, on which the children of Israel were to offer up sacrifices—oxen, lambs, and goats—of wood covered with brass. Then he made the laver of brass, which was a great basin, or bowl, to hold water, for Aaron and his sons to wash their hands and their feet in, because God had commanded them always to wash their hands and their feet before they went into the tabernacle or went to the altar of burnt offering to offer up a sacrifice there.

Bezaleel made the brass posts, or pillars, which were to stand around the tabernacle to make a court, or yard, around it; and he made the curtains that were to hang between those pillars, for a wall, or fence; and the curtain that was to hang down in front of the court for its gate.

Bezaleel and Aholiab made the clothes for Aaron: his linen coat, and a coat called the ephod. They took gold, and beat it very thin, and cut it into little strips, and worked these strips in among the purple, the blue and the scarlet of the cloth, to make this coat more beautiful. And with it they made a belt, or girdle, of the same cloth as the ephod itself. This was to be fastened around Aaron's body over the ephod. They made the breastplate with twelve precious stones upon it. Each stone was set in a piece of gold. Aaron was to wear this on his breast. It was to hang there by two chains of gold coming down from his shoulders.

Moses (shown at the left) sets up the tabernacle, by God's command.

Then they made the robe, or coat, which Aaron was to wear under the ephod. It was all of blue, and around its lower edge were hung pomegranates of blue, and purple, and scarlet, and between them golden bells that would ring as Aaron went in and out of the tabernacle. They made coats of fine linen for Aaron's sons, and linen trousers as well, and the mitre for Aaron's head, with a plate of gold bearing words that said it was sacred to the Lord.

So the different parts of the tabernacle were finished, and were ready to be put together. Bezaleel and Aholiab and the other workmen took them to Moses, and Moses looked at all the work and saw it was done as God had commanded.

God spoke to Moses then and told him to set up the tabernacle. So Moses set up the boards covered with gold, for its sides, and spread over them the curtains that had been made for the roof, and these curtains covered the tabernacle, and hung down on each side of it. He put the two tablets of stone with the Ten Commandments written on them into the ark and covered the ark with its golden throne. Then he took the ark into the tabernacle, and hung up the curtain called the Veil, so that it made two rooms, and he left the ark in the innermost room.

He stood the golden table, the golden candlestick and the golden altar in the other room, and he hung up the curtain that was made for a door in front of the tabernacle. Outside this door, but not far from it, he placed the altar of burnt offering, and he offered up a sacrifice upon it. He set the laver near to the altar and put water in it, and Moses and Aaron and his sons washed their hands and their feet at the laver. Then Moses set up the brass pillars around the tabernacle, and hung up the curtains between them for a wall, and made the court around the tabernacle. He hung up the curtain of blue and purple and scarlet and fine linen, which had been made for the gate of the court.

So the tabernacle was set up, and the court; and everything was put in its place inside the court, and in the tabernacle. Then the pillar of cloud, that went before the children of Israel to show them the way, came over the tabernacle and covered it. And the glory of the Lord filled the inside of the tabernacle, so that no one could go into it, not even Moses.

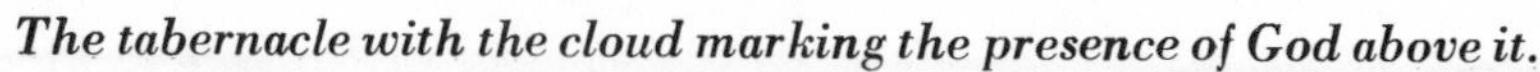

The tabernacle with the cloud marking the presence of God above it.

43

The story of the priests of Israel

After the tabernacle was finished God did not call Moses up on Mount Sinai again to speak with him. Instead, God called Moses into the tabernacle. God came into the tabernacle in a cloud, over the Mercy Seat, where the golden cherubim spread out their wings. He spoke with Moses there and gave Moses many new laws for the people of Israel.

God told Moses to bring Aaron and his sons to the door of the tabernacle, where Moses would consecrate them, or make them priests. Moses obeyed, and he called all the people to come and see what the Lord had commanded him to do.

While the people stood around the door of the tabernacle, Moses took Aaron and his sons and washed them with water; and he put on Aaron the beautiful garments that had been made for him. Then he poured oil on Aaron's head and anointed him. On Aaron's sons also Moses put their new garments. Afterward Moses offered up sacrifices to God.

So Aaron and his sons were made priests, to stay at the tabernacle and burn incense and offer up sacrifices for the children of Israel. Before this time men had offered up their own sacrifices, as Abel, Noah and Abraham had done. Now that God had chosen Aaron and his sons to be priests, no one else was allowed to offer up a sacrifice; every man had to take his offering to the tabernacle, and let the priests burn it for him on the altar there.

After being made high priest, Aaron took a lamb and killed it, and laid it on the altar as an offering for the sins of all the people, but he put no fire under it. The Lord sent fire that burned up the lamb. When the people saw the fire they shouted for joy, for now they knew that the Lord was

The blinding glory of the ark of the covenant and the Mercy Seat.

pleased with their priests and with their offering. Afterward the priests always kept the same fire burning on the altar, and would not let it go out, because the Lord had sent it there for them. It was sacred fire.

The priests were commanded to offer up two lambs every day, one in the morning and the other in the evening, for the sins of all the children of Israel. God told Moses that if any man who was sorry for his sins wanted to bring an offering for himself alone, he might bring an ox, or a sheep, or a goat to the door of the tabernacle. There he was to lay his hand upon its head. This was as if the man transferred his sins from himself to the animal. Then he was to kill the animal and Aaron's sons, the priests, would burn it for him on the altar, and God would be pleased with it for an offering.

The burnt and peace offerings

There were different kinds of offerings. When a man brought one because he repented of his sins and wanted to be forgiven, the priests took it and burned it all on the altar. This was called a burnt offering. When a man brought one because he was thankful for some blessing God had given him, or because he wanted some blessing he was praying that God would send him, then the priest took the animal and burned only part of it on the altar, not all. Some of it the priests kept for themselves to eat, and some of it they gave back to the man for him to eat. This kind of offering, part of which was burned and part eaten, was called a peace offering.

The man who made the peace offering, after the priest had given him back his part, invited his family and his friends, and perhaps his poor neighbors, to feast on it. The man was not allowed to put away his part and keep it to eat later. It had to be eaten that same day or the next day. The Bible often mentions the feasts that the people held with their peace offerings.

Aaron had four sons and they were all made priests when he was made high priest. It was their duty to attend to the worship of God at the tabernacle in the way that God commanded. There was a special way for incense to be burned on the golden altar. The incense was placed in a censer, which was something like a cup, made probably of brass. The priest first put coals of fire in the censer. Afterward he carried the censer into the tabernacle and set it on the golden altar. He then sprinkled the incense on the coals so that it might burn and send up its sweet smoke.

Punishment of Nadab and Abihu

Two of Aaron's sons were named Nadab and Abihu. They were priests, and one of their duties was to burn incense in their censers, using the sacred fire from the altar. Only coals from that sacred fire were to be used, and only incense made of certain spices, leaves, and herbs were to be its ingredients. To use another incense, or to use a coal from any fire but the altar fire, was in direct disobedience to God's command.

Nadab and Abihu took coals from a "strange fire"—which means that they used a fire other than the holy one—and placed the coals in their censers to burn incense.

That act of disobedience angered God, for it was a sin to disobey God's commands. In punishment for their sin, God sent down fire from the sky, and killed both Nadab and Abihu. The "fire from the sky" was probably lightning, for it killed the two priests without burning them.

"Come and remove these bodies from the tabernacle," said Moses. "Take them far away from here, and out of the camp, for God has killed them as punishment for their sin.'

Nadab and Abihu are killed by fire from the sky.

God commanded Aaron and his two remaining sons not to grieve or mourn for the two who were dead, because their death was due to their sinning against God.

Clean and unclean meat

The Lord told Moses what animals, and birds, and fishes the people of Israel might eat after they reached the land of Canaan, for they were not to eat every kind. They were allowed to eat cattle, deer, sheep, and goats, but not camels, rabbits, or pigs. They were allowed to eat all fish that had fins and scales but they were not allowed to eat those whose skins were smooth and without scales. They were allowed to eat some kinds of birds, such as the dove, the pigeon, and the quail, but there were many other kinds which they were forbidden to eat, such as the eagle, the raven, the owl, and the swan. Those that they were allowed to eat were called clean animals, and those they were not allowed to eat were called unclean.

At that time, the skin disease that was called "leprosy" was believed to be sent as a punishment for a man's sin, and the people believed that only

The laws on leprosy

God could cure it. This was the disease that God made to appear on Moses' hand, and then removed, so that it might be a wonderful miracle to show the people of Egypt, to help Moses convince them that he had spoken with God.

God seems to have used leprosy, in those times, as a punishment for the people's sins; at least He allowed them to believe so. Today doctors know that leprosy can usually be cured by proper treatment, just like any other skin disease.

Still, because the people thought it was a disease of punishment, God gave Moses instructions for the priests to follow when people appeared to have leprosy.

God told Moses and Aaron that when a man had a spot or sore on his skin that seemed like the beginning of leprosy, he must go to the priest, so that the priest might look at it and decide whether or not it were leprosy. If it were, the man had to go away from the camp, from his family, and from all the rest of the people, and live in some place alone until he was cured. When God cured him, he had to go and say that he was cured. After that he might come back and live in the camp. But he must take three lambs (or, if he were poor, and could not bring so many, he could take one lamb and two doves or young pigeons) to the tabernacle as offerings to the Lord, who had cured him.

The room in the tabernacle where Moses had left the ark and where God came and lived in a cloud, over the golden throne, was the most holy part of the tabernacle. It was called the Most Holy Place, or the *Sanctum Sanctorum*. The Lord told Moses that no one but Aaron, the high priest, must ever go there, and even he should not go there often. He could go only once a year, and then he must go very carefully. Before entering he was to wash himself thoroughly so that he might be clean, and he was to take off his splendid high priest's dress and put on a plainer dress of pure white linen. He must go in humbly dressed before the Lord. He was to offer up sacrifices before going, for his own sins and the sins of all the people, and he was to take the blood of those sacrifices into the Most Holy Place and sprinkle it, with his finger, before the throne. There Aaron was to pray that the Lord would forgive him and all the people.

The Sanctum Sanctorum

On the day when Aaron went into the Most Holy Place the people of Israel were commanded to do no work, but to remember the sins they had committed. God said they should "afflict their souls for their sins," which meant they should think of them and repent, with great sorrow. Whoever did not do this, God said, would be punished. That day was to be the most solemn day of all the year to the children of Israel. It was called the Day of Atonement. Now it is called Yom Kippur.

God said that when the children of Israel reached Canaan and went into the fields, to cut down their grain and store it in their barns, they must not gather it all, but must leave a little. And when the grapes were ripe on their vines, and they went out to gather them, they must not take every grape but must leave a few. They had to do this so that poor persons and strangers, who had no fields or vineyards of their own, could come and take what was left.

The Lord said that the people of Israel must not steal, or deceive, or lie to one another. When a man had been working for them they should not make him wait until the next day to be paid for what he had done, but they should pay him on the same day.

If a person were deaf, they must not say unkind things about him because he could not hear; or if he were blind, they must not put things in his way to make him stumble and fall. If any one knew evil of another, he must not go about telling it. In other words he must not be a tale-bearer.

The people of Israel were told not to hate one another, but they were to love one another as they loved themselves. If one of them saw another do wrong, he should reprove the wrongdoer kindly for what he had done. Perhaps then the man would repent and not do it again.

If a stranger from another country came to live among them, he must not be treated unjustly, nor should they take away what belonged to him. They must be as kind to him and love him as much as though he had always lived with them and was one of their own people.

On the day when Aaron went into the Most Holy Place the people of Israel were commanded to do no work, but to remember the sins they had committed.

'HE FALL OF MANNA

Molech, the idol made of bras

The feast of the Tabernacles.

44

The story of the feasts and the year of Jubilee

THE HEATHEN NATIONS AMONG WHOM the people of Israel were to live worshiped an idol named Molech. This was an idol made of brass. It had the face of a calf. It was very large and hollow, so that a fire could be lighted inside it. After it became very hot those wicked people put their little children into its arms, where they were burned to death. While they were being burned the people beat drums, so that their cries could not be heard. They burned their children in this way to please the idol, and they called it "giving their children to Molech."

God told Moses that if any man among the Israelites gave his children to Molech, that man must be put to death. The people were ordered to stone him till he was dead. If they let him go without punishment, pretending not to know what he had done, God said that He Himself would punish that man.

The Lord commanded the people of Israel to hold three feasts to Him every year. The first was called the feast of Passover.

The Passover was held in memory of the night when the Destroying Angel traveled through Egypt, killing the firstborn in Egyptian houses but passing by the houses of the Israelites where there was blood on the door. The blood was the sign that the people of that house had killed a lamb and eaten it during the night, according to the instructions God had given Moses before Pharaoh had finally let the Hebrews leave Egypt.

Now, the Lord said, the people should remember this once every year, eating lamb in the night as they did then and for seven days afterward eating unleavened bread. All those seven days were called the Feast of the Passover. While the people were holding this feast they would remember how God had punished Pharaoh for their sakes and had set them free when Pharaoh was determined not to let them go.

Seven weeks after the Passover, the people were to hold a Harvest Feast, called also the Pentecost. This was to last only one day and was to begin after the grain had been gathered into the barns. Then the people would thank God for sending the rain and the sunshine, which had made their seed grow in the field and bear food for another year. At this feast, the Lord said, they should be glad and rejoice.

At the end of the year, when all the grain had been gathered in from the fields, all the fruits taken off from the trees, and all the grapes picked from the vines, the people were to keep the Feast of Tabernacles, or Tents. This was to last seven days. Then, the Lord said, they should cut off branches from the trees and make booths, or tents, of them. They should leave their houses and live in those booths for the seven days of the feast, because the people of Israel had lived in tents while they were journeying through the desert. The Lord wanted the Israelites to remember that time after they settled in Canaan and had houses there to live in.

At each of these three feasts every man among the Israelites was to visit the tabernacle and give an offering to the Lord.

God told Moses that the people should give olive oil for the lamps in the tabernacle. Olives grew plentifully in Canaan and people made olive oil by pressing them. It was this oil that the people were to bring for the seven lamps that belonged to the golden candlestick. The Lord said that every day Aaron and his sons should trim the lamps, which were to burn all night in the tabernacle. Only the priests were allowed to trim them.

God also commanded Moses to take fine flour and bake twelve cakes, or loaves of bread. These were to be placed on the golden table that stood in the tabernacle near the golden candlestick. Moses was to put the loaves there on the Sabbath day and leave them a whole week, until the next Sabbath. Then the priest was to take them away and put fresh loaves in their place. The priests were to do this every week. Aaron and his sons could eat the old bread when it was taken away, but they could not take it home to eat it. They must eat it at the tabernacle, because it was holy bread; it had been set on the golden table before the Lord. These twelve loaves were called show-bread, because it was placed in the tabernacle to show that the people realized that all things came from God, including the grain that provided bread for the people. In ancient writing this was spelled "shew bread," but the "shew" is pronounced "show."

The stoning of the Egyptian

There was, at this time, a man in the camp whose father was an Egyptian, but his mother was one of the children of Israel. He quarreled with an Israelite, and in his anger he blasphemed God's name. That is, he spoke wickedly of God. He was brought to Moses.

"This man has spoken evil of the Lord, our God," the people said to Moses. "What shall be his punishment?"

"The Lord will tell me," Moses replied. "Until the Lord makes His wishes known, lock this man up, so that he may not escape."

The order of Moses was obeyed, and the man was locked up until such time as Moses would learn what God wanted his punishment to be.

The Lord spoke to Moses and commanded him to take the man out of the camp and to have the people throw stones at him. The Lord said that whoever blasphemed His name, whether it were one of the people of Israel or a foreigner who had come to live with them, must be put to death. The people should stone him till he was dead. Moses told the people, and they took the man out of the camp and did as the Lord commanded.

The twelve loaves of bread on their golden table: The show-bread.

The sabbath year

God said that after the children of Israel were settled in the land of Canaan they must plant seed in the fields and when it had grown they should cut it down and put it in their barns. They could do this for six years, but in the seventh year they must not plant any seed at all, but must let the land alone. If any grain grew by itself, without being planted, they must not cut it. If any grapes grew on the vines, they must not pick them. This year, God said, would be a sabbatical year, or year of rest, for the land. Every seventh year, He said, would be so. The people were never to plant seed nor take grain into the barns, nor gather grapes from the vines, in the seventh year. If any of the people were afraid they would not have food to eat, because they could not plant that year, the Lord would make enough grow the year before to last until the seventh year had past and the time had come again for them to sow their seed and reap their grain.

The year of Jubilee

Once in fifty years was to come the Year of Jubilee. This was to be a glad and happy year. On the first day of that year, trumpets were to be blown through all the land. The people were not to sow or reap in that year. God promised that He would give them enough food the year before to last through the Year of Jubilee. Then, if any man had been very poor, so that he was forced to sell the land his father had left him, when the Year of Jubilee came he was to have it back. The person who had bought it must give it back. Or, if any poor man among the children of Israel had been sold as a slave, when the Year of Jubilee came he must be set free, and all his children must be freed with him.

God told the people that if they obeyed His commandments, He would send rain on their land, their grain would grow well, their trees would bear fruit, they would have plenty of bread to eat, and no man could hurt them. The Lord would destroy or drive away from Canaan the wild beasts that might do them harm. He Himself would take care of them, and make all their enemies afraid of them.

If they did not obey His commandments, God warned that they would have sickness and trouble. They would sow their grain, but it would do them no good, for when it had grown up their enemies would come and take it from them. Wild beasts would carry off their children and kill their cattle. In the streets and roads where there used to be a great many people, only a few would be left. The Lord would send famine upon them, and they would have disease, and they would die. Their enemies would make war on them also, and the people of Israel would be carried away from their own land to other lands, where the people would hate them. There many of them would die. But if those who were left alive confessed that they had been wicked, and that it was God Who had punished them, He would punish them no more, but would be kind to them and take them back to the land He had promised to Abraham, and Isaac, and Jacob.

45

The story of the journeys through the desert

MORE THAN A YEAR HAD PASSED SINCE the Israelites had left Egypt, and they were still at Mount Sinai, where their camp had been so long. First, they had waited there forty days and forty nights, while Moses was on the Mount, when God gave him the two tablets of stone with the Ten Commandments written upon them. These were broken because the people worshiped the golden calf. Then they waited forty days and forty nights more, while Moses went up with the two new tablets that the Lord commanded him to make. Afterward they waited still longer while the tabernacle was being built, and when God spoke to Moses inside of the tabernacle, giving him many new laws for the children of Israel to obey. Now the time was near when they must leave Mount Sinai and continue their journey toward the land of Canaan.

The people of Israel were divided into large groups called tribes. There were thirteen of these tribes. Each tribe was descended from one of the sons of Jacob or of Joseph. These were their names: the tribes of Reuben, Simeon, Levi, Judah, Zebulun, Issachar, Dan, Gad, Asher, Naphtali, Ephraim, Manasseh, and Benjamin. As they would have to fight against their enemies when they came into Canaan, the Lord commanded Moses and Aaron to number, or count, the men in the different tribes who could become soldiers and go out to war. Moses and Aaron did so and found there were 603,550.

The men of the tribe of Levi were not counted with the others, because the Lord did not want them to go out to war. He chose them to be His priests, to stay near the tabernacle and take care of it. When the people of Israel went on their journeys, the men of this tribe were to take the tabernacle down and carry the different parts of it. When the people stopped to rest and make a camp, these men were to set the tabernacle up again.

The tabernacle and all the things in it were holy, and no one, except the priests and Levites, was allowed to come near them or touch them. If any other man did so, except when he came to offer up a sacrifice, or to worship, the Lord said he must be put to death.

After the other tribes had been counted, the Lord commanded Moses to take all the men of the tribe of Levi to Aaron. God said that the Levites should help Aaron and his sons.

The Levites appointed by God

They should not only take down the tabernacle, and carry it and set it up again, on their journeys, but all the time that it stood in the camp they must do the work there; for there was much work to be done. In addition to the two lambs that the priests were to offer up every day, the people would bring many other offerings. Wood must be cut in order to burn them. Water must be brought for the laver, or basin, where Aaron and his sons were to wash their feet and their hands whenever they went into the tabernacle or to offer up a sacrifice. The ashes must be taken away from the altar, and the court where

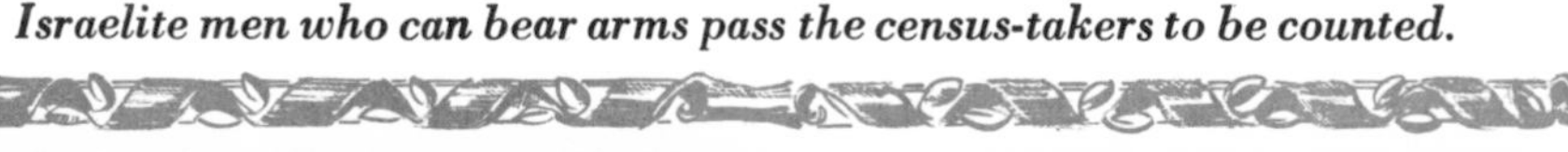

Israelite men who can bear arms pass the census-takers to be counted.

the offerings be killed must be kept clean of their blood. Aaron and his sons could not attend to all these things, and God chose the Levites to do it. He commanded Moses and Aaron to count the Levites, and they did so and found there were eight thousand five hundred and eighty men in that tribe. After they were counted, the men of the tribe of Levi went to wait on the priests and do the work at the tabernacle. Aaron himself was of the tribe of Levi, but he and his descendants had been separated to be priests.

Twelve princes, or tribal leaders, came from the other twelve tribes, bringing presents to the tabernacle. They brought six covered wagons and twelve oxen to draw them; also dishes, bowls, and spoons, made of silver and gold, to be used at the tabernacle. Moses gave the wagons and oxen to the Levites, so that there would be carts in which they could carry the different parts of the tabernacle when the people of Israel again set out on their journey. Two wagons were to carry the heavy curtains, and the other four would carry the boards covered with gold that made the sides of the tabernacle, and the brass pillars that stood around the court. Moses gave no wagons to carry the ark, the golden table, the golden candlestick, the golden altar, and the brass altar, for these were to be carried on the Levites' shoulders, not in wagons.

The pillar of cloud was still over the tabernacle. In the day it looked like a cloud and in the night it looked like fire. The day that Moses set up the tabernacle it came and stood over the Most Holy Place. Afterward it stayed there always, except when the Lord wanted the children of Israel to proceed on their journey, when it was lifted up higher. As soon as it was lifted up the people knew they were to go, and as the cloud moved on they followed after it. As long as it moved they followed, but whenever the cloud stopped they stopped and made their camp there.

How the Israelites traveled

When the Israelites had made their camp, they stayed until the cloud rose up again from over the tabernacle. If it stayed only one day, they stayed one day. If it stayed two days, they stayed two days. If it stayed a whole year, they stayed a year. Whenever the cloud rose, whether it was in the day or in the night, they went on their journey. For it was the Lord Who made it stay or go, and in this way He guided them through the wilderness.

The Lord commanded Moses to make two silver trumpets for the priests to blow upon, when Moses wanted to call all the people together, and also when they were about to start on their journey. Silver trumpets have a beautiful tone.

While on their journey the people of Israel carried standards, or banners, with them, and marched like an army. Each tribe kept in its own place, and each one had a leader. In the midst of the other tribes went the Levites, carrying the different parts of the tabernacle. As soon as the people stopped anywhere to make their camp, the Levites set up the tabernacle. Next to it they set up their own tents, and the other tribes set up theirs farther off. This was the way the children of Israel always made their camp. The tabernacle was in the middle of it, the tents of the Levites were next, and the tents of the other tribes were farther off. They did not move their tents until they took them down to set out again.

The Pillar of Cloud leads the Israelites on their way.

46

The story of Miriam's affliction

NOW THE TIME HAD COME FOR THE ISRAELITES to leave Mount Sinai. The Lord spoke to them, through Moses, and said they had been there long enough and that they should continue their journey toward Canaan. Then the cloud rose up from over the tabernacle and moved on before them; and they followed it for three days, until they came into the desert of Paran. There it stopped and they made their camp.

With the pillar of cloud always before them, the people of Israel knew that God was watching over them and taking care of them. Still their faith was not sufficient to keep them from worrying and complaining to Moses. This time their complaint concerned their food.

"We want meat to eat!" they exclaimed. "Where are we going to find meat?"

"Can you not trust God, who has always provided the things you need?" asked Moses.

"But we are tired of eating this manna!" they cried. "We have eaten nothing else for many days. At least, in Egypt we had fish, and melons, and vegetables. Here we have none of these things."

Each day Moses could hear them weeping inside their tents and complaining bitterly about their misfortune. Moses was very sad because the people were not properly grateful to God for the care and protection He had already given them; and the Lord was very angry with them.

Moses was discouraged. The care of the people was too much for him, Moses said, and if the Lord was going to send him such great trouble, he begged he might die, so that he would have it no more.

Moses sinned in speaking so. The Lord had always helped him when he was in trouble before and was willing to help him now. Moses should not have complained, but should have trusted in God.

The Lord commanded Moses to tell the people that they would have meat, for He had heard them weeping. They would have it, He said, not only for one day, nor five days, nor twenty days, but for a whole month, until it would become loathsome to them—that is, until they could not bear to taste it or see it. God would make it loathsome to them because they had been so wicked as to complain of the manna, without which they would have starved.

When the Lord told Moses that the people would have meat for a whole month, Moses could hardly believe it.

"There are six hundred thousand men here," murmured Moses. "How can meat possibly be provided for so many men and their families? Perhaps we are to kill all the flocks and herds that we brought out of Egypt."

God knew what Moses was thinking, and Moses was rebuked for his doubt. The Lord asked him if he thought the Lord no longer had power to do anything and everything He wanted to do, and Moses was ashamed for his doubt. Moses then told the people that they should merely wait and see how the Lord would provide them with meat.

God sends meat for a month

Then the Lord sent a wind that brought millions of quails from the sea coast, and they fell all around the camp. There were so many that the ground was covered with them. The people went out and gathered them all that day, and all that night, and all the next day.

However, when the quails were cooked, and the people started to eat greedily, many became ill. The Lord had decided to punish them by means of the very meat for which they had cried. It was a severe punishment, for great numbers of the Israelites died for the sin of complaining against the Lord's care. They were buried there in the wilderness.

At length the cloud was lifted up again and the people followed it until it stopped at a place called Hazeroth, where they stopped and made their camp.

Aaron and Miriam rebel

Now, Moses was the chief of the Israelites, because the Lord had chosen him to rule over them and had talked with him and given him the laws they were to obey. Yet the Bible says Moses was more meek and humble than any other man who was then living.

In spite of this, Miriam, who was Moses' sister, and Aaron, his brother, became angry at him because he had married a woman who was not one of the people of Israel.

"Why should our brother be the ruler of the people?" Miriam said to Aaron. "He did not even marry a woman of his own nation, but a foreigner!"

"That is true," said Aaron. "And has not God spoken to us, telling us what to do, as well as to Moses?"

"Surely we have as much right to rule as he!" said Miriam.

The Lord heard what Aaron and Miriam said, and He commanded them to go with Moses to the tabernacle. When they had gone there the Lord came down in the pillar of cloud and stood by the door. Then He called to Aaron and Miriam, and they came before Him; and the Lord told them that Moses was His servant who was obedient in doing His will, and He asked how dared they speak against Moses. Then the Lord's pillar of cloud rose up from the tabernacle. After it was gone Aaron looked at Miriam, and she was afflicted with leprosy, the skin disease, which made her skin as white as snow. God had caused it as a punishment for their wickedness.

Punishment of Miriam

When Aaron saw this, he was greatly troubled and he spoke to Moses.

"My brother, we have sinned in questioning God's work, and His selection of you as ruler over the people," said Aaron. "I know we have sinned. But this punishment of Miriam is a dreadful one. Will you pray to the Lord, that He may heal her?"

Moses felt great pity for his sister and he saw that Aaron's repentance was real. He prayed to the Lord, asking that Miriam's leprosy be cured.

"I beg You, Lord," Moses prayed, "heal her."

The Lord granted Moses' prayer and after seven days He healed Miriam's leprosy.

Shortly afterward, the people left Hazeroth and traveled to the desert of Paran.

47

The story of the spies sent to Canaan

At last the people of Israel were near Canaan. By the Lord's command, Moses chose twelve men, one from each tribe, to go ahead as scouts, or spies.

"Go into Canaan, and look over the land," Moses instructed them. "See whether the soil appears to be rich and good. Find out what kind of people are in this land—whether there are a great many, or just a few."

The twelve scouts listened carefully as Moses spoke.

"Notice whether they seem to be a powerful people, or weak," he continued. "We should also know whether they live in tents, or in houses within walled cities. Have no fear, while you are in this strange land, for the Lord will protect you. And when you return, bring back some of the fruit of the land, so that we can see what it is like."

The twelve men went into Canaan and walked through it from one end to the other, and the Lord protected them, as Moses had said He would. At a place called Eschol, where grapes were growing, they cut off a branch with a single cluster on it. This cluster was so large that it took two men to carry it. They hung it on a pole, or staff, and one man carried one end of the staff and another the other end, so that the cluster was carried between them. They also gathered some pomegranates and figs.

The spies remained forty days in Canaan and then returned to Moses and Aaron, and to the people of Israel, with the fruits they had gathered.

Of the twelve who had gone into Canaan, ten men were frightened and did not want the Israelites to enter the land. Two of the scouts, Caleb and

Cowardly spies fool the people

Joshua, were not afraid. They wanted the people to take the land that God had promised to give them. Caleb and Joshua had faith in God's promise, but the other ten were too filled with fear. They made up stories to tell Moses and the rest of the Israelites.

"Is the land rich and good?" Moses asked them.

"It seems to be very good," they answered. "The grain and the vines grow well, and there is plenty to eat and drink. But the cities have walls around them and the people are very numerous and powerful."

"But the people of Israel are well able to take this land," exclaimed Caleb. "Let us go at once into Canaan!"

"No, it is too dangerous!" declared the cowardly scouts. "The Canaanites are so big that we Israelites looked as small as grasshoppers compared to them! They would kill us all."

"But we have the promise of the Lord," said Joshua and Caleb. "We surely need nothing more to protect us."

At that point the people of Israel began to weep, for they believed the words of the cowardly spies, rather than the words of Caleb and Joshua, who were willing to act upon God's promise to them.

"We should go back to Egypt!" cried the people. "We should never have left there. It is because of Moses that we are here, and now what shall we do? What will happen to us?"

"Yes," agreed others. "Why has the Lord brought us to this place? Are we all to be killed by our enemies—even our wives and children?"

At last some of them entered into a conspiracy.

"Why do we not choose another captain, instead of Moses?" they whispered. "We can choose someone who will lead us back to Egypt!"

These complaints and murmurings were greatly disturbing to Moses and Aaron. Joshua and Caleb still tried to convince the people that Canaan was a good land and that they should enter it immediately.

"Do not be afraid of the men of Canaan," they begged. "The Lord will not help those men, but He will help the Israelites. He has promised!"

The people were angry at Caleb and Joshua for saying this, and wanted to stone them.

The Lord was greatly displeased with the people of Israel, and He told Moses that He would send a plague, or disease, to destroy them, and would

The spies return with samples of the rich fruit of the land of Canaan.

no longer have them for His people. However, He would make Moses' descendants even a greater nation than the Israelites were. But Moses prayed that the Lord would not destroy the people of Israel, but would keep them for His people.

The Lord granted Moses' prayer and promised not to destroy the people; but because they had disobeyed Him so often, and would not believe His promise in spite of all the wonderful things He had done for them, they could not yet go into Canaan but must turn back into the desert. There they must wander for forty years, until all the men who had refused to go in were dead. After the forty years were ended, and all those men had died, God said he would take their children into Canaan. He promised that Caleb and Joshua, the two good spies, would live until that time and go with them.

The people must wander forty years

When the people of Israel heard this they were very sorry for what they had done. They told Moses that now they were willing to go.

"No, you must not go now," said Moses sadly. "The Lord will not protect you if you go now. He would have, if you had been willing to enter Canaan before, but now it is too late. If you go into the land of Canaan, your enemies will kill you, and drive you out."

The Israelites disobeyed Moses and went into Canaan anyway, and the people of the land came and fought against them, and chased them away, as bees chase a person who goes near their hive. The Israelites returned to their camp and stayed there many days. Then they all returned to the desert again.

Death for a Sabbath-breaker

While they were in the desert, some people saw a man at work gathering sticks on the Sabbath day, which was against the Lord's commandment. They locked him up, waiting to learn how the Lord wanted him punished.

The Lord told Moses that the man should be put to death. The people should take him out of the camp and stone him (that is, throw stones at him) until he died. The people did as the Lord had commanded. For many years, those who "broke the Sabbath" were stoned by the Hebrews.

The punishment for these offenses seems very harsh to us today, but in the early days the people's faith in God was not very strong and—as you have read in these stories—they were constantly turning away from God's commandments to the wickedness and idol-worship of other tribes. Quite often, therefore, a wrongdoer was given very severe punishment as an example of the importance of obeying the commandments.

48

The story of the false priests

SOME TIME AFTER THE EXECUTION of the man who had violated the Sabbath, three men approached Moses, and with them were two hundred and fifty of their followers. The men were named Korah, Dathan, and Abiram. They were dissatisfied with the leadership of the Israelites.

"Aaron has no right to be high priest," they said, "and Moses ought not to be the ruler over the people."

Korah was a member of the tribe of Levi, so one of his duties was to help the priests in the tabernacle. Korah was not content with this task. He wanted to be a priest himself. That was why he had persuaded the others to go with him and stand by him when he accused Aaron of having no right to the high office he held.

Moses decided upon a method to convince everyone as to which man was rightfully entitled to be high priest.

"Bring censers and incense tomorrow," he said. "Aaron will do the same. Then you will all light your censers, and the Lord will show us which man should be high priest."

The next day Korah, Dathan, and Abiram, and the two hundred and fifty men, took censers and put fire in them, and sprinkled incense on the fire, as the priests did at the tabernacle. Many more of the people of Israel came out with them to rebel against Moses and Aaron. But the Lord was greatly displeased with the people for coming and commanded them to leave Korah, Dathan, and Abiram. The people obeyed.

Then Moses spoke.

"If the ground opens up and swallows these men, all of you will know that you have offended the Lord," he said.

As soon as Moses had spoken, the ground opened and swallowed up Korah, Dathan, and Abiram. They cried in anguish as they went down alive under the ground, but the earth closed over them. All the people near them ran away, when they heard their cry, for they feared the earth would swallow up them also. At the same time that Korah, Dathan and Abiram were swallowed up, the Lord sent lightning from heaven and it killed the two hundred and fifty men who had come out with them.

The next day the people again murmured against Moses and Aaron, saying it was they who had killed Korah, Dathan, and Abiram, and the two hundred and fifty men. "These were good men," they said.

The Lord was again angry with the Israelites, and He told Moses and Aaron to go away, so that He could destroy all of the other people in a single instant without destroying Moses and Aaron at the same time.

Moses and Aaron fell to their knees and prayed for the people of Israel, but the Lord would not listen, for even while they were praying He sent a disease upon the people and many were already dying in the camp.

As soon as Moses heard of this plague, he spoke to Aaron.

"Take a censer," he said. "Put fire from the altar of burnt offerings in it, for this is sacred fire and will be acceptable to the Lord. Go out quickly, and burn incense, offering it up to the Lord for the sake of the people. Already they are dying of the plague the Lord has sent to punish them!"

Aaron did as Moses had told him. He ran out with his censer, containing the burning incense, and stood between those who had already died and those who were still living. The Lord accepted the offering and put an end to the plague. Before it ended, however, fourteen thousand and seven hundred people had died, in addition to the three who had wanted to be priests and the two hundred and fifty men who had died with them.

Some time later the Lord told each of the tribes of the children of Israel to send Moses a rod. He commanded Moses to write on each rod the name of the man who brought it. Then Moses was to take the rods to the tabernacle, to the Most Holy Place, and leave them there before the ark, all night. One of them, God said, would grow in the night, and bear blossoms, as if it were still on the tree. The man whose name was found written on that rod would be the one whom God had chosen for His high priest.

Aaron's rod blossoms

The people sent their rods to Moses. After he had written the names on

The earth opens up and swallows Korah, Dathan, and Abiram.

them, Moses took them into the tabernacle and left them before the ark all night. The next day he went and looked at them, and one of them had grown blossoms and borne almonds. On this rod Aaron's name was written.

Moses brought out the rods and the people saw that Aaron's had grown blossoms.

Then Moses brought out the rods to all the people, and they saw that none had grown blossoms but Aaron's. God commanded Moses to take that rod and put it in the tabernacle again, to be kept there so that the people of Israel would remember that God had chosen Aaron for His high priest.

When Aaron and his sons died, their sons who lived after them were to be priests, and the men of the tribe of Levi would help them and do the work at the tabernacle.

The Lord said that all the other tribes of the children of Israel must give the priests and the Levites a part of their grain, of their fruit, and of their cattle. This was because the Levites were to stay at the tabernacle, attending to the worship of God.

49

The story of the brass serpent

THE PEOPLE OF ISRAEL TRAVELED ON and reached the desert of Zin. Miriam, the sister of Moses and Aaron, died and was buried there.

Again a time came when there was no water for the people. As they had done before, on occasions when they found no water, they complained bitterly against Moses and Aaron.

"Why have you brought us out into this waterless desert?" they cried. "Do you want us all to die of thirst, and our cattle as well?"

As He had done before, the Lord told Moses to call the people together at a rock nearby and take his staff in his hand. With Aaron beside him, Moses was to speak to the rock, in the name of the Lord, and the water would come out of the rock as it had before when Moses struck a rock at God's command.

This time both Moses and Aaron were angry at the people. They were tired of the way in which the people complained whenever there was any test of their faith in God. When they reached the rock, Moses addressed his people angrily.

"Listen to me!" he cried. "Must my brother and I get water for you out of this rock to make you remember that the Lord has always taken care of you?"

And with that he struck the rock twice with the staff that God had blessed, and water came out. There was plenty for all the Israelites, and for their cattle as well.

Moses and Aaron sinned, however, when they spoke in anger to the people and also when they led the people to think of God as cruel and not as the merciful Father of His people.

The Lord was displeased with Moses and Aaron for what they had done,

Moses (seen in the distance) again brings forth water from a rock.

and He said that as their punishment Moses and Aaron would not lead their people into the land of Canaan. The Israelites would go into that land, after the forty years they must spend in the desert, but Moses and Aaron would both die before then.

Soon the people reached Edom, the country where Esau had gone to live when he parted from his brother Jacob, or Israel. It had been hundreds of years since Esau went there, but his descendants were living there still; it was their land. Now the Israelites wanted to pass through it on their journey to Canaan, and Moses asked permission of the king.

"You know about the years our people spent in Egypt," he said. "You know also how cruelly we were treated by the Egyptian people. At last the Lord has taken pity on us and has brought us out of that land. Will you give us permission to pass peaceably through your country, on our way to Canaan? We will not damage the grain in your fields, and we will not drink the water that your people need. We will travel by the main highway through your country. We will hurt nothing."

But the king of Edom would not let them pass through, and he came out with his army to fight them. So the people of Israel turned and went by a different way.

They finally came to Mount Hor. There the Lord spoke to Moses and Aaron. He told Moses to take Aaron and Aaron's oldest son, Eleazar, up on Mount Hor. There Moses should take the high priest's garments off Aaron and put them on Eleazar, for Aaron was to die there.

Moses did as the Lord commanded. He and Aaron and Eleazar went up on Mount Hor, and the people watched them go. Moses took the high priest's garments off Aaron and put them on Eleazar, and Aaron died there on the top of the mount. So Eleazar was made high priest in the place of his father, and Moses and Eleazar came down from the mountain. When the people learned that Aaron was dead, they mourned him for thirty days.

The Israelites had a long way to go still, and they were tired of traveling.

"There is no bread here for us," they said. "Nor is there any water. And after all these years, we cannot stand this manna any longer!"

The Lord was angry at this, and sent fiery serpents (poisonous snakes) into the camp. They bit the people, and many of the people died.

The people appealed to Moses for help.

"We were wicked in speaking against you, and against God," they confessed. "We realize that now. But will you pray to the Lord for us, so that He will take away these serpents that bite and kill us?"

Moses prayed for them; and the Lord commanded him to make a serpent of brass, like those that bit the people, and set it up on a pole. If whoever was bitten would look at that serpent of brass, he would be made well, the Lord said.

Moses places a serpent of brass on a pole.

So Moses made a serpent of brass and put it upon a pole, and when anyone who had been bitten looked at it, he was cured. The serpent of brass did not do this, of course. It was the Lord, who used the serpent only as a sign.

50

The story of Balaam and the talking ass

THE ISRAELITES TRAVELED ON AND REACHED the plains of Moab. People called Moabites lived there, and their king was named Balak. When Balak saw the Israelites he was afraid, because he thought they had come to make war against him and there were too many of them for his soldiers to fight. He sent for a man named Balaam to come and curse them. The king of the Moabites wanted a great evil sent upon the children of Israel, and he thought that if Balaam asked for it God would send it, because Balaam pretended to have power with God.

The king told Balaam he would give him silver and gold, and make him rich and great, if he would come and curse the children of Israel. Balaam loved riches, and although the children of Israel had done him no harm he was willing to curse them for the silver and gold the king promised to give him. He rose early in the morning, and saddled his ass to go with the men the king had sent for him.

God was very angry with Balaam for this and sent an angel to stand before him, with a drawn sword in his hand. Balaam could not see the angel, but the ass saw him and turned out of the way into the field. Then Balaam struck the ass to make it go back.

The angel went on farther and again stood in Balaam's path, at a place where there was a wall on each side of it. When the ass reached that place it pressed close to the wall to get by; but it hurt Balaam's foot in doing so, and he struck it again.

Then the angel went on farther still and stood in a narrow place where there was no room to pass either to the right or to the left. The ass, because it was afraid, fell down on the ground under Balaam. At this Balaam was very angry and struck it with the staff that he had in his hand.

The ass speaks to Balaam

Then the Lord gave the ass power to speak to Balaam. "What have I done to you to make you strike me three times, as you have done?" it asked.

"You have disobeyed me," answered Balaam. "You turned aside when I wanted you to go straight on. I only wish I had a sword instead of a stick. If I had I would kill you—not merely strike you!"

The ass spoke again. "You have ridden on my back for a long time," it said. "Have I ever disobeyed you before?"

"No," Balaam admitted. "You have not."

Then the Lord let Balaam see the angel before him, with the sword in his hand, and Balaam bowed down to the ground.

"Why have you struck the ass three times?" the angel asked. "The animal saw me, and turned aside. I am here because you are planning to do a wrong. If the ass had not turned aside, I might have killed you and let the ass live."

Balaam listened to the angel as he continued to speak.

"Go with these men the king sent to accompany you, but tell the king only those things that I will say to you when the time comes."

Balaam obeyed, and went with the men. When the king learned of their coming, he went to meet them.

The next day the king took Balaam up on a hill, from which they could look down and see the camp of the Israelites. Here, as instructed by the angel, Balaam told the king to build seven altars and to prepare seven bullocks and seven rams to offer up as burnt offerings. The king did as Balaam said. He built seven altars, and offered up a bullock and a ram on each altar. Then Balaam asked the king to stay there while he went away alone, to see whether the Lord would let him curse the people of Israel.

Balaam went away alone, and the angel of the Lord came to him. Balaam told of the altars he had built, and of the animals he had offered, but the Lord would not let him curse the people of Israel. Instead he must say good things of them.

Then the king told Balaam they would go to another place. He took Balaam up to the top of a mountain, and there he built seven more altars and prepared seven bullocks and seven rams, and soon they offered a bull-

The angel with his sword stops Balaam and his ass: Doré's engraving. Balaam's back is shown, the other man being one of his attendants.

ock and a ram on every altar. Balaam thought that by building so many altars and offering up so many sacrifices he might persuade the Lord to let him curse the Israelites. But it was wicked of Balaam to think so, for the Lord cannot be persuaded to let anyone do wrong.

Balaam told the king once more to stay by the burnt offerings while Balaam went away alone to speak with the Lord and ask permission to curse the Israelites. The Lord came and spoke to him, and still would not let him curse the people of Israel.

Then the king said to Balaam,

"Come, we will go to still another place; perhaps the Lord will let you curse them from there." He took Balaam to a mountain called Peor and they built seven altars, as they had done before. Still the Lord would not let Balaam curse the Israelites. When Balaam spoke with the king the Lord made him say good things about the Israelites, and bless them.

The king became angry at Balaam and said, "I sent for you to curse my enemies, and instead you have blessed them three times." Then the king sent Balaam away without the silver and gold he had wanted so much.

When the Moabites found that they could not bring trouble to the people of Israel by getting Balaam to curse them, they tried another way to hurt them.

There were both Moabites and Midianites in that country, and Balaam told them both that they might be able to tempt the Israelites and make them sin. This would offend God and so it would do great harm to the Israelites.

"Invite them to the feasts that you hold to your idols," Balaam suggested.

The Moabites and Midianites did as Balaam said. They invited the Israelites to their feasts, and the Israelites came and ate with them. They even bowed down to the idols. The Lord was of course very angry with the people of Israel and sent diseases that killed thousands of them.

But the Israelites, with God's protection and help, finally overcame their enemies and Balaam too, though this did not happen until the Israelites had wandered in the desert for forty years, as the Lord had commanded.

When those forty years were ended God led the Israelites near the land of Canaan again. He commanded Moses and Eleazar to count the Israelites, to see how many were able to be soldiers and go to war. Moses and Aaron had done this before, while their camp was at Mount Sinai.

When Moses and Eleazar went out and counted the Israelites, they found that all of the men who had refused to go into Canaan the first time had died in the desert, as the Lord had said they would. But Caleb and Joshua were living still, for God had promised that they would live to go with the people into Canaan.

Balaam dies in battle

The Lord then commanded Moses to make war against the Midianites, because they had tempted the Israelites to sin and worship idols. Moses sent twelve thousand men, a thousand from each tribe, against the Midianites. The men of Israel defeated the Midianites and killed their kings. They killed Balaam also, who had taught the Midianites how to tempt the Israelites. The men of Israel took everything that belonged to the Midianites, including their cattle. There were seventy-two thousand oxen, sixty-one thousand asses, and six hundred and seventy-five thousand sheep. The Israelites burned the cities of the Midianites and all their great castles.

After the battle was over, the officers of the Israelites said to Moses, "We have counted the men that went out with us to fight, and all of them are here. Not one was killed."

The officers were grateful to the Lord for protecting their men in battle, and gave all the gold and jewels they had taken from the Midianites to Moses and Eleazar, as an offering of thanks to the Lord. Moses and Eleazar, who had become the high priest after Aaron's death, took them all into the tabernacle, to be placed there as an offering to the Lord.

The Lord led the people of Israel to the River Jordan, and there they made their camp. They waited until God should command them to pass over, for on the other side was the land of Canaan.

While they were waiting there, two of the tribes of Israel came to Moses and told him that they did not want to pass over the Jordan. They wanted to stay in the land where they were then (which was called the land of Gilead), because it was a good land for feeding cattle and they had a great many cattle.

Moses was displeased with these two tribes. He thought they wanted to stay in Gilead because they were afraid to fight the wicked people of Canaan.

"Do you expect the others to fight for you, while you stay here safely?" he asked them severely.

"No, we do not expect that at all," they answered. "We will build shelters for our cattle and houses for our wives and children, and then we men will go over to the other side of the Jordan to fight with the rest. When our brother tribes have made their land secure for themselves and their families, we will come back and live on this side of the river."

The two and one-half tribes

"If that is what you wish, and you will do as you say, you may do this," said Moses. He spoke to the rest of the people and told them that those two tribes should be allowed to live there. This was the land of Gilead, and the tribes that were the descendants of Reuben and Gad settled there. Half of the tribe of Manasseh decided to stay there also, and were given permission to do so, so there came to be two and one-half tribes in Gilead.

The Lord spoke to Moses and told him that when the Israelites went over into Canaan they must drive out all the heathen nations there. They must break down the idols and destroy the places that had been built to worship the idols. They must take the land from those people and keep it for themselves, because the Lord meant them to have it. Every man among the people of Israel was to have land given to him, where he could build his house, and sow his grain, and feed his cattle.

The Lord told Moses how large the land was that He would give the people of Israel, and how far it would reach. The priests and the Levites were to have no land given them. They would need houses to live in, and therefore they were to have forty-eight cities. The priests and Levites were to take their wives, their sons and their daughters into those cities. There they would make their homes.

MOSES STRIKING WATE
FROM THE ROCK

51

The story of Moses at the promised land

WHILE THE PEOPLE OF ISRAEL WERE CAMPED near the River Jordan, Moses spoke to them for the last time. God had told him that he could not go with them into Canaan but would die before they reached there. Moses was afraid that after he was dead the people of Israel would forget the things that God had told them and had done for them. So Moses made a long speech to the Israelites and told them again about many of those things.

Moses was now one hundred and twenty years old. The Israelites were close to Canaan, and soon they were to go there; but Moses could not go to the good land that God promised to his people. This was the punishment God pronounced on Moses for his sin at the rock, which is told about on page 223. The Lord said that Moses should go up on a high mountain from which he could see the land far off, but he must not cross the Jordan and actually enter Canaan.

Moses asked the Lord to choose the man who would go over with the people and lead them as Moses had done. God told Moses to make Joshua the leader of the people, to guide them when Moses was dead. Moses did as God commanded. He laid his hands upon Joshua and blessed him. God made Joshua wise and holy, so that he would know how to command his people in the right way.

Then Moses called all the people together, to speak to them for the last time.

These were the children who had grown up in the desert; the rebel-

The last speech of Moses

lious ones were dead. Moses spoke to them of all those wonders that God had done for them, and for their fathers, for forty years. He told them all their past history, since they went from Egypt. He reminded them of God's kindness, and of their sins and rebellions, and of all the laws that God had given them; and then, when he had finished, he taught them a beautiful song of praise to God.

Moses told the people that very soon they would cross the Jordan, and the Lord would go before them. They would have to fight against the nations that lived there, but the Lord would give them the victory. When God had given them the victory, the Israelites must not say that it was because they were righteous that He had done it. It was not because they were righteous but because those other nations were wicked that God would drive them out, and because He had promised Abraham, Isaac, and Jacob that He would give the land to the people of Israel. Actually, the people of Israel had not always been righteous.

Certain other rules were given in Moses' last talk with the people.

"If a man is poor, and in need of money or goods, you must lend him whatever he needs," said Moses, describing more of the Lord's commandments to the people. "Even though it seems that he may never be able to pay you back, you must lend to him willingly and generously, never with a feeling that you begrudge him that which you give. If you are kind to the poor, the Lord will bless you for it."

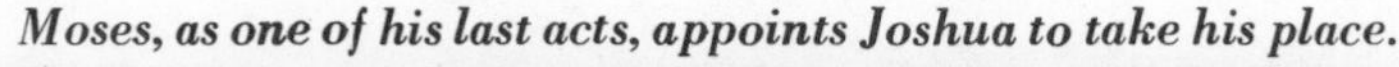

Moses, as one of his last acts, appoints Joshua to take his place.

The cities of refuge

Some cities in the land of Canaan must be cities of refuge. This meant cities where a man might go and be safe from punishment if he had killed another by accident. God had said before that any person who killed another on purpose should be put to death, for he would be a murderer. But sometimes a man might kill another without intending it. He might go to the woods to cut down a tree, and while he was doing it, the head of the axe might fly from the handle and strike someone who was standing near and kill him. The man with the axe would not be a murderer, but for fear that the dead man's brother, or his son, or some relation of his might come to kill him, he should go to the city of refuge.

When he reached the gate of the city, he should tell the elders there what he had done. The elders would take him into the city and give him a place to live. If the brother or the son of the man he had killed came to ask for him, they would not give him up because, although he had killed the man, he had not meant to do him any harm.

If a wicked murderer should come there, however, the elders would not take him into the city to save him from punishment. They would give him up to be put to death for his crime.

The Lord said that when the Israelites lived in Canaan and had the land for their own, each man must take the first of the grain, and the first of the fruits that ripened in his fields, and put them into a basket and take them to the tabernacle. The priest at the tabernacle would take the basket from the man and set it down before the altar of burnt offering. Then the man should say,

"I have brought the first fruits of the land that You, Lord, have given to me."

The basket with the first fruits in it would go to the priest, because the priests would have no fields or orchards in which to raise grain and fruit for themselves. The Lord commanded each man among the children of Israel to give his first fruits, every year, in this way, as an offering to the tabernacle.

Moses wrote down in a book the laws that God had given him. He told the priests and the elders to gather all the people together every seven years and read those laws to them so that they would learn to obey them. He gave the book to the Levites who carried the ark, and told them to take it and put it in the side of the ark, where it would always be kept.

Moses views the promised land and dies

After these things, the Lord spoke to Moses and told him to go up on a mountain called Mount Nebo and to look from there across the Jordan River into the land where the Israelites were going. Then, when he had seen that land, the Lord said, Moses would die on the mountain, as Aaron had died on Mount Hor.

Moses went from the place where the Israelites had their camp, up onto the mountain that the Lord had named. When Moses came to the top of it, the Lord let him see far over the land of Canaan and told him that this was the land He had promised Abraham, and Isaac, and Jacob, to give to their descendants.

Moses himself could not go to that promised land, and he knew it. He lay down on the mountain and died, and the Lord buried him; no one

Moses views the promised land and dies.

Moses dies in the mountains and is buried by angels of the Lord.

knows where, or how. When the people knew that Moses was dead, they wept for him in the plains of Moab for thirty days.

After Moses was dead, Joshua ruled over the people, and they obeyed him as they had obeyed Moses. The Lord gave Joshua wisdom and made him able to teach the people and guide them as Moses had done before. But there was never again any man among the people of Israel whom the Lord talked with face to face, as he did with Moses. Nor was there ever again a man sent to perform such wonders as God had entrusted to Moses, to be worked in Egypt and in the desert.

52

The story of Joshua and crossing the Jordan

CANAAN WAS THE LAND WHERE ABRAHAM, Isaac and Jacob had lived, and God had promised them that it would belong to their children's children. At this time there were other nations living in Canaan. There were the Ammonites, the Amorites, the Hittites, the Jebusites, and many others.

God told the Israelites that they were to go to the cities of these people. If the people would let the Israelites in, then their lives could be spared and they would afterward pay tribute or taxes to the Israelites. If the people would not agree to do this, then the Israelites were to fight against them and destroy them entirely.

God told the Israelites to destroy them because these nations were exceedingly wicked. They had gone on from bad to worse, till their sins seemed to cry to heaven for punishment.

The Lord spoke to Joshua in a dream and told him to lead the people of Israel across the Jordan into Canaan. Joshua was warned to be very strong and brave, and to obey all of God's commandments. If he did this, the Israelites would prosper. God also promised Joshua that He would always be with them to help if they neeeded it.

The first city the Israelites would come to, the city across the Jordan nearest to the place where they were encamped, was Jericho.

It was about April now. The sun had melted the snows of the mountains of Lebanon, and these mountain torrents had made the River Jordan swell to twice its usual size. The people of Jericho knew this, and they thought that they were safe for several weeks to come, as the Israelites could not cross to fight them yet.

However, very soon after the death of Moses Joshua had secretly sent two men to Jericho, to spy out the state of the city and see how the Israelites could best get into it. It was a city with a strong wall all around it, and the people of Jericho kept careful watch at the gates to keep out the Israelites.

Spies are sent to Jericho

The two spies somehow managed to get into the city, and they went to the house of a woman named Rahab. They had not been there long before they found out that the king of Jericho had learned that they had come into the city and that they had gone into that very house.

The king sent messengers to Rahab and said to her, "Give up the spies that are in your house, for they have come to search out the country."

Rahab protected the spies by answering, "The men did come here, but I did not know where they came from, and they are not here now. They went out through the city gates just before the gates were shut at dark. I do not know where they have gone, but if you hurry I think you can catch them."

Rahab saves the spies

The king's messengers believed Rahab and hurried away through the city gates, which were closed after them. They hurried in the direction they believed the spies to have taken, and went as far as the River Jordan. Of course, they did not find or catch Joshua's spies, because the spies were still at Rahab's house.

When Rahab was sure the king's men had gone away, she spoke to the two men.

"I must hide you," she said. "Come with me to the roof."

The roofs of houses in Jericho were flat, so that people could walk on them. That was the place where, in the cool of the day, the people sat for fresh air, and often in hot summer nights they slept there. Here, too, they would lay things they wanted to be dried by the heat of the sun, and it was there that Rahab had laid out stalks of flax to dry.

These stalks she meant to place over the men, so that they might be hidden, and that is why she took them to the roof. Before the men lay down she told them the reason she wanted to save them from the king of Jericho.

"I know that the Lord has given you this land," she said. "All the people

Rahab helps the Israelite spies to escape.

who live here are afraid of you. We have heard how the Lord dried up the waters of the Red Sea for you, when you came out of Egypt. We have heard how you have overcome all your enemies on the other side of the Jordan. I know, too, that God will give you the city, and I want you to promise me that you will protect me and all my relations just as I have protected you, by not giving you up to the king's messengers."

"We promise to do as you ask if you will keep our secret, and tell no one that we have been here," said the spies. "There is something you must do, however, so that we will know which is your house, and not destroy it with the others. Hang this piece of scarlet cloth in the window, and we will see it. Then we will be able to tell which house is yours."

"I will do that," said Rahab.

"And if you have any relatives whom you want spared, be sure that they are in this house with you," the spies warned her. "Otherwise we can do nothing for them."

"This shall be done," promised Rahab.

The house of Rahab was directly beside the city wall, and there was a window in her house directly above the wall. This was fortunate, because she could lower the spies by means of a rope and they would reach the ground outside of the city wall. The gates had all been closed and locked after the king's messengers had departed on their search for the spies, and there was no other way for the two men to get out of Jericho.

With the assistance of Rahab, they were lowered over the wall and were able to escape, and they hid for three days in the mountains, waiting for the messengers who were looking for them to return to the city.

When the messengers had given up the search and had returned to Jericho, the two spies crossed the River Jordan again and reported to Joshua everything that had happened to them.

Then Joshua spoke to the leaders of the people of Israel. He said to them, "Go through the camp and tell all the people to make food ready to take with them, for within three days you shall cross the Jordan."

Joshua reached the Jordan with all the people of Israel, and after three days the officers went among the tribes and told them to follow the ark of the covenant, which the Levites would carry before them. This ark was a sign of God's presence among them and a sign also that He was their chief guide.

The day following, the priests and the Levites "took up the ark of the covenant and went before the people." God told Joshua that He would now honor him by a wonderful miracle, which would show the people of Israel that God had chosen Joshua to lead them, as He had before chosen Moses.

The waters of Jordan stand aside

Joshua told the people of Israel what God would do for them. As soon as the priests who bore the ark touched the brink of the river with their feet, the waters of the River Jordan would stand in a heap on one side, so as not to flow down the channel. The waters on the other side would continue running without any fresh supply; then the bottom of the river would be dry for the people of Israel to pass over, as the Red Sea had been for their fathers with Moses. Joshua also ordered twelve men to be selected, to witness this miracle so that the rest would be convinced.

The priests moved forward and stood in the River Jordan, and the waters dried up as Joshua had foretold, although this happened at the time of harvest, when the river usually overflowed its banks because of the great quantity of water; this made the miracle even more wonderful.

When the priests came to the edge of the river, as soon as their feet touched the water, the water parted before them, and they walked out on dry ground into the middle of the river. There they stood with the ark, and waited while all the children of Israel passed over to the other side, into the land of Canaan.

The men of the two and a half tribes, who had asked to have their homes in the land of Gilead, went over also, as they had promised Moses to do, forty thousand of them, armed, to help the other tribes fight against the nations of the land. After the people had gone over, the priests, carrying the ark, followed them. As soon as the priests came up out of the river and stood on the shore, the waters flowed in the river again, filling it as full as it had been before.

At this time the Israelites numbered six hundred thousand men besides women and children, which was, indeed, a vast army. Still the Canaanites did not try to stop their crossing of the Jordan. Perhaps the Canaanites thought the Israelites could not cross the river. If the Canaanites saw that the waters stood aside, that would have been quite enough to frighten them, alarmed as they already were, and to make them run away.

The crossing of the Jordan was a great event, and Joshua therefore commanded twelve men, one from each tribe, and probably the same men spoken of before, to take twelve stones from the spot where the priests' feet had stood, and to carry them to their first lodging-place over Jordan, where they were to leave them. When at any future time their children asked, "What is the meaning of those stones?" they would be told "that the waters of the Jordan were cut off before the ark of the covenant of the Lord, when it passed over the Jordan, and that the stones were a memorial of the children of Israel forever."

God then commanded Joshua to give the Israelites of the new genera-

The Israelites, led by Joshua, cross the Jordan.

tion a sign of God's covenant with them. The Israelites then solemnly celebrated the Passover, for this was the proper time of the year for it.

The Israelites made their camp at a place called Gilgal. The country people fled away from the invading armies, and all their grain in the field and in barns became the property of the Israelites, who took it and ate it as part of their promised possession given them by God, Who made it grow. The day after they had eaten the corn, the manna stopped coming. For forty years the Lord had sent manna to them in the wilderness, where no grain grew. Now they were in Canaan, where there was plenty of food for them, and the Lord no longer sent manna.

53

The story of Joshua and the walls of Jericho

JOSHUA LEFT THE CAMP AND APPROACHED the walls of Jericho. Suddenly he looked up and saw a man standing before him, with a drawn sword in his hand.

"Are you a friend of the Israelites, or of the people of Canaan?" Joshua asked.

The man said he had come as the captain of the Lord's army. By saying this he let Joshua know that he was an angel of the Lord. The angel was there to show the Israelites how to capture the city and defeat their enemies.

Perhaps this was the same angel of the Lord that had appeared to Abraham, warning him of the destruction of Sodom and Gomorrah, and the same one that had wrestled with Jacob on his way to Canaan, and the same one that had appeared to Moses in the burning bush, all as told in Volume 1. Joshua was encouraged with the assurance that God would fight for him and give him the promised land for his people.

The people of Jericho had shut up the gates of the city, so that no one could go out or come in, because they were afraid of the children of Israel.

The Lord said he would give Joshua the victory over the king of Jericho, and he told Joshua how the Israelites should take the city. All their men of war, or soldiers, should march around the city once every day for six days, and some of the priests should carry the ark around with them. Seven more priests were to go before the ark, and to blow on trumpets made of rams' horns. On the seventh day the Israelites were commanded to march around Jericho seven times and the priests were to blow on the trumpets. Then, when the men of Israel heard a long blast on the trumpets, they were all to give a great shout, and the Lord said that the wall would fall down flat, so that they could go into the city.

Joshua told the people of Israel that only Rahab and the persons who were in her house with her should be spared. The Lord had commanded that all the rest of the people of Jericho should be put to death for their

The angel, captain of the Lord's army, speaks while Joshua kneels.

sins. Joshua also said that all the silver and gold, and all vessels made of brass and iron that were found in the city, belonged to the Lord and must be put into the treasury where the Lord's things were kept. Joshua warned the people not to take any of the silver or gold, or brass or iron, for their own, or the Lord would punish them for their disobedience.

The people did as the Lord commanded. On the first day they marched around the city once, and after them came the priests blowing on the trumpets. Then followed the priests who carried the ark. On the second day they marched around the city again. They did this for six days. On the seventh day they got up early, before it was light, and marched around the city seven times. The last time, when the priests blew with the trumpets, Joshua said to the children of Israel,

"Shout, for the Lord has given you the city."

Then the people shouted, and as they did so the wall of the city fell down flat before them. Then the Israelites marched in. They completely destroyed every living thing in the city—men, women, and children, and all the animals.

The walls of Jericho fall.

The city itself they set afire, and destroyed it also, but not until after the spies had kept their promise about Rahab, who had hidden them. Joshua told the spies, who had been at Rahab's house before, to go and bring out all the persons who were there, as they had promised to do. They went and brought out Rahab and her father, her mother, her brothers, and all others who were with her. Afterward the Israelites burned the city; but the silver and gold, and the vessels of iron and brass, were put into the treasury of the Lord.

Rahab lived thereafter with the people of Israel.

Upon Joshua's command, the spies brought out all persons that lived in Rahab's house and the promise to spare them was kept.

The silver and gold of Jericho was put into the treasury of the Lord.

54

The story of the battles for Ai

SOME TIME LATER, JOSHUA SENT SPIES to another city of Canaan, a city called Ai. Soon the spies came back with their report.

"Not many people live there," they told Joshua. "Only a small army of Israelites will be needed to take that city."

"Yes, two or three thousand will be enough," one of them added.

Joshua believed them and sent an army of only three thousand to capture Ai. However, when the men of Ai came out to defend their city, the Israelites suddenly became terrified and ran away. About thirty-six of them were killed.

This caused Joshua great distress.

"When the other people of Canaan hear how the Israelites ran from an enemy, they will all join together and surround us. All of the Israelites will be killed!" he cried.

As Joshua and the priests were praying for courage and help, the Lord told Joshua why this thing had happened to the Israelites at Ai. There was sin among them, and that sin had made them afraid to face the army of their enemies. One of their number had hidden some of the treasure taken in Jericho and had kept it for himself, instead of giving it to the Lord, as he had been commanded to do. Unless the sinner were punished, the Israelites would no longer have the protection of the Lord.

In the morning Joshua called all the people together and waited for the Lord to point out the guilty man. His name was Achan.

"What have you done, that the Lord should be angry with the children of Israel?" Joshua asked him.

Achan knew it was useless to try to conceal what had happened, and he confessed what he had done.

"I saw a beautiful garment in Jericho," said Achan. "It was so beautiful I wanted to keep it for my own. I also saw a piece of gold, and some silver money that I wanted to keep, and so I did. I hid them all in the ground under my tent."

Joshua sent messengers to Achan's tent and they found the things hidden there as Achan had said. They took the things to Joshua, who laid them out before the Lord.

Achan's punishment was severe, like every punishment for disobedience to the Lord's commands. Achan and all his family were taken into a valley and put to death by stoning. Their possessions and their dead bodies were then set afire, and a great heap of stones was piled on them, to mark the spot where they had died.

The Lord was no longer angry with the children of Israel on account of this sin, because they punished the man who had done it. The valley was called Achor, which means "trouble."

The second attack on Ai

Then the Lord told Joshua to attack the city of Ai once more, and this time the Israelites would be victorious because the Lord was with them. The people of Ai were to be put to death, like the people of Jericho, because they too were very wicked and sinful people. This time, however, the gold and silver and other treasures that were captured with the city need not be given to the Lord. The people were to be allowed to keep them all.

Joshua and the soldiers went to attack Ai, but they did not all go together. Joshua chose thirty thousand brave soldiers, whom he sent away in the night to go around the city and hide where the people of Ai could not see them. The rest went with Joshua in front of the city. When the king of Ai saw the men with Joshua, he thought they were all that had come, and he marched out with his army to fight against them. Then those who were hidden behind the city went in and set it on fire. When the men of Ai looked back and saw their city burning, they did not know which way to go. Joshua and his men were in front of them, and those who had set the city on fire were behind them, so they could not escape. Joshua put them to death, as the Lord had commanded. The gold, the silver and the cattle in Ai the people of Israel took for their own.

Joshua built an altar of great stones on the mountain called Ebal. He

The army of Ai is trapped when their city burns behind them.

covered the stones with plaster and wrote on the plaster the words of God's law, as Moses had commanded the people of Israel to do before they crossed over Jordan.

55

The story of how the sun stood still

WHEN THE OTHER KINGS IN CANAAN heard how Joshua had destroyed Ai, they joined together to make war against him. But the people of a city called Gibeon acted more cunningly. They did not want to make war against Joshua, for they knew that the Lord would give him the victory. Instead they sent messengers who wore very old clothes and worn-out shoes and carried dry and moldy bread with them, to pretend they had come from another country and had been a long time on the journey.

The men from Gibeon approached Joshua in the camp.

"We have come from a distant country, far from Canaan," they said. "We have heard of your God and of all the great things He has done for you. Our people would like to make a covenant with you and be your friends."

Joshua and the Israelites did not ask the Lord what they should do, but they promised at once to be friends with the men of Gibeon. Three days later they heard that these men had not come from a far country at all, for they lived nearby, in Canaan, and were among the wicked nations whom the Israelites were commanded to destroy.

Joshua called the men of Gibeon to him.

"Why have you come here and deceived me in this manner?" he asked them.

"We were afraid for our lives," they confessed. "We had heard how the people of Canaan are to be destroyed and all the land given to the people of Israel."

The Israelites did not put the people of Gibeon to death, because they had promised, before the Lord, to let them live. But Joshua said they

The sun stands still at Joshua's command, and the battle goes on.

should be bondsmen, or slaves, and work for the priests and the Levites, cutting the wood and carrying the water that would be needed in the tabernacle.

The people of Gibeon united with the people of Israel, which greatly angered the king of Jerusalem, whose name was Adonizedec. He called together some of the other city kings in Canaan and declared that they must attack Gibeon for making friends with the Israelites.

The kings united with Adonizedec and marched against Gibeon. When the people of Gibeon saw so great an army against them, they were frightened again and they sent for Joshua, saying,

"Come to us quickly, and save us."

Now, as Joshua had given his word, he would not kill the Gibeonites; and he would not, if he could help it, let others kill them. So he marched all night to Gibeon, with all his army, and God told him to fear nothing.

The Gibeonites are killed by "a hail of stones." This is Gustave Doré's interpretation, in which he shows actual stones falling from heaven. Many authorities believe that the Bible means actual hailstones, composed of ice; these often are so large (perhaps as large as apples) that in falling they can kill or injure men.

Joshua defeats the five kings

Joshua and his men attacked the five kings. The kings were surprised and fled, and Joshua pursued them.

As the kings were fleeing the Lord cast down great hailstones upon them, out of heaven, so that more died from the hailstones than the Israelites killed with the sword.

While the men of Israel followed the fleeing kings, the sun was going down and night was coming on. Joshua feared that his enemies would escape in the darkness, and he spoke to the sun, commanding it not to go down, and to the moon, commanding it to rise no higher in the sky. The sun stood still, and did not go down for many hours after the time when it went down on other days. That day was longer than any other day.

The Israelites continued to pursue the fleeing armies, and the five kings hid themselves in a cave. When Joshua heard of this, he told the people what to do.

"Roll large stones in front of the cave, and continue to follow those who are still trying to escape from you."

After the battle was over and the soldiers of Israel had returned to the camp, Joshua told them to open the cave where the kings were held prisoner.

"Let out the five kings and bring them to me," he said. When this was done, Joshua spoke again to his people.

"Never be afraid," he said. "Always be strong and brave, for the Lord will treat all of your enemies as he has treated these five kings."

All five kings were put to death, as the Lord had commanded. Their dead bodies were placed in the very cave in which they had hidden, and the Israelites once more sealed up the mouth of the cave with rocks.

After this, Joshua gained the victory over twenty-four more kings, and yet there was a great deal of land left for the men of Israel to take in Canaan. These kings did not rule over whole countries, but only over cities or over small portions of the land.

The tabernacle is set up in Shiloh

Joshua had grown old; he could no longer lead the people of Israel out to war as he had done. The people went to the city of Shiloh, to set up the tabernacle. They had carried the tabernacle all the way from Mount Sinai, taking it down when they traveled and setting it up when they made their camp. Now they had come into Canaan to stay and

Joshua casts lots to decide, with God's help, how to divide the land.

would journey no more. They took the tabernacle to Shiloh, which was in the middle of the land, and set it up to let it stand there, because that was the place the Lord had chosen for it.

So far, the Israelites had taken only a part of Canaan but they had grown tired of going out to war and they chose rather to rest and be quiet. The Lord was not pleased with them for this, for it seemed as though they did not care to have all the good land that He was willing to give them. The Lord spoke to Joshua and said that a large part of the land that he had given to the people was not yet taken from the Canaanites.

Then Joshua asked the people how long it would be before they went out again to conquer the heathen nations that were still living in Canaan.

"Choose some men whom I can send out to investigate the land that the people of Israel have not yet taken," he said. "Let them go and look over the land, and then they can come back with a description written in a book. Let them return to me here in Shiloh."

Joshua casts lots to divide the land

The men did as Joshua had told them and walked through the land. They wrote down in a book the description of it, and they took the book to Joshua in Shiloh. Joshua then cast lots for the different tribes, so that the Lord might show what part of the land each tribe should have. After the Lord had shown them this, Joshua told the men of Israel to go and drive out the heathen nations and take the land as their own. He promised that the Lord would help them.

The Lord told the people to choose the cities that were to be the cities of refuge, where any person who had killed another by accident might flee and be safe from punishment. The people chose six cities in different parts of the land.

Because the Lord had commanded it, Joshua and the people gave the priests and the Levites forty-eight cities in which to live with their wives and children and have their homes.

56

The story of the first judges of Israel

After Joshua was dead, the men of Israel went out to war against the heathen nations, as Joshua had commanded; and the Lord helped them and let them win. But they did not persevere until they had driven out all those nations from Canaan. They allowed some of them still to live in the land.

The Israelites were reminded often that the Lord had given them the land He had promised them, and that they were supposed to destroy the idols of that land, which they had not done. They were also reminded that they had been forbidden to make friends with the heathen peoples who lived in Canaan, and once again they had disobeyed.

The Lord sent a warning to the people of Israel and told them that from this time on He would not drive out their enemies. Instead, the heathen people would remain in the land and would tempt the Israelites to sin. This, the Lord said, would be the cause of great trouble to the children of Israel.

When the people heard these words they wept. But they soon forgot what the Lord had said, for they not only allowed many of the heathen peoples to stay in Canaan but they also treated them as their friends and often married among them. The men of Israel took heathen women for their wives and the daughters of the Israelites married heathen men. Then the people of Israel began to worship the idols called Baal and Ashtaroth, which the people of Canaan worshiped. The Lord was very angry with them and sent enemies who fought against them and enslaved them.

When the people of Israel finally repented and asked the Lord for help, He heard them and gave them rulers called judges, who led them out to war against their enemies and set them free.

The same thing happened many times. The Israelites soon forgot about the Lord and His goodness to them, after they were freed, and began to sin again. In time, they again repented, and once more the Lord took pity on them and set them free. For more than three hundred years they repeated this pattern of sinning and repenting, freedom and enslavement. During that time fifteen judges ruled over them.

Foreign kings rule Israel

The Israelites were conquered at one time by the king of Mesopotamia (the land we now call Iran) and were his servants for eight years. The first of the judges led the armies of Israel against the king of Mesopotamia and God gave them the victory. The name of the judge was Othniel, the younger brother of Caleb. (Caleb was the man allowed to enter Canaan with Joshua because, as a spy, he had trusted in the Lord.)

For forty years, the Israelites did not go to war, while Othniel was at their head. After the death of this judge, the people began sinning again.

The king of Moab brought an army against the Israelites and made them his servants for eighteen years. The people cried to the Lord for help, and the Lord made Ehud judge over them. Ehud was a man of the tribe of Benjamin and was left-handed. The Lord sent Ehud to set the Israelites free from the king of Moab. Ehud made a dagger and hid it under his garment on his right thigh.

Ehud then went to the house of the king of Moab, where he found the king sitting in his summer parlor. Ehud spoke to the king.

"I have a secret message from God for you, your majesty," he said.

The king's attendants were all sent out of the room and the king and Ehud were left alone. When Ehud was certain that no one was near, he reached around with his left hand for his dagger and stabbed the king. Because he was left-handed, the king probably had no suspicion that the motion of Ehud's hand was any threat of danger. Had Ehud made the same motion with his right hand, as most men would have done, the king might have tried to jump out of the way or defend himself in some fashion. The king might even have called loudly for help, recalling his guards before they were too far away to hear. This may be the reason the Bible mentions the fact that Ehud was left-handed.

Ehud kills the king of Moab

After Ehud had killed the king, he ran from the house and locked the doors after him. Of course, the king's attendants had no idea of what had

Ehud, left-handed, kills the king of the Moabites with a dagger while the king's attendants wait outside.

happened, and when they returned to the house and found the doors shut they supposed the king had shut them himself.

"The king probably wishes to be alone," they said. "That is no doubt why he has closed the doors. We should not disturb him."

They waited a long time, and finally began to wonder why the king had not opened the doors by then.

"I think we should take one of our keys and open the doors," said one of the servants. "It has been a long time since we left our king alone with that man."

They let themselves in, and found their king dead on the floor, where Ehud had left him. By then, however, Ehud was far away, and there was no chance of catching him.

When Ehud had escaped, he went to Mount Ephraim, which is in the land of Canaan, and blew a trumpet to call the men of Israel together.

"Follow me," he said. "We go to fight the soldiers of Moab. The Lord will give us the victory!"

The battle took place by the River Jordan, and there the Israelites killed ten thousand Moabites, although the Moabites were brave men and strong soldiers. As Ehud had promised, the Lord gave the victory to the Israelites.

For eighty years after the people of Israel were set free from the Moabites, they were at peace.

The victory of Shamgar

Shamgar became the judge over the people after the death of Ehud. While Shamgar was ruling, he fought single-handed against the Philistines, who were enemies of his people. The Lord helped Shamgar wonderfully. With only an ox-goad as a weapon, Shamgar killed six hundred men.

57

The story of Deborah, the woman judge

IN SPITE OF THE LESSONS THEY HAD HAD, with punishment following surely each time they became sinful, the Israelites slipped again into the way of evil after the death of Shamgar.

God sent Jabin, king of Canaan, to fight against Israel and conquer the people. He was very cruel, and the Israelites suffered under his power for twenty years. God did not fight for them because they had rebelled and made Him angry with them. The Israelites realized this. They remembered their sins, and they repented and cried to the Lord to forgive and help them.

The Lord had chosen a woman to be judge over Israel at this time. Her name was Deborah and she was a very good woman. She lived in a house that stood under a palm tree between Ramah and Bethel. There she prayed, and sang praises to God, and talked to and taught all the people who came to see her. She was a very wise woman. God had given her the best wisdom, the knowledge of Himself. He taught her to prophesy and to know the future, so that she could tell the Israelites what they must do and how they could be delivered from their cruel enemy, Jabin.

When the Israelites began to cry to God, Deborah, at His command, sent for a brave man, whose name was Barak. She told him that the Lord had given her a command for him.

"You must take ten thousand men from the tribes of Zebulun and Naphtali, and go to fight against Sisera," she said. Sisera was the captain of Jabin's army. "You need not fear, for the Lord has promised to give us the victory."

Nevertheless, Barak was afraid.

"I will go only if you go too," he said.

Heber delivers the sleeping Sisera to his enemies.

Then Deborah's gift of prophecy showed itself.

"I will go with you," she agreed. "But I warn you that you will not have credit for the victory that will be ours. You will not have the honor of killing Sisera yourself, for the Lord will give him into the hands of a woman, and that woman will kill him, but you will not."

Barak took ten thousand men and went to fight against Sisera, and Deborah went with him. Sisera assembled all the army of the king of Canaan, his soldiers and his war chariots made of iron, nine hundred of them, and came to fight with the Israelites.

Soon the Israelites were victorious, because the Lord was with them and helped them. Barak followed after Sisera's army and killed the men as they ran away. Sisera himself, however, left his chariot and tried to escape on foot. He ran to the tent of a man named Heber to hide, because Heber was not at war with Jabin. Heber's wife was named Jael, and when she saw Sisera coming toward their tent she went out to meet him. Jael was a friend of the Israelites, although Sisera did not know it, because her husband was a friend of Jabin, Sisera's king.

"Come in," she said. "Do not be afraid."

Sisera entered the tent and lay down on the floor, where Jael covered him with a robe to hide him.

"Will you give me some water, please?" Sisera asked. "I am very thirsty."

Jael gave him good milk to drink, and he was grateful to her. Then he lay down again to rest.

"If anyone comes to the door of your tent and asks if I am here," he told her, "say that I am not."

He soon fell asleep, because he was very tired after fighting and then running so far. While he slept, Jael took a great nail that was used in fastening the side of the tent to the ground. She went softly to Sisera while he was sleeping, and drove the nail into his forehead, and he died. Soon afterward Barak came by, looking for Sisera, and Jael went out to meet him.

"Come," she said, "I will show you the man you are looking for."

Jael took Barak into the tent, and there Sisera lay dead. So it was that the people of Israel were set free from Jabin, king of Canaan, that day, but Barak did not get credit for the victory because Sisera, the captain of the king's army, was killed by the hand of a woman, as Deborah had predicted.

Barak and Deborah knew that it was the Lord, not themselves or their soldiers, who had gained the victory, and they sang a beautiful song of praise to Him.

Deborah sings her beautiful song of praise to the Lord.

The fleece was so wet that Gideon could wring the dew out with his hands. In fact, he filled an entire bowl with the dew (*p. 264*).

58

The story of Gideon

AFTER THE CANAANITES UNDER KING JABIN had been conquered, the people of Israel had no further warfare for forty years. After the forty years were ended, they again began to behave sinfully and God became displeased with them.

The Midianites then attacked the Israelites and defeated them, for God was not helping the sinful Israelites at that time. The Midianites enslaved the Israelites and treated them very cruelly. The Israelites were driven from their cities and their homes, and had to live in caves or dens in the mountains. The grain that they had planted and grown was taken by the Midianites, and there was nothing left for the people of Israel to eat. The Midianites also took the Israelites' oxen, and goats, and sheep. The Israelites became very poor and lived in misery because of what the Midianites did.

In their distress, the Israelites remembered the Lord, Whom they had forsaken, and prayed to Him for help. God heard their prayers, as He had done so many times before, and as He had also done before, He answered those prayers. He sent a prophet to them, a man who would make them understand that they had been wicked and who would then deliver them from their cruel masters, the Midianites.

In a place called Ophrah, a brave young man of Israel made his home. His name was Gideon.

One day Gideon was busy threshing wheat under a tree, intending to hide the grain from the Midianites, so that his own people might have at least that little bit to eat. As he was working, an angel of the Lord appeared to him.

"The Lord is favorable to you and your people," said the angel. "You are a brave and strong man, and the Lord has noticed it."

"If the Lord is favorable to my people," answered Gideon, respectfully but somewhat puzzled, "then why do we suffer so from the Midianites, whom the Lord allowed to conquer us?"

"The Lord has chosen you to set the Israelites free from these people," said the angel.

"But how could I possibly set the people of Israel free?" Gideon asked in amazement. "I come from a poor family, and I am the least important in my father's house! How can I do anything?"

"The Lord will be with you," replied the angel. "And with the help of the Lord, you can destroy the entire army of the Midianites with no more trouble than if you fought against a single soldier."

"Please stay here until I can go fetch a sacrifice for an offering to the Lord," Gideon begged the angel.

"I will stay here until you return," the angel promised, and Gideon went away to do as he had said.

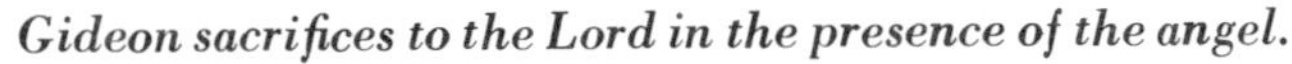

Gideon sacrifices to the Lord in the presence of the angel.

He took a kid, or young goat, and he killed it and made it ready for the sacrifice, and he put the meat into a basket. He also took some cakes. He gave the entire offering to the angel, who told him to place it on a rock that stood nearby. Gideon obeyed, and the angel touched his staff to the rock.

Suddenly fire burst forth from the rock, and Gideon's offering was burnt in honor of the Lord. Then the angel disappeared. This had been such a wonderful experience for Gideon that he built an altar on the spot where the angel of the Lord had made fire appear from the rock.

Soon after this had happened, the Lord made known to Gideon that he was to tear down an altar that Joash, his father, had built to the false god Baal. Many other of the Israelites had also learned to worship the false god Baal and had visited the grove where the altar stood in order to do their worship. Gideon cut down the trees of that grove, so that the place as well as the altar was no longer there to encourage the people in the sin of worshiping wrongly.

The spirit of the Lord entered into Gideon, and when the army of the Midianites made a camp in the valley of Jezreel, Gideon blew a trumpet and called the men of Israel to go with him and fight the Midianites. For the benefit of those who lived too far away to hear his trumpet, he sent messengers throughout the land. Many of the Israelites came at his call.

Still Gideon wanted some reassurance that he was doing the right thing and that God truly wanted him to lead the Israelites into war and conquer the people of Midian. So Gideon prayed to the Lord, and begged for a sign to show that he was doing the right thing and doing the Lord's will. He asked the Lord to perform a miracle, so that he would know certainly that God would be there to help him when he went out to fight the Midianites.

In his prayer, Gideon said that he would take a fleece of wool, and leave it out on the ground overnight.

"If the fleece has dew on it in the morning," Gideon said in his prayer, "and all the ground around it is dry, then I will know surely that the Lord will help me to set the children of Israel free."

Gideon did exactly as he had said. He left a fleece of wool out-of-doors on the ground overnight. Early in the morning, he arose and went to look at his fleece. It was drenched with dew. It was so wet that Gideon could wring the dew out with his hands. In fact, he filled an entire bowl with the dew that he wrung from the fleece. In spite of all that moisture on the fleece, however, the ground around it on all sides was completely dry.

Once again Gideon prayed to the Lord, and begged God not to be angry if his timid servant asked for one more sign—another miracle to make him even more sure that he was truly intended to be the deliverer of the Israelites, under God's protection.

In his prayer Gideon said that he would put the fleece out for a second time, and asked that God would keep the fleece dry this time, and let the ground surrounding it be wet. If this happened, then Gideon would have no slightest question in his mind that the Lord would most certainly be with him and the people of Israel in their battle with the Midianites.

Gideon left out the fleece overnight again, as he had said, and in the morning it was totally dry, while all the ground surrounding it was drenched with heavy dew. These two miracles reassured Gideon completely, and he knew that he had been chosen to deliver the Israelites and that the Lord would be with him when he went out to fight the oppressors of his people.

Gideon and all the army of Israel arose early in the morning and marched toward the camp of the Midianites. However, this was not the way in which the Lord had planned it. The army of the Israelites was vast, and the Lord knew that if such a large army of Israelites succeeded in defeating the Midianites, the soldiers would doubtless boast and brag that it had been their number and strength that had won the victory. They would take all credit to themselves, and give none to the Lord, who was actually responsible.

The Lord had a plan to reduce the number of men in the army of the Israelites, before they had a chance to go into battle. He made Gideon understand that he should tell all of the men who were afraid, or timid, or uncertain of their bravery, to return to their own homes and leave the rest of the Israelite army to do the fighting.

Gideon told the men what the Lord had commanded and twenty-two thousand men left the camp. This left ten thousand soldiers.

This was still too many, and the Lord spoke to Gideon again. He told Gideon to take the ten thousand men down to the water, and the Lord would indicate which of them were to go into battle, and which were not.

Gideon did as the Lord directed him, and took the men to the edge of the water. The men were thirsty and began to drink. Some drank by putting their mouths down into the water, stooping so that their mouths could reach it. Others scooped up water in their hands and drank that way. The Lord told Gideon to notice those who drank from their hands and set them apart. These amounted to a total of three hundred.

The Lord had made the men drink in these different fashions because he wanted to send only a small army into battle under Gideon's leadership and this was a good way to select Gideon's army. The Lord then told Gideon that only those three hundred men should take part in the battle against the Midianites.

On that same night, the Lord told Gideon that now he must attack the Midianites with his army of three hundred. Gideon need have no fear, the Lord told him, because the army would fight under God's protection and God would give them the victory.

But if Gideon still felt doubtful about going into battle with so few soldiers, the Lord was willing to give him a sign that would remove all fear from his mind.

Gideon was told that he should go under cover of darkness, alone except for one helper, and approach the camp of the Midianites. This was not to be any kind of attack, but Gideon was merely to go where he could listen to what the Midianites were saying among themselves.

Gideon went with one helper toward the valley where the Midianites were camped. There were so many of them they seemed to cover the ground like grasshoppers, and they had so many camels with them that it was impossible to count the camels.

As Gideon and his servant approached the camp, they could hear two of the Midianite soldiers talking together.

"Last night I had a very strange dream," said one of them. "I dreamed that I saw a loaf of barley bread come tumbling into our camp. It struck a tent, and the tent was knocked over and lay flat on the ground."

"That dream had an important meaning," said the other man. "The loaf of barley bread represents the sword of Gideon. The Lord is going to put all of us, and all our army, under his power."

When Gideon heard this he knew that he and the Israelites had nothing to fear, just as the Lord had said, for they would win victory with God's great powers helping them. It was nighttime, but when Gideon reached his own camp again he called together the three hundred men.

Gideon selects his soldiers by the way they drink.

"Wake up and come with me," he said. "We go to fight the Midianites, and the Lord is going to give us the victory."

He divided the men into three different companies of one hundred each, and he gave each man a trumpet and a jar or pitcher. Inside each jar or pitcher was a light, made by a lamp or torch.

"When we draw near to the camp of the Midianites, you must all watch me, and do the same thing I do," he told them. "When I blow my trumpet, each of you must also blow his trumpet, and everyone will shout out loudly, 'FOR THE LORD AND FOR GIDEON!' "

The three hundred soldiers did as Gideon had commanded. They reached the camp of the Midianites in the middle of the night, and when Gideon blew on his trumpet they all joined in and blew theirs also. Then, again following Gideon's example and lead, they broke the pitchers in their hands, so that the light of the lamps inside could be seen, and shouted loudly the words that Gideon had told them to shout.

"For the Lord and for Gideon!" they shouted.

The sound of the sudden noise, and the sight of those three hundred lanterns suddenly shining in the night, filled the Midianites with terror and they ran from the men of Israel. The Lord made them mad with fear. They were afraid of the Israelites, and even afraid of each other. They fought among themselves as they ran to escape the soldiers of Israel, and many of them were killed, both by the Israelites and by their own countrymen.

The Israelite army followed the fleeing soldiers to the river Jordan and crossed over the river pursuing the two Midianite kings, who fled before the soldiers of Gideon with the fifteen thousand remaining Midianite soldiers—all that was left of their huge army. Gideon and his three hundred soldiers overtook them before very long, and destroyed their cities of Succoth and Penuel. He made the two kings captive.

As the Lord had promised, Gideon had driven the Midianites out of Canaan and had set the Israelites free. The people were grateful to Gideon and wanted him to rule over them as their king.

"I will not rule over you," he said. "It is the Lord who rules over you.

The lamps of the Israelites terrify the Midianites.

But there is something I would like you to do, if you really would like to please me."

The people were more than willing to do anything that Gideon wished. So he told them that he would like to have for himself the golden earrings and beautiful robes and ornaments that had been captured from the people of Midian. After these had been given to him, Gideon made a splendid ephod, or robe of state, decorated with gold and precious stones, to be worn by the high priests and to be kept in Ophrah, Gideon's home.

There were many golden earrings and other treasures that had been taken from the Midianites after their defeat by the men of Israel, and Gideon became a very rich man when he owned all these things.

Although Gideon did not wish to be a king, he was willing to serve his people as judge and rule over them in that office. He was a wise and able ruler, and the country lived in peace for the forty years that Gideon ruled as judge over Israel.

Gideon had seventy-one sons, and he lived to a good old age. When he died, he was buried in his father's sepulchre at Ophrah.

59

The story of Jephthah and his daughter

AFTER GIDEON'S DEATH, ONE OF GIDEON'S SONS—a man named Abimelech—became the judge over Israel, but Abimelech was not a good judge. Not only did he fail to lead the Israelites away from the worship of idols, he even worshiped idols himself. The two judges who came after Abimelech, one of them named Tola or Thola and the other named Jair, were unable to keep the people of Israel from worshiping idols.

It seems that the Israelites were always easily tempted. Unless they had a judge who was both a good man and a powerful leader, they slipped away from the worship of God and became idolators. And when they did this, God did not protect them against their many enemies.

This time they began to serve the idols called Baal and Ashtaroth, just as their fathers and grandfathers had done before Gideon led them back to worship of the true God.

Soon the Philistines and Ammonites began to make war against the people of Israel. The Philistines were a people that lived in Canaan but did not worship the one true God. The Ammonites were a people that were descended from one of the daughters of Lot, the nephew of Abraham.

The Philistines and the Ammonites won mastery over the Israelites, and the Israelites served these new masters for eighteen years.

In their trouble, the Israelites cried to the Lord for help, but the Lord answered that He had set them free several times before, when their enemies had enslaved them, and still they had not remembered His goodness to them and had returned to idol worship without much delay. If their idols were so powerful, why did the Israelites not ask the idols to save them?

Still the people of Israel cried to the Lord for help.

"We will confess our sins, and we are willing to take whatever punishment the Lord has for us. Only let us be set free from the enemies who now rule over us." This was the manner in which the Israelites prayed.

They stopped worshiping idols and once more returned to the worship of the one true God. After a time, the Lord pitied them in their sufferings and decided to help them.

The Ammonite armies had their camp in the land of Gilead, on the east side of the Jordan. The Israelites assembled an army and made a camp at a place called Mizpeh. Now they needed a captain for their army.

"Whom shall we get to lead us in our fight against the Ammonites?" they asked one another. "Whoever that man is, he shall rule over all the people of Gilead."

There had been a man in Israel named Jephthah, whom the people remembered as a brave and valiant soldier. He had moved to a land called Tob, because his family had treated him badly.

Now, in the hour of need, the people of Israel remembered Jephthah. The elders of Gilead went in search of him, and when they found him, they pleaded with him.

"Come and be our leader," they begged. "We need someone like you to free us from the Ammonites."

But Jephthah remembered how he had been treated, years before.

"You are the very people who sent me away from my father's house," he exclaimed. "Now do you come and ask me to serve you?"

"What you say is true," the elders admitted, "but if you will come and deliver us from the Ammonites, who are stronger than we are, we will make you leader over all the people."

"If I go with you, and the Lord does indeed allow me to win a victory for the people of Gilead," said Jephthah, "do you promise that you will make me ruler over all the people?"

The elders promised, before the Lord, that they would do exactly as he said. Jephthah then agreed to go with them, and the people made him their captain.

First Jephthah sent messengers to the king of the Ammonites, asking why the king had come to fight against the people of Israel. The king answered that it was because they had taken away his land when they came out of Egypt.

"Now I want my land back," the king said.

"The land the Israelites have taken was given to them by the Lord," said Jephthah. "Whatever the Lord gave the children of Israel, they will keep for their own. They have done the Ammonites no wrong, but the Ammonites wrong the Israelites greatly in making war against them."

The king of the Ammonites paid no attention to what Jephthah said. He continued with his plans to make war upon Jephthah's people.

At length Jephthah collected all the forces of the Israelite army. He marched to the place where the Ammonites had their camp.

Just before the battle, he made a sacred oath to the Lord. He promised solemnly that if the Lord would give him and Israel the victory, he would offer as a sacrifice to the Lord the first thing that came out of his door to meet him, when he returned to his own home.

The Lord did allow the Israelites to defeat the men of Ammon, and the people of Israel were again set free from their oppressors.

After the battle was over, Jephthah returned to his home, and as he approached his daughter came out, delighted to see him, and singing for joy. She was his only child, and Jephthah loved her dearly. When Jephthah remembered his vow he was desperately unhappy at the thought that he must sacrifice this lovely child.

When Jephthah's daughter heard what her father had vowed, she reassured him.

"If you have made a vow to the Lord, our God," she said simply, "then you must of course keep it. Do with me as you promised the Lord. But first let me go to the mountain and mourn, for two months, that I can never marry and have children."

Jephthah granted this request, and after two months his daughter returned to be sacrificed.

After this, Jephthah was judge over the people of Israel for six years; then he died.

60

The story of Samson and the lion

THE PEOPLE OF ISRAEL HAD OVERTHROWN THE AMMONITES during Jephthah's lifetime, but after Jephthah's death they gradually began to sin again, worshiping idols, which displeased the Lord. Once again the Philistines attacked and overcame the Israelites, and the people of Israel were enslaved by the Philistines for forty years.

In a place called Zorah some of the descendants of Dan had settled. (Dan was one of Jacob's sons, and so had founded one of the tribes of Israel.) One of these descendants was a man named Manoah. He and his wife had been married for many years, but they had no children. They were good people and worshipers of the one true God. They had not turned to idolatry as so many of their neighbors had done.

One day an angel of the Lord appeared to Manoah's wife and told her that she was going to have a son.

The angel told her many other things as well, and when Manoah returned home that day his wife recounted all that the angel had said.

"A man of God appeared to me," she told Manoah. (At that time, Manoah's wife did not realize that it was an angel.) "He said that I am to have a son!"

Manoah was astonished at this news, but there was even more to come.

"This son is to be a Nazarite, dedicated to the service of the Lord," said his wife. "I am to eat nothing unclean, and I am to drink no wine, for he will be a Nazarite from the moment he is conceived until the day of his death."

A Nazarite was a man who lived in God's service. Nazarites were not allowed to drink any wine or liquor, or to cut their hair at any time. It was then the custom among the Hebrew people for men to shave their heads, but the Nazarites were forbidden to do so.

Manoah then prayed to the Lord and asked that the man of God be allowed to return and explain fully to him and his wife what they must do for the son who would be born to them.

The Lord granted Manoah's prayer and sent his angel once again to the woman as she was seated in the field, away from the house. Manoah was not with her, and she ran swiftly to find him, so that he might come and see the man of God, who had returned. They still did not know that this was an angel of the Lord.

They returned to the field, and the angel was still there.

"Are you the same man who spoke to my wife before?" Manoah asked.

"I am," said the man.

"If what you told her comes true," Manoah continued, "in what manner should we train the boy?"

The angel repeated the instructions he had given Manoah's wife and also told them that this child, when he grew to manhood, would take the lead in saving Israel from the Philistines.

"Won't you stay awhile with us, and let me prepare food for you, so that you may eat before you continue your journey?" Manoah asked.

"I will stay awhile with you, but I will not eat," said the man. "If you wish to make a burnt offering, offer the food that you prepare for me instead to the Lord."

Then Manoah asked the man's name, so that he and his wife might know whom to honor when their son was born.

"Do not ask my name; it is a mystery," the stranger said—and soon Manoah and his wife learned that it was indeed a mystery.

The angel is revealed by the lord

Manoah had prepared a burnt offering with the kid that he had killed and some cereal grain. He offered it up on a rock, and as it burned the Lord performed a miracle that Manoah and his wife could see. In the flame and smoke rising from the altar, the angel of the Lord rose heavenward also, and disappeared from sight. Manoah and his wife fell on their faces in worship, for now they knew that this had been an angel of the Lord. Never again did the angel appear to them.

Manoah was frightened, for he knew that no man could see God and

Manoah and his wife make a sacrifice to the Lord while the angel of the Lord rose heavenward in the flame and smoke rising from the altar.

live, and he felt certain that they had indeed seen God.

"We are surely going to die!" he exclaimed to his wife.

His wife had greater faith than Manoah in the promise of the Lord, and she was not frightened.

"No," she said. "If the Lord had intended us to die, He would not have accepted our offering. Furthermore, He would not have told us that our son is to be a Nazarite, in God's service, nor would He have allowed us to witness the wonder of the angel ascending to heaven in the smoke from our burnt offering. No, we have nothing to fear."

And Manoah's wife was right.

She obeyed all the instructions the angel had given her, and in due time a son was born to her. His hair was never to be cut, nor his head shaved. He was never to drink wine or liquor, nor eat any unclean thing. Manoah and his wife named their son Samson, and the Lord blessed him, so that

Samson kills the lion: Gustave Doré's famous interpretation.

he grew big and strong. Soon he became the strongest man in the world, though they did not know it.

When he was a young man, and at an age when he thought of marrying,

Samson visited a place called Timnath, which was not far from Zorah. There he saw a woman of the Philistines whom he liked very much. When he returned home he spoke to his father about her.

"There is a Philistine woman in Timnath whom I want to marry," he said. "Will you please arrange a marriage between us?"

This was the custom at the time. A man's parents approached the woman's parents, and the marriage was arranged by the two families.

"Why do you not marry a girl of our own people?" his parents asked Samson. "Must you go to the Philistines for a wife? There are plenty of fine young women of Israel. It would be far better if you were to marry one of them."

"No, I wish to marry the Philistine woman," Samson insisted. "She pleases me very much."

None of them knew at the time that the Lord permitted this so that Samson would later have reason to be angry and fight against the Philistines. This was during the period when the Israelites were subject to the rule of the Philistines, and Samson was to be the means of setting the people of Israel free.

Samson and his parents went to Timnath, and as they reached the vineyards outside the city a young lion attacked Samson. The Lord gave Samson great strength, and with his bare hands Samson seized the lion and killed it, tearing it open as if it were a tiny lamb or kid, and with no more difficulty. He did not tell his parents what he had done.

When they talked to the woman of Timnath she agreed to marry Samson, and the family of Manoah went home again, to prepare for the marriage feast.

61

The story of Samson's riddle

ON HIS WAY BACK TO TIMNATH FOR THE WEDDING, Samson passed the place where he had killed the lion on the previous trip. He turned aside to look at the carcass, and to his amazement he found that a swarm of bees had made a hive and were making honey in the lion's body.

Samson scraped out some of the honey with his hands and ate it as he walked. He took some home to his father and mother also, but he did not tell them that he had found it in the carcass of the dead lion.

Samson then prepared a feast which was to last seven days. This was the custom of bridegrooms at the time. Thirty Philistines, men of Timnath, attended the feast, and Samson offered them a challenge.

"I will tell you a riddle," he said. "If you can guess the answer, I will give you thirty linen robes and thirty festival robes. If you cannot guess the answer, you must give me thirty linen robes and thirty festival robes."

"Tell us the riddle," the men aswered. "We will try to guess it, and the rewards will be just as you said."

Samson made up a little riddle in the form of a verse, which he recited to the men.

"Out of the eater came something to eat.
"Out of the strong came something sweet."

The men thought it over for a time, but no one could figure out the answer immediately.

"You must guess the answer before the seven days of the feast are over," said Samson. "If you do not, then I win the robes."

After three days, the Philistine men had been unable to guess the answer to the riddle. On the fourth day, they spoke to Samson's wife, because they were afraid they would lose the wager and they did not want to give Samson the costly robes that were the prize.

"Speak to your husband; coax him and tease him until he tells you the answer to the riddle," one of the Philistine men said to Samson's wife. "We must have the answer! If we have to give him all the things he will demand as a prize, we will all be poor!"

"You find out what the answer is!" said another. "If you don't, we'll burn down your father's house!"

The woman tried to persuade Samson to tell her the answer.

"Please tell me," she begged. "I am your wife, and if you really cared about me you would tell me the answer!"

"I have not even told my own mother and father the answer," said Samson. "If I have not told them, why should I tell you?"

The woman kept pleading with him, and she cried bitterly that he did not love her. Still he would not tell her, and she had to report to her kinsmen that Samson would not be swayed by her pleas.

"Persuade him!" they insisted. "We are your kinsmen and you owe it to us. Besides, as we said, we will burn up your father's house if you do not get us the answer. You can coax your husband so that he will tell you. There is still time before the seven days of the feast are over."

The woman tried again to win Samson's confidence. She wept on his shoulder, and sobbed as if she were heartbroken, pretending that she would think he did not love her if he would not tell her the answer to his riddle.

Finally, on the very last day of the feast, Samson could no longer resist her tearful pleas and he foolishly told the riddle's meaning.

Quickly, she ran out to her kinsmen—those who had made the wager with Samson—and told them the answer.

When the men of the city saw Samson about to enter his wife's tent that day, they triumphantly told him they could answer his riddle.

"What is stronger than a lion, and what is sweeter than honey?" they cried, tauntingly.

Samson immediately knew that only his wife could be responsible for their knowing the answer. They could never have guessed it if she had not told them, and Samson was wildly angry.

The Lord had given Samson great strength, far beyond that of ordinary men. In his rage, Samson killed thirty men of Ashkelon, another Philistine city, and paid his wager with the dead men's garments. Then he departed from his Philistine wife in Timnath, and returned to his father's house.

Shortly after Samson had left her, the Philistine woman became the wife of another man—one who had been the "best man" at Samson's wedding.

62

The story of Samson and the jawbone

SAMSON REMAINED AT HIS FATHER'S HOUSE for some time, and his anger at his wife cooled. After a while he decided that he would go back to Timnath and make up the quarrel. To please her, he killed a kid to give her as a present and as a sign that he wanted to be on good terms again with her.

When he reached her father's house, his father-in-law would not let him go in.

"I have given her in marriage to another man," he said. "I thought surely you must hate her and would never want to see her again. Why don't you marry my younger daughter? You will like her."

This time Samson's anger was even greater than it had been before, and he determined to have vengeance for the loss of his wife to another man.

He caught three hundred foxes and tied their tails together in pairs. Then he tied burning torches to each pair and set the terrorized foxes loose in the fields of the Philistines. As the foxes ran, trying to escape the torches that were tied to their tails, the flames set fire to the corn in the fields and to the grain that had already been cut and was standing in shocks. The vines in the vineyards caught fire and were destroyed, and even the olive trees burned up. The land of the Philistines suffered badly, and great quantities of precious food were lost to the people.

Of course this infuriated the Philistines and they wanted to find out who was responsible.

"It was Samson, the son-in-law of the man from Timnath, who did it," they were told.

"He was angry because his father-in-law gave his wife to another man in marriage, while Samson was back at his own father's house for a time," the people explained.

The Philistines seek to capture Samson but cannot overcome his strength.

When the Philistines learned that it was because of Samson's treatment by his father-in-law and his wife that their fields had beeen destroyed, they determined to punish the man who had made Samson angry.

Both Samson's wife and his father-in-law were burned, and their houses burned with them. That was the vengeance of the Philistines, but it made Samson angrier than ever. Each time Samson grew angry, he became angrier than the time before, and his strength was so mighty that this meant great trouble indeed for those against whom his anger burned.

"Did you imagine that you could do such a thing as to kill my wife and father-in-law without being punished?" he demanded. "I must have vengeance for what you have done, but when I have had my vengeance, I will leave you alone. When I have punished you for this, I will stop."

With that Samson killed a great many of the Philistines, and then went to live in the mountains on a crag called Etam.

After Samson had moved to the crag Etam, the Philistines sent an army of soldiers to attack the tribe of Judah.

"Why have you attacked us?" asked the men of Judah.

"We want to take Samson as our prisoner," said the Philistines. "We intend to do exactly the same things to him that he has done to us!"

With that, three thousand of the tribe of Judah went up to where Samson was living and told him that the Philistines were causing them trouble.

"You know that they are our masters," they said to Samson. "Why have you put us in a position where they may decide to punish all of us because of you?"

"I did to them only the things they had done to me," replied Samson.

"We have come here to take you prisoner," said the men of Judah. "Then we must turn you over to the Philistines."

"I will let you do that if you will promise me one thing," said Samson. "Promise me that you yourselves will not attempt to harm me along the way. If you will promise, I will allow you to bind me and turn me over to the Philistines if you wish."

"We promise not to hurt you ourselves," they swore. "We will only take you prisoner, and then turn you over to them. We ourselves will not harm you."

"Very well," said Samson. "You may do so."

The men of Judah then bound Samson with two new ropes, and took him to where the Philistines were waiting. When they saw him, and realized that he was securely bound, they gave shouts of triumph and ran toward him. This time they were certain that they had him in their power.

Samson is bound

As the shouting Philistines approached, the Lord sent great surging power into Samson's muscles, and he burst his bonds as if they were no more than wet paper. He saw the jawbone of an ass on the ground before him, and picked it up to use it as a weapon against the hundreds of armed Philistines.

With only the jawbone of an ass to serve as a club, Samson made use of the tremendous strength the Lord had given him and killed a thousand Philistine men single-handed.

Samson uses the jawbone of an ass as a weapon and fights the Philistines.

As soon as they were dead, he threw the jawbone away from him. Suddenly he was very thirsty, and he asked himself if the Lord were going to allow him to die of thirst, after giving him such a wonderful victory over his enemies.

Even as he thought these things, the Lord made water gush forth in a sweet, cool spring, and as Samson drank gratefully, his spirits revived, and he felt well rested.

After his slaughter of the thousand Philistines with the ass's jawbone, Samson was made judge of the people of Israel, and he ruled them for twenty years, during the time of the Philistines.

63

The story of Samson and Delilah

WHILE SAMSON WAS JUDGE OVER ISRAEL the Philistines feared to attack him openly. Everyone knew of his unbelievable strength, and no one was a match for him. The Philistines waited impatiently for a chance to come upon Samson when he suspected nothing. After a long time their opportunity arrived, or so it seemed to them.

Samson spent the night in a city called Gaza on one occasion, and the Philistines heard about it.

"This is our opportunity to kill him!" declared one of their leaders. "We will wait till morning at the gates of the city and be sure that they are all locked and barred, so that he cannot get away from us. We will attack and kill him when he tries to leave!"

Samson did not remain in the city until morning, however, but decided to leave at midnight. When he found the gates locked and barred, he summoned his great strength and pulled up the gateposts with his bare hands. The entire gates, with the doors and heavy bars, he carried away with him. He left them at the top of a hill near the town of Hebron.

This additional proof of Samson's great strength made the Philistines hate and fear him more than ever. The only solution, they decided, was to discover the secret of his strength. If they could only learn what he needed to maintain that strength, they would be able to make him weak.

The Philistines knew that Samson loved a woman named Delilah, and they knew also that Delilah was a bad woman. Such a woman as Delilah could be bribed, they thought; for a large enough reward she would be willing to betray the man who loved her.

Samson carries the huge gate of Gaza to the hills above Hebron.

Delilah listened to their proposal and agreed that she would persuade Samson to reveal the secret of his strength.

She flattered Samson, telling him how wonderfully strong and powerful he was. She doubtless thought that all men liked to be complimented on their strength, and that Samson would find it as pleasant as any other man would.

Then she tried to learn his secret.

"What gives you this wonderful strength, Samson?" she said. "You must have some secret source of your power. Tell me, is there nothing in the world that you are not strong enough to break? No bonds with which you could be tied that you could not snap with your mighty muscles?"

Samson did not quite trust her, and in fact he felt sure that she was trying to trick him in some fashion—for what reason he did not know. However, he answered her, merely to satisfy her.

"Surely there is something with which I can be bound," he said, laughing. "And if I am bound with this substance, I shall be as helpless as a baby—quite unable to break loose."

"And what is this?" asked Delilah softly.

"If I am bound with seven fresh thongs that have never been dried, I shall be quite helpless to release myself," he said.

Delilah was triumphant. Quickly she told the men of the Philistines that she had learned his secret.

"Hide yourselves," she said. "I will bind him with the substance that he cannot break. When he is helpless I will call you."

While Samson was asleep Delilah bound him with seven fresh thongs that had not been dried. Then she believed him helpless.

"The Philistines are here to take you," she cried.

With that, Samson leaped up and snapped his bonds as if they had been made of rotten thread.

Delilah was a wicked and a deceitful woman. She pretended that she had been testing Samson, to learn if he trusted her.

"You did not trust me!" she sobbed. "You deceived me, because you do not truly love me. Why did you lie to me? I shall never believe in you again unless you tell me the truth about the secret of your strength."

"Very well," Samson agreed. "If I am bound with new ropes that have never been used, and have never touched anyone else, that will destroy my strength, and I shall be helpless."

Once more Delilah thought he was telling the truth and she hastened to inform the Philistines.

"Come and hide yourselves in my inner room," she said. "Samson has told me the secret of his strength, and I shall deliver him to you, helpless! When I call you, come in and take him."

Delilah returned to her house, and when Samson was there she persuaded him to let her bind him with the new rope she had obtained. As soon as Samson was fully bound, the Philistines hidden in the other room heard her cry out.

"The Philistines are here to take you, Samson!" she exclaimed.

Samson then exerted his great strength and snapped the ropes as easily as if they had been delicate threads, and for the second time the Philistines were disappointed.

Now Delilah was becoming more and more impatient. For the third time, she tried to find out what gave Samson his strength, and what could cause him to lose it.

She pretended to be very angry with Samson because he had not trusted her enough to tell the truth about the secret of his strength.

"Twice you have lied to me!" she exclaimed. "How can I believe anything you tell me, if you lie so? Why do you not trust me? Why do you not tell me what makes you so strong?"

Samson supposed that each time she had called that the Philistines were about to attack him, she had done so to give him a chance to escape. He still did not realize that she had plotted for his capture and destruction. Still, he did not wish to reveal the secret of his powers to anyone, and once again he deceived Delilah, thinking it was just a woman's curiosity that made her seek the information she kept demanding.

"All right," said Samson. "I will tell you. If you take seven locks of my hair, and weave them into the cloth on your loom, my strength will depart from me."

At that time, women usually wove the cloth that made their own clothes, and Delilah had a loom in her house that she used for that purpose.

While Samson slept, she wove seven locks of his hair in with the cloth on her loom, and when this was done she awakened him again with the cry that the Philistines had come to take him.

Samson leaped up, and with him went the part of the cloth that had been woven with his hair, and a piece of the loom as well. Still Samson believed that Delilah's cries had been intended as a warning to him, instead of as a signal to the Philistines that he was helpless.

Samson reveals his secret

Day after day Delilah plagued Samson, asking him over and over to tell her his secret. She asked so many times, and over such a long period, that Samson was sick to death of hearing her ask. Finally he decided that he would tell her, merely for the sake of having some release from the constant questioning.

One day when Delilah had asked him once again to tell her the secret of his great strength, Samson answered her truthfully.

"I am a Nazarite," he said. "A Nazarite spends his life in dedication to the Lord, and it is forbidden to cut off his hair. If my hair were cut off, I would lose the spirit of the Lord that gives me strength when I need it."

This time Delilah knew from the manner in which he spoke that Samson was telling the truth, and that in the length of his hair lay the secret of his strength.

Triumphantly, she told her news to the Philistines, and assured them that this time there was no question but that she knew the secret of Samson's power.

"Come and pay me the rewards you promised," she said. "Then I will deliver Samson to you, shorn of his power."

The Philistines did as Delilah demanded, and when she had received their money, she went back to Samson and caressed him gently until he fell asleep with his head on her knees. He slept very soundly and did not awaken when a man whom Delilah had summoned shaved off his hair. When Samson was completely stripped of his hair, Delilah called again that the Philistines were there to take him.

For the fourth time, Samson leaped up, thinking that as usual he would be protected by his great strength—the strength that the Lord gave him as a Nazarite whenever he needed it.

This time, however, the Lord had left him, because his hair had been shaved off, and it was forbidden for the hair of a Nazarite to be cut.

Samson was no stronger than an ordinary man, and the Philistines overcame him swiftly. They bound him, and put out his eyes, and took him away from the house of the wicked woman who had betrayed him.

Samson eyeless in Gaza

Samson was put in prison in Gaza. He was bound with heavy chains of brass and was set to grinding wheat. The Philistines were gay and triumphant, for they thought that they had Samson forever in their power. How could a poor old blind man, deprived of the great strength he once had, do them any damage?

The Philistines proceeded to hold a great feast to their idol, Dagon—the false god that the Philistines worshiped. They offered sacrifices to Dagon and praised the senseless image for having given Samson into their hands. They truly believed that Dagon had helped them. They did not even suspect that the only reason they had captured Samson was because the Lord had decided to punish the strong man for revealing to a bad woman the secret of his strength.

Samson, betrayed by Delilah, sleeps, while his hair is shaved off.

Perhaps it may seem that Samson's punishment was greater than he deserved, when his eyes were put out; but many years before, the Lord had promised Manoah and his wife that Samson would be the leader in releasing the Israelites from their slavery to the Philistines, and this promise was still to be fulfilled. Samson's blindness in the prison at Gaza was a part of it.

During all the time when Samson was forced to grind wheat for his enemies, the Philistines, his hair was growing. Perhaps the Philistines believed that once Samson's hair had been cut, the new growth would not give him the same strength again; perhaps they did not even think about it, for Samson was blind and seemed to be helpless in his chains of heavy metal. At any rate, in the midst of their feasting and celebrating, in honor of their false god, the Philistine people demanded that Samson be brought out before them.

"Bring him out," they cried. "Bring out the strong man who now is blind and helpless. He will be very amusing to watch."

In their mood of celebration, the leaders of the Philistines did as the people wished. Samson was brought out of the prison by an attendant, who led him to the center of the temple where the people were celebrating. As he stumbled along, the people laughed and mocked him. At length Samson spoke to the lad who was guiding him.

"Let me feel the two pillars in the middle of the building, so that I can place one hand upon each one, and hold myself upright," said Samson.

The attendant saw no harm in this, and did as Samson asked. Samson steadied himself on the two pillars for a moment, and all who saw him supposed that he was merely maintaining his balance thereby.

The building was filled with men and women. All the tyrants of the Philistines were there, celebrating, and there were about three thousand more men and women on the roof, all watching and laughing as Samson stumbled and wavered.

Samson prayed with all his heart to the Lord.

"Lord, hear me!" he cried in his prayer. "Give me strength just this once, and let me avenge myself upon the Philistines!"

Samson grasped the pillars firmly, one with each hand. He then prayed again to the Lord.

"Let me have strength enough to pull down these pillars," he prayed. "Let all who are in this building die as it crashes down, and let me die with these Philistines!"

With that he gave a mighty push to each of the pillars.

As Samson prayed, his wonderful strength—such as no man has had before or since that time—came back to him, and the great pillars that supported the house collapsed. The temple fell in a heap of ruins. All that were in it were buried in the wreckage, and the three thousand who were on the roof fell and died.

Samson died with his enemies, the Philistines, as he had prayed to the Lord that he might do. Samson took with him when he died more Philistines than he had killed in his entire lifetime. The Philistines, who had lost all their leaders at this one moment, could no longer enslave the Israelites.

Thus it was that the Lord's promise was fulfilled. Samson was the leader in releasing the people of Israel from the bondage of the Philistines.

When Samson's brothers and other relations learned of his death they went to Gaza to claim his body. They placed it in the sepulchre of his father, Manoah.

64

The story of Ruth and Naomi

AFTER SAMSON, ELI BECAME JUDGE over all the people of Israel. During his reign there was a famine in the land of the Israelites. To find food, a man named Elimelech went from the city of Bethlehem, where he lived, to stay for a while in the land of Moab. With him he took his wife and their two sons. The wife of Elimelech was named Naomi.

Elimelech died just a short while after the family had moved to Moab, and Naomi was left a widow. Both of her sons married women of Moab, but her sons also died about ten years later. Naomi decided to leave Moab and return to Canaan, for she had heard that there was no longer a famine in that land, and plenty of food was available.

When Naomi was ready to leave, both of her daughters-in-law wanted to go with her. They were both very fond of Naomi, and she was fond of them. They were both widows, just as Naomi was. But Naomi thought the two younger women would be happier if they remained in Moab.

"You should stay here, where all your relatives live," she told them kindly. "After all, this is your home, and you have lived here all your lives."

"We feel just as if you were our own mother, rather than our mother-in-law," they answered her. "We want to go with you."

Naomi kissed them both, because she could see that they were sincere in wanting to stay with her. But again she urged the two younger women to return to their homes.

"If you come with me, you may never find other husbands," she said.

One of her daughters-in-law decided at last that she would stay in the land of Moab, instead of going to Bethlehem. Her name was Orpah. The other daughter-in-law was Ruth, and Ruth refused firmly to leave her mother-in-law.

"Do not ask me to leave you," Ruth begged. "Wherever you go, I will go. Where you live, I will live. Your people shall be my people, and your God shall be my God. Where you die, there I also will die and be buried."

Then Ruth asked the Lord to punish her if she ever left Naomi, as long as they both were alive.

Naomi knew now that Ruth was determined to go with her, and no longer tried to persuade her daughter-in-law to return to Moab. They traveled until they reached Bethlehem. There Naomi's friends came out to meet her—the women she had known years before. They were happy to see her and gathered around to greet her.

"Is this really Naomi?" they asked delightedly.

"You should not call me *Naomi* any more," said the sad widow. "Instead, you should call me *Mara. Naomi* means *pleasant,* and *Mara* means *bitter.* I have had a bitter time. When I left here, I had a husband and two sons. Now I have none."

Ruth stays with Naomi while the other daughter-in-law sorrowfully returns home.

When Naomi and Ruth arrived in Bethlehem, it was at the time of the barley harvest.

"May I go to the barley field and glean grain for us?" Ruth asked her mother-in-law.

Ruth gleans in the fields of barley

Gleaning was a custom among the poor people of the countryside. As the reapers went through a field of grain, they always missed gathering many stalks of grain, and gleaners were allowed to go after them to take what had been left. Gleaning was hard work, but it gave very poor people a chance to obtain some grain for bread without paying for it.

"Go, if you wish, my daughter," said Naomi.

Ruth did so, and it happened that the field in which she gleaned belonged to a rich man named Boaz, who was a relative of Elimelech's. Boaz was a good man and lived according to the laws of God.

As Ruth was busily gleaning the grain after the reapers, Boaz came to his field and saw her.

"Who is that young woman?" he asked one of his men.

"She is the young woman who came from Moab with Naomi," the man answered. "She asked us to let her glean after the reapers, and we gave her permission to do so. She has been working since early this morning."

Boaz then spoke kindly to Ruth, and told her that she need not look for any other fields in which to glean, but she could glean as often and as much as she wanted in his field. He had instructed his men not to do her any harm, but to treat her with respect and courtesy.

"And when you are thirsty, help yourself to the water my men keep on hand to drink," said Boaz to Ruth.

Ruth was amazed at his kindness and generosity to her.

"You are most kind," she said. "But why should you be so good to me? You have never seen me before, and I am a stranger in your land."

"I have heard of your kindness to your mother-in-law," said Boaz. "I know that you unselfishly left your own land and came with Naomi so that she would not be lonely. The Lord will reward you for your goodness, for you have entrusted yourself to Him."

Then Boaz told her when mealtime came she might eat with the reapers. She did so, and enjoyed bread and parched corn with them. She ate all

HANNAH WITH HER CHILD AT SILOM

she wanted, then returned to gleaning. All afternoon she gathered grain, and she collected a good amount.

Boaz told his men to let her take all she could find, and not to speak harshly to her for any reason.

"You might also let a few handfuls of grain fall on purpose, so that she will have plenty to take home," he instructed his men.

At the end of the day, Ruth took all she had gleaned home to Bethlehem. It was more than a bushel. When Naomi saw how much Ruth had gleaned, she was very pleased and asked the Lord's blessing on the man who had been so kind.

"What was the name of the man who owned the field in which you worked?" Naomi asked Ruth.

"His name is Boaz," Ruth replied.

"He is one of our kinsmen," said Naomi. "He is a good man."

"He has told me that I may come and glean in his field until the end of the barley harvest," said Ruth.

"By all means, do so," said Naomi.

Ruth gleaned in the fields of Boaz throughout the barley and wheat harvests.

One day Naomi told Ruth that Boaz would be winnowing barley that night.

Threshing and winnowing are two steps in separating the grain from the stalks in which it grows. First it is threshed, on a threshing-floor. At the time of Boaz, the threshing-floor was a large circle of level ground that had been beaten until it was as hard and smooth as a floor. The sheaves were spread out on this floor after being brought in from the fields, and cattle walked back and forth over the stalks to separate the grain from the stems or stalks on which it grew. That was the threshing. Then it was necessary also to winnow it, in order to separate the individual grains from the small, broken pieces of straw that were left mixed with it after the threshing. These pieces could not be picked out by hand, because there were too many of them, and they were often very small.

Instead, the reapers tossed the grain and straw in the air with pitchforks, while a wind was blowing, and the breeze would carry away the light straw. The heavier grains of barley would fall to the ground, separated from the scraps of straw. That was winnowing.

Ruth asking Boaz to continue to be kind to her.

Naomi told Ruth to go to the threshing-floor that evening and say what Naomi told her to say. Ruth washed and dressed herself, and went to watch the winnowing of the barley. When it was done, Boaz held a feast, and Ruth waited until he had eaten and drunk all he wanted, and until he had slept for a while. When, after a few hours, he awoke, Ruth spoke the words that Naomi had told her to say.

"You are a near relation of ours," she said. "I have come to ask you if you will continue to be kind to me."

"Bless you," said Boaz. "You need have no fear. I will see that you have everything you need. Everyone in Bethlehem knows that you are a very good woman. Here, bring me your veil."

Ruth did as Boaz said, and he poured a generous quantity of grain into the veil as she held it out.

"You must not leave here without taking something back to your mother-in-law," said Boaz, as he filled her veil.

Ruth thanked him, and took the grain home to Naomi. Naomi was pleased to receive this gift, and told Ruth to be patient.

"Let us see what Boaz is going to do now," she said.

Boaz loved Ruth and wanted to marry her, but under the customs of the Israelites the nearest relative of a widow's husband had the first right to marry the widow. Boaz was related to the man Ruth had first married, but there was another man who was a closer relative than Boaz.

The day after Boaz had winnowed his barley, he went to the gate of the city wall. All the cities of Canaan had walls around them, and the people gathered at the gate to tell each other any news they had heard, or to judge people who had broken a law, or to sell their goods. The gates were a kind of market place, as well as a meeting place.

Boaz seated himself at the gate and called ten of the elders of Bethlehem to come and listen to what he had to say. He called also the man who was a nearer relative and had the first right to marry Ruth.

To the delight of Boaz, this man was already married and did not want to marry Ruth. So Boaz announced that, as the next-closest relative, he now had the right to marry Ruth.

"I have called you here to witness what I am saying," he said. "I intend to marry Ruth, the daughter-in-law of Naomi."

The people approved this and prayed that the Lord would bless Ruth and make Boaz even richer and greater than he was.

Boaz then made Ruth his wife, and Naomi was happy that her daughter-in-law had such a fine husband. The Lord sent Boaz and Ruth a son, and they were all very happy. The son was named Obed, and Naomi was glad to have a grandson to care for.

The descendants of this boy Obed were to be far more famous than they could have imagined. They included not only the great kings David and Solomon but also, many years later, Joseph, the husband of Mary whose son was Jesus Christ.

65

The story of Samuel, who was given to God

THERE WAS AN ISRAELITE NAMED ELKANAH who went every year from the city of Ramah, where he lived, to offer up a sacrifice at the tabernacle in Shiloh. His wife, whose name was Hannah, went with him.

Hannah was unhappy, because the Lord had given her no child. In the tabernacle she prayed and made a vow to the Lord that if he would give her a son she would give that son back to him as a Nazarite, who would serve the Lord all the days of his life.

Eli was the high priest as well as the judge of Israel at that time. When Hannah prayed at the tabernacle she wept while she prayed. Eli saw her lips moving but could not tell what she said, she spoke so softly.

At first Eli thought she was drunk and muttering words to herself, and he said to her,

"You know you should not drink."

But Hannah answered, "No, my lord, I am a woman in trouble. I have not drunk any strong drink. I have been praying with all my heart to the Lord."

Then Eli answered her kindly, "May God give you what you ask Him for." Hannah was glad at the high priest's words, and when she left the tabernacle she no longer looked sad. After this she and her husband went home to Ramah.

The Lord remembered Hannah's prayer and sent her a son, and she named her son Samuel, which means "asked of God," because she had asked God for him and God had given him to her.

As long as Samuel was a baby, Hannah would not go to Shiloh to offer up the sacrifice each year. She said she would wait until Samuel was a little boy, and then would take him to the tabernacle and leave him there, to stay there always. For she had given Samuel to the Lord, and he would live at the tabernacle and wait on the priests and serve the Lord as long as he lived.

As soon as Samuel was old enough, Hannah took him to the tabernacle. She and her husband offered a bullock as a sacrifice, then they took the child to Eli and Hannah said to Eli,

"My lord, I am the woman that stood here, praying to the Lord for this child; and the Lord has given me what I asked Him for. Therefore I have given the child back to the Lord, as long as he lives." And she left Samuel to stay with Eli at the tabernacle.

Eli had two sons, whose names were Hophni and Phinehas. They were priests at the tabernacle. But though the Lord had said that the priests should be holy, Hophni and Phinehas were not holy, they were wicked men.

We have read that when any man offered up a peace offering, only a part of it was burned on the altar; of the rest, some was given to the priest, for him to eat, and some to the man who brought the offering, for him to eat. Hophni and Phinehas took more than their share of the peace offerings, and when a man was unwilling to let them have so much, they would take it from him by force. Therefore the people did not wish to come to the tabernacle with their offerings.

As Samuel grew up, he did what was right and pleased the Lord. Each year his mother made him a coat and brought it to him when she came with her husband to offer their sacrifice. Eli always spoke kindly to them and asked the Lord to bless them, because they had given Samuel to the Lord.

Eli was becoming very old. He heard of the evil things that his sons did, and he was grieved at their wickedness, but he did not punish them. He allowed them to remain priests and go on in their sin. It seemed that Eli cared more to please his sons than to please the Lord. Therefore the Lord declared that he would not have Eli or one of his sons as high priest, but would choose another man; and both of Eli's sons, the Lord said, would die in one day.

Samuel stayed at the tabernacle, doing as he was bidden by the high priest. One night, while Samuel and Eli were both asleep, Samuel heard

Hannah brings the child Samuel to Eli at the tabernacle.

a voice calling to him. He rose and ran to Eli, saying that he had come because Eli called him (for he thought it was Eli's voice). But Eli said,

"I did not call; go back to sleep."

Samuel went and lay down and he heard the voice again. He rose and went to Eli, and again Eli answered,

"I did not call you, my son; lie down again."

When Samuel heard the voice a third time, and went to Eli again, Eli knew that it was the Lord who had called the child. This time Eli said to him,

"Go, lie down; and if He calls you, say, 'Speak, Lord, for I hear."

So Samuel went and lay down, and the Lord called as before, "Samuel, Samuel!" And Samuel answered, "Speak, for Your servant hears." Then the Lord told Samuel that He was going to punish Eli and his sons, because the sons had made themselves wicked and Eli had not kept them from doing so.

When the Lord had finished speaking, Samuel lay still until the morning. Then he rose and opened the doors of the tabernacle. He was afraid to tell Eli of what the Lord had said. But Eli called him, and asked,

"What did the Lord say to you? May God punish you if you hide anything from me."

Then Samuel told Eli every word. When Eli heard it he said,

"It is the Lord Who has said He will punish me. Let Him do to me whatever He thinks best."

Samuel grew, and the Lord blessed him, and all the people knew that he was chosen to be a prophet.

The words that God spoke to Samuel came true. The army of Israel went out to fight against the Philistines, and the Philistines killed about four thousand men. When the army of Israel came back to their camp after the battle, the elders said to one another,

"Let us bring the ark out of the tabernacle to save us from our enemies." Perhaps they remembered how the ark was carried around Jericho, when the Israelites took that city. But on that occasion the Lord had commanded them to carry it. He did not command them to send for it now, and it was foolish of them to think that the ark could save them. Only the Lord could do that.

Yet they sent to Shiloh for the ark, and the two sons of Eli, Hophni and Phinehas, came with it. When it was brought into the camp, the people were glad and gave a great shout, and the noise was heard far off. The Philistines heard it, and said,

"What does it mean, this great shout in the camp of the Hebrews?"

They were told that the ark had been brought into the Israelites' camp, and they were afraid; but then they said to one another,

"Let us be brave, and fight like men, so that we will not be made servants of the Hebrews."

So the Philistines fought again with the men of Israel, and killed thirty thousand of them. They took the ark away from the Israelites, also, and the two sons of Eli, Hophni and Phinehas, were killed.

A man from the Israelite army ran to Shiloh that same day. His clothes were torn and he had put earth on his head to show his grief. Eli, the high priest, was sitting on a seat by the road, for he was afraid, since the ark had been carried to the battle, that some harm might come to it, and he waited to hear what had happened.

Eli had become very old, and weak, and almost blind. The man went to him and said,

"The men of Israel have fled from the Philistines, and a great many of them have been killed. Your two sons, Hophni and Phinehas, are dead, and the ark of God has been taken."

When the man spoke of the ark, Eli fell from his seat backward, down to the ground, and his neck was broken and he died; for his grief was greater than he could bear, when he heard that the ark had been taken.

The Philistines carried the ark to one of their cities, called Ashdod, where they had a temple for their idol, whose name was Dagon. They took the ark into the house of Dagon, and set it down by the idol and left it there all night. When they rose the next morning, and went into Dagon's house, they found that the idol had fallen on its face on the ground.

They lifted up the idol, and set it in its place, and left the ark there an-

The Philistine idol Dagon falls and is broken before the ark.

The Philistines return the ark of the covenant to the land of Israel.

other night. But when they came the next morning, Dagon had fallen down before the ark, and this time Dagon's head and hands were broken off, only his body being left.

After that, there came to be great sickness among the people of Ashdod, and many of them died. Then they said to one another,

"The ark of the God of Israel must not stay with us." They said this because they believed it was God Who had sent the sickness among them and had thrown down their idol.

The Philistines called all their leaders together and asked them,

"What shall we do with the ark of the God of Israel?"

"Carry it to Gath," the leaders answered. Gath was another city of the Philistines. So the people carried it to Gath, but a great sickness came among the people of that city also. The Philistines kept the ark for seven months, but during all that time the Lord sent them great trouble. At last they called for their wise men, and asked how they should send the ark back to the land of Israel.

Now, in that country cows were used for drawing carts. The wise men told the Philistines to make a new cart, and hitch two cows to it, but not to let the cows' calves follow them. Then the people should put the ark in the cart and send it away, letting the cows draw it wherever they chose, without anyone to guide them. If the cows went away from their homes and their calves, and took the ark into the land of Israel, it would show that the Lord made them go there; but if the cows did not take the ark to the land of Israel, it would show that the Lord did not want it sent back, and that he had not punished the Philistines for keeping it, but that their troubles had come by chance.

The Philistines did as their wise men said. As soon as the cows were let loose they went straight into the land of Israel, lowing as they went, until they came to a city called Beth-shemesh. The Israelites who lived there were reaping their wheat harvest in the valley near the city. They looked up and saw the ark, and rejoiced to see it.

The cows took the ark into the field of a man named Joshua, and stood still beside a great stone there. Then some men of the tribe of Levi came, and took the ark down from the cart and laid it on the stone. They broke up the cart for wood to burn, and killed the cows for a burnt offering to the Lord. The Levites took the ark from the cart because, as we have read, the Lord had chosen them to take care of it, and of all the things in the tabernacle. If the men of any other tribe came near those sacred things, God had said, they must be put to death. Some of the men of Beth-shemesh disobeyed God, because they were curious and wanted to see the ark. They went near it and looked into it, and many of them died for their sin.

Later the ark was taken to the city of Kirjath-jearim, into the house of a man named Abinadab, and was left there for many years.

66

The story of the anointing of Saul as king

When Eli died, the Lord made Samuel judge over the people. Samuel lived in the city of Ramah, where his father and mother had lived.

We have read that after the tabernacle was finished, every man of Israel was commanded to make his sacrifices there; but at the time we are now reading about the ark was not in the tabernacle, for the people had never brought it back to Shiloh. So Samuel built an altar at Ramah, where he lived, and offered up sacrifices himself.

Soon the people of Israel sinned again by worshiping the idols Baal and Ashtaroth. Then the Philistines made war upon them. Samuel said to the Israelites,

"If you will put away your idols and serve the Lord, He will save you from the Philistines."

The people obeyed Samuel. Then he said to them,

"Come to the city of Mizpeh and I will pray for you." They went to Mizpeh, and there they confessed their wickedness and said,

"We have sinned against the Lord."

When the Philistines heard that the Israelites were at Mizpeh, they went there to fight against them. The men of Israel were afraid, and they said to Samuel,

"Pray to the Lord for us."

Samuel took a young lamb and offered it up as a burnt offering; and he prayed to the Lord for the people. While Samuel was offering up the lamb the Philistines came; but the Lord sent a great storm of thunder and lightning that made them run away in fear. The men of Israel left Mizpeh and chased them, killing many of them. Thus the Lord gave the men of Israel the victory. And Samuel set up a stone at the place where the Lord helped them, and called it Ebenezer, which means "the stone of help."

When he had grown old, Samuel made his two sons judges, to help him in ruling over the land. They did not rule justly, as their father had done. If two of the people disputed about anything, and came to them to decide which was right and which was wrong, they would say that the one was right who paid them for saying so. That is, they took bribes from the people, allowing anyone to do wrong who would pay them money for it.

The elders of Israel went to Samuel, at Ramah, and told him that his sons were doing wrong; and they asked him to choose a king for them so that they might be like the other nations around them. It was right in them to tell Samuel that his sons did wickedly, but Samuel was displeased when they asked him to choose a king, because the Lord should have been their only king. Samuel prayed to the Lord for guidance.

The Lord commanded Samuel to tell the people what their king would do to them, and how cruelly he would treat them, if they had a king like

The stone of help: Samuel calls the Israelites back to God.

the other nations. Samuel did so. He told the men of Israel that the king would take their sons to be drivers of his chariots and workmen in his fields, and their daughters to be cooks and bakers in his kitchen. The king would take the best of their lands and their vineyards and give them to whomever he pleased. He would take away their cattle and their sheep also; and they would cry out, Samuel said, for the trouble their king had brought upon them, but the Lord would not hear them.

Still the people said, "We want to have a king like all the other nations, to rule over us and to lead us when we fight our battles." So the Lord commanded Samuel to do as they asked, and choose them a king.

There was a man among the Israelites named Kish, who had a son called Saul. The Bible tells us that Saul was a "goodly" young man. He was well formed and handsome to look at, and he was taller than any of the rest of the people.

One day the asses that belonged to Kish, Saul's father, strayed away. Kish said to Saul,

"Take one of the servants and go look for the asses." Saul took a servant and went to look for the asses, but he went a long way and could not find them.

By this time Saul and the servant had come near a city, and the servant told Saul that in the city there was a prophet whose words always came true. The servant meant Samuel. He said,

"Let us go and ask him; perhaps he can tell us where we should look for the asses."

As Saul and his servant went up the hill to the city, they met young maidens going out to draw water, and they asked them if the prophet were there. The maidens answered,

"Yes, he came today, for there is to be a feast. As soon as you go into the city you will see him." And when they had come into the city, Samuel met them.

The Lord told Samuel He would reveal to Samuel that day the man who should be king over Israel. When Samuel saw Saul, the Lord said to him,

"This is the man."

Saul did not know Samuel, and he went to him and said,

"Tell me, please, where the prophet's house is."

Samuel answered, "I am the prophet." Then he told Saul to bring his

Samuel anoints Saul to be the first king of the Israelites.

servant and come to the feast, and stay there that day; the next day, Samuel said, Saul could resume his journey. And as for the asses that had been lost, Saul need think of them no more, Samuel told him, for his father had found them.

Samuel took Saul and his servant into his parlor and made them sit in the best place among those who were invited to the feast. So Saul stayed with Samuel that day.

The next morning, very early, Samuel took Saul to the roof of the house, where they would be alone, and talked with him; afterward Samuel went with him toward the gate of the city. As they were walking together, Samuel said to Saul,

"Tell your servant to go on while you stay here with me. I want to show you what the Lord has commanded me to do."

When the servant had gone on, Samuel took a bottle of oil and poured it upon Saul's head. This was called anointing him. We have read that Moses anointed Aaron when he was made high priest; they used the same custom with one who was made king. Now Samuel anointed Saul to be king over the people of Israel, because the Lord had commanded him to do it. But no one knew of it except Saul and Samuel. The Lord did not mean to let the people know of it until the time came to choose Saul again, before them all, for their king.

After this, Samuel spoke to the people and told them to come to the city of Mizpeh, so that they might have a king set over them. When the people saw Saul as he stood among them, he was taller than any of them; they came only to his shoulders. Samuel said to them,

"See the man whom the Lord has chosen; there is no one like him among all the people."

And they all shouted and said,

"God save the king!"

Then Samuel sent them away, every man to his own home, and Saul went to his home in the city of Gibeah.

After this the Ammonites came to fight against the city of Jabesh-gilead. The men of Israel who lived there were afraid and promised that if the Ammonites would treat them kindly, they would be their servants. But the Ammonites would not; they said they would take every man and put out his right eye.

When the men of Jabesh-gilead heard this, they asked the Ammonites to give them seven days. They would send messengers to the Israelites in other parts of the land. If, by that time, no one had come to help them, they promised to give up their city and let the Ammonites do to them as they pleased.

They sent messengers to Gibeah, where Saul lived, and the messengers told the people what the Ammonites said. The people wept when they heard it, and they told Saul what the messengers had told them. Then Saul took two oxen and cut them in pieces, and sent the pieces through all the land of Israel, saying to the people,

"Whoever does not come to fight against the Ammonites, this shall be done to his oxen."

When the people heard these words, more than three hundred thousand men came to Saul. Early the next morning he led them out against the Ammonites, and they fought the Ammonites and killed almost all of them. The rest of the Ammonites fled and were scattered, so that no two of them were left together. The Israelites rejoiced over their victory.

67

The story of Saul and Jonathan

AFTER SAUL HAD BEEN KING TWO YEARS, he chose three thousand men for soldiers. Saul himself was captain over two thousand of them and his son Jonathan was captain over the other thousand.

Jonathan and his men fought against some Philistines, who had come into the land of Israel, and drove them out. Then the Philistines gathered a great army and came into Israel with thousands of chariots and horsemen and with so many soldiers that they could not be counted.

When the people saw what a great host had come against them, they were afraid. They hid in caves and thick bushes, and among the rocks, and on the mountains, and in pits in the earth. Some of them fled over the Jordan into the land of Gilead, where the two and a half tribes lived. The few who were left followed Saul, their king, but they trembled with fear.

Saul went to Gilgal, for Samuel had promised to meet him there and had commanded him to wait. When Samuel came he would offer up burnt offerings and peace offerings, and afterward he would tell Saul what he should do.

Saul waited seven days; then, when Samuel did not come, he grew impatient and said,

"Bring the burnt offering to me."

Then Saul offered up the burnt offering himself. As soon as he had done it, Samuel came, and Saul went out to meet him. Samuel said,

"You have done wrong"—for only Samuel, the prophet, should have made the offering.

Saul began to make excuses for offering up the sacrifice. He said that he was afraid to wait any longer, for fear the Philistines would attack him. But Samuel said that Saul had done wickedly, for he had disobeyed the Lord. Therefore the Lord would not let him remain king, but would choose another man in his place. Samuel did not mean that Saul would be removed at once, but that the Lord had determined to replace him some time and that it was as certain to be done as if it were done that very day.

Saul counted the soldiers who were with him and found that there were about six hundred men. He and Jonathan led these men to the city of Gibeah. The Philistines were at Michmash.

The Philistines had for a long time had power over the people of Israel, and they would not let the men of Israel have swords or spears, for fear they might rise up and fight against them. The Philistines had sent away all the smiths who could make these weapons for the people. So when the day for the battle came, it was found that among the Israelites no man had either a sword or a spear except Saul and Jonathan.

In those days soldiers wore armor made of iron or brass. They carried shields made of strong boards covered with leather, the skin of oxen. These shields they held up before them while they were in battle, so that the arrows and darts of their enemies would not wound them. Jonathan, Saul's son, wore armor, and he had a soldier to carry his shield and spear for him, when he did not want to use them. This soldier was called his armor-bearer.

The Philistines had their camp near the camp of the Israelites. Jonathan asked his armor-bearer to go with him to the camp of the Philistines.

"For," said Jonathan, "the Lord may help us, even you and me alone, to fight against all the Philistines' great army; because the Lord can give the victory to whomsoever He chooses, either to many or to few." The armor-bearer said he would go.

Then Jonathan told the armor-bearer that this was the way they would know whether or not the Lord intended to help them: They would go and stand where the Philistines could see them. If the Philistines called out to them and told them to wait, then, Jonathan said, they would go no farther, for the Lord was not going to help them. But if the Philistines said, "Come up to us," they would go; for this would mean that the Lord would give them the victory.

Jonathan attacks the Philistines

So Jonathan and his armor-bearer went and stood at a place where the

Jonathan fights the Philistines and defeats them.

Philistines could see them. The Philistines made fun of them, and said,

"See, the Hebrews are coming out of the holes where they were hidden." The Philistines called out, "Come near to us and we will show you something."

When Jonathan heard the Philistines say this, he told his armor-bearer to follow him and the Lord would give the Israelites the victory. Jonathan climbed up over the rocks, on his hands and feet, to reach the Philistines' camp, and his armor-bearer climbed after him. When they came to the camp, they fought the Philistines and killed about twenty men. The Lord made the earth shake under them, so that all the Philistines were afraid and trembled.

Saul and the men who were with him did not know what Jonathan had done; but Saul's watchman looked out toward the camp of the Philistines and saw fighting there, and he told Saul of it. Saul counted his men, to learn which of them had gone against the Philistines; and when he counted his men he found that only Jonathan and his armor-bearer were missing. Saul and his men then went over to join in the battle. Many of those who before had been afraid, and had hidden in the mountains, came with them.

The Lord helped the Israelites and the Philistines fled from them. Yet the men of Israel suffered on that day, for Saul commanded that no man should eat any food until the evening, because he wanted them to go on pursuing their enemies. So none of the people had any food.

While they were pursuing the Philistines, the Israelites came to a wood where honey was dropping on the ground, from a nest in the trees where the wild bees had made it. The men were hungry but were afraid to eat, because of Saul's command. But Jonathan did not know what his father had said, so he reached out the end of the staff he had in his hand, and dipped the staff into the honeycomb, and put the honey into his mouth.

Jonathan is condemned by his father

When Saul heard of this, he said,

"You must die, Jonathan"; for he was angry, and would have killed Jonathan for disobeying his command.

But the people objected, saying,

"Shall Jonathan die, who has caused us to gain this great victory?" And they insisted that no harm should come to Jonathan. So they saved Jonathan from being put to death.

After this, Samuel told Saul that the Lord remembered the wickedness of the Amalekites, in making war against the Israelites when they came out of Egypt, although the Israelites had done them no harm. Now, Samuel said, the Lord commanded Saul to fight against the Amalekites, and destroy them, and their cattle, and save nothing of theirs alive.

Saul gathered a great army of more than two hundred thousand men. He fought with the Amalekites and conquered them and killed their people, but their king he let live. Also the best of their sheep, their oxen, their lambs, and all that was good, Saul and the men of Israel saved alive. Only what was poor and worth nothing did they put to death.

The Lord was displeased with Saul, and he said to Samuel,

"I am sorry I made Saul king, for he has not obeyed my command."

After the battle, Samuel went to Saul and Saul said to him,

"I have done as the Lord commanded me."

But Samuel heard the bleating of the sheep, and the lowing of the cattle,

Saul against the Amalekites.

which Saul had taken from the Amalekites, and Samuel said,

"Then why do I hear the bleating of sheep and the lowing of oxen?"

Saul began to make excuses; he said that the people had saved them alive to offer them up as sacrifices to the Lord. But Samuel asked Saul whether the Lord was better pleased to have sacrifices offered up to him, than he was to have his commands obeyed.

"It is better to obey than to offer up sacrifices," Samuel said. "To do what the Lord has commanded you not to do is as wicked as to worship idols."

Then Samuel told Saul again that because he had disobeyed the Lord, the Lord would remove him from his place as king.

God told Samuel that he should go to the city of Bethlehem, to a man named Jesse, and should anoint one of Jesse's sons to be king.

Samuel answered, "How can I go? If Saul hears of it he will kill me."

Then the Lord said that Samuel should take a heifer to offer up as a sacrifice there, and should ask Jesse to come to the sacrifice. Afterward, the Lord said, He would show Samuel what to do.

Samuel did as he was commanded. He went to Bethlehem and made ready his sacrifice, and he invited Jesse and his sons to come to it.

When they came, Samuel thought that Jesse's oldest son must be the one whom the Lord had chosen for king; but the Lord told him this was not the one. Then Jesse called another, but the Lord did not choose him. And Jesse caused seven of his sons to pass before Samuel, but still Samuel said, "The Lord has not chosen any of these."

Then Samuel asked Jesse, "Are these all thy children?"

Jesse answered, "There is yet one left, the youngest, but he is keeping the sheep."

Samuel said, "Send for him."

They sent for this youngest son and brought him to Samuel. Now, he had been out in the field; and when he came in and stood before them, his cheeks were red and his face was beautiful to look at. And the Lord said to Samuel,

David is anointed by Samuel

"Arise, anoint him, for this is he."

Samuel took oil and poured it on the young man and anointed him, in the presence of all his brothers.

That is how the Lord chose David (for that was his name) to be king over Israel. Yet David was not to be king at once, nor for a long while afterward, but only when the Lord decided to remove Saul from being king.

And after David had been anointed, the Lord sent his Holy Spirit into David's heart, to make David good and wise; and the Lord took his Spirit away from Saul.

We have read of the angels—those good spirits that serve God. The Bible tells us there are evil spirits also, that serve Satan. Now one of these evil spirits went into Saul and troubled him. Saul's advisers told him that he should look for a man who could play well on the harp, and when the evil spirit troubled him, that man, they said, should come and play before him, for then the evil spirit would go away. So Saul said to his advisers,

"Get me a man that can play well on the harp, and bring him to me."

One of the advisers answered that he had seen such a man. "This man is

Samuel anoints David to replace Saul, in the presence of David's family.

the son of Jesse, of Bethlehem," he said. It was David of whom he spoke; for David knew well how to play on the harp.

David plays the harp for Saul

Therefore Saul sent messengers to Jesse, and told him to send David, his son, who kept the sheep. Jesse took an ass and loaded it with bread, and a bottle of wine, and a kid, and sent them by David as a present to Saul, but he did not let Saul know that Samuel had anointed David to be king.

So David came to Saul, and stayed with him and waited on him, for he pleased Saul well. When the evil spirit troubled Saul, David took a harp and played sweet music that comforted Saul. Then the evil spirit left Saul. But after a while David left Saul's house and returned to his own home. Saul had many other servants, and he forgot David.

68

The story of David and Goliath

THE PHILISTINES GATHERED THEIR ARMIES together to fight against Israel. Saul and the men of Israel made ready for the battle.

The camp of the Philistines was on a mountain on one side of a valley and the camp of the Israelites was on a mountain on the other side.

There came out of the camp of the Philistines a giant, named Goliath of Gath. On his head was a helmet made of brass, and he wore a coat of armor; pieces of brass also covered his legs, so that no sword or spear might wound him. He came into the valley between the two armies, where the men of Israel could see him, and he stood and cried to them,

"Choose a man out of your army, and let him come down to me. If he can kill me, then we will be your servants; but if I kill him, then you shall be our servants." The Philistine giant also said, "I dare the armies of Israel to send a man who will fight me."

When Saul and the men of Israel heard these words, they were greatly afraid; for no man in Saul's army was willing to go out and fight with the giant. And every morning and evening for forty days, Goliath came out and defied all the men of Israel.

David was taking care of his father's sheep at Bethlehem, but three of his older brothers had gone with Saul to fight against the Philistines. Jesse said to David,

"Take this parched corn and these ten loaves of bread, and run to the camp, to your brothers, and carry these ten cheeses as a present to their captains and find out how they are doing."

David rose up early in the morning and left the sheep with a servant, and went to the camp as his father had told him to do. He reached the camp just as the army was going out to fight, and all the men were eager for the battle. For the Philistines and the Israelites had made ready for battle and their armies stood facing each other.

David left the things he had brought with a man, to take care of them, and he ran into the army to speak with his brothers. While he talked with them, Goliath came out between the two armies and spoke the same words that he had spoken before, and David heard him.

The men of Israel fled from Goliath in fear, and David heard them say that if any man would kill the Philistine giant, Saul the king would give him great riches and he could have the king's daughter to be his wife.

David asked the Israelite soldiers to tell him again what would be done for the man who killed the Philistine giant Goliath. Eliab, David's eldest brother, heard him asking and was angry with him, and said,

"Why did you come down here? And whom have you left at home to take care of the sheep? I know the wickedness of your heart; you have come down to see the battle."

"What wrong have I done?" David asked. Then David said, "Who is this Philistine, that he should defy the armies of the living God?" David called the armies of Israel the armies of God, because the children of Israel were God's chosen people; and he called God the living God, because all other gods are only dead idols.

When the men who were near David heard the words that David spoke, they told Saul, and Saul sent for David. David went to Saul, but Saul did not remember him as the boy who had played the harp.

David told Saul that he would go out against the Philistine giant. David said,

"Let no man be afraid because of him; I will go and fight with this Philistine."

Saul said to him, "You are not able to fight him, for you are only a boy, and he has been a man of war from his youth."

David kills a lion and a bear

David answered, "While I was keeping my father's sheep, there came a lion, and a bear, and took a lamb out of the flock; I went after the lion and knocked him down and set the lamb free from his mouth. When the lion rose against me, I caught him by the beard and killed him. I killed both the lion and the bear; and this wicked Philistine shall be like one of them, because he has defied the armies of the living God." David said also, "The Lord who saved me from the paw of the lion and the paw of the bear will save me from the hand of this Philistine."

Then Saul said to David, "Go, and the Lord be with you."

Saul wanted to give David his own armor, his helmet of brass, and his coat of mail, and his sword. But David said, "I cannot go with these"; and he took them off. Then he took his staff, such as shepherds carried; and he chose five smooth stones out of the brook and put them in his shepherd's bag; and his sling was in his hand, and he walked out toward the Philistine giant, Goliath.

At first, Goliath also walked toward David; but when he saw David, he thought him not worth fighting with for David did not look like a soldier, strong and brave, such as Goliath expected would come out against him; but like a shepherd boy, gentle, and with a beautiful face, who had never seen a battle.

"Am I a dog," said Goliath, "that you approach with a staff?" And Goliath

A stone from David's sling strikes and fells the Philistine giant Goliath.

called on the idols that he worshiped to curse David, and he told David to come nearer, so that he might kill him. David answered,

"You come to me trusting in your sword, your shield, and your spear; but I come to you trusting in the God of Israel. For this day He will give you into my power, and I will kill you and cut off your head, and the army of the Philistines will be slain, and their dead bodies will lie on the ground; the birds of the air and the wild beasts of the field will eat them."

When the Philistine giant came near, David ran toward him, and put his hand in the shepherd's bag, and took out a stone and put it in his sling, and slung it and struck the Philistine in the forehead, so that the stone cut into his forehead; and Goliath fell down on his face. So David overcame the Philistine with a sling and with a stone, for there was no sword in his hand.

Goliath's head is cut off

Then David ran and stood upon the Philistine giant, and took the giant's own sword from him and cut off his head with it.

When the Philistines saw that the man in whom they trusted was slain, they fled. The army of Israel rose up and shouted, and followed after them

Saul tries to kill David with his spear.

and killed them, and many Philistines died as they fled. Afterward the men of Israel turned back from pursuing them, and went into the Philistines' camp, and took all the gold, silver and other possessions that they had left in their tents.

David came back from the battle with the head of Goliath in his hand. Abner, the captain of the army of Israel, took him to Saul. Saul said,

"Whose son are you, young man?"

David answered, "I am the son of Jesse of Bethlehem."

Jonathan, Saul's son, was there, and when he saw David and heard him speaking with his father, he loved him; the Bible says he loved him as his own soul, that is, as much as he loved himself. It was the Lord who made him love David, so that David might have Jonathan for his friend in all the troubles that were coming afterward upon him.

Saul took David that day to live with him, and would not let David go home to his father's house. Jonathan made an agreement with David; he promised to be kind to David, because he loved David as his own soul. To show his love he took off his robe and the garments that he wore and gave them to David; and his sword also, and his bow, and the girdle that was fastened around his waist. David obeyed the commands of Saul, and behaved himself wisely in all things, and Saul made him a captain in his army.

The love of David and Jonathan

After the battle with the Philistines, as Saul and David passed together through some of the cities of the land, the women came out with songs and dances, to praise them for their victory. But they praised David more than Saul; they sang "Saul has slain thousands but David had slain ten thousands of the Philistines."

Saul was greatly displeased at their words, and from that time he was jealous of David.

Saul tries to kill David

The next day an evil spirit came into Saul's heart and troubled him, and David played for him on the harp, as he used to do. Saul held a javelin, or spear, in his hand, and he cast it at David, intending that it should go through his body and fasten him to the wall, for he wanted to kill him. But David saw it, and stepped aside out of the way, and it did him no harm. Saul cast it at him again, but David stepped aside this time also.

Saul was afraid of David because he saw that the Lord was with David and was not with Saul any more. So Saul sent David away from his house, with the soldiers that he had made him captain of. The Lord helped David to do all things well, and all the people loved him.

Soon afterward Saul said to David,

"I will give you Merab, my daughter, to be your wife, if you will go out and fight against the Philistines." Saul said this because he hoped the Philistines would kill David, but David went and fought with the Philistines and was not killed. When the time came that he should have been given Merab, Saul gave her to be the wife of another man.

After that, Saul's younger daughter, Michal, loved David, and Saul was told of it. Then Saul said that if David would go and kill a hundred Philistines, he could have Michal for his wife. Saul hoped that this time the Philistines would kill David. But David went with his soldiers and fought against the Philistines and killed five hundred of them, and David himself was not harmed. This time Saul had to give Michal to David, and she became his wife.

Saul could see that the Lord was with David and was helping him. This made Saul even more afraid of David, and Saul came to be David's enemy, and hated him. He spoke to Jonathan, his son, and to all his ministers, and commanded them to kill David. But Jonathan loved David, and told David of what Saul had said.

"My father wants to kill you," Jonathan told David. "You must go to some secret place and hide yourself. I will talk with my father, and what he says I will tell you."

Jonathan talked with Saul and begged him not to harm David, for Jonathan said that David had done no evil to Saul, but only what was good. David had risked his own life to kill Goliath, the Philistine, and after he had killed him, the men of Israel gained a great victory. Saul knew of all these things, and was full of joy when they happened. Why, then, Jonathan asked, would Saul do so wicked a thing now as to kill David, although David was a good man and had done nothing for which he deserved to die?

Saul listened to Jonathan's words and promised, before the Lord, that David would not be killed. Then Jonathan called David from the place where he was hiding and told David what his father had said. He brought David to Saul, and David stayed at Saul's house as before.

David escapes from the murderous plans of Saul when his wife Michal, who is Saul's daughter, lowers him from a window of Saul's palace: See the story on the following page. This is one of the celebrated interpretations of Gustave Doré.

Again there was war in the land, and David went out and fought with the Philistines, and won a victory over them. But Saul was not pleased that David had won the victory, because it made the people love David even more. The evil spirit came into Saul's heart, as he sat in his house with his javelin in his hand, while David was playing on the harp before him. Then Saul cast the javelin again at David, to kill him, but David saw it and slipped away, as he had done before, and the javelin went into the wall and did him no harm; and David fled that night.

David is saved by his wife

Saul sent soldiers to David's house to make sure he did not escape during the night, and then to kill him in the morning. But Michal, David's wife, knew of it, and told David,

"If you do not save your life tonight, tomorrow you will be killed." So she let David down through a window, where Saul's men could not see him, and he escaped from them. Then she took an image and laid it in his bed, and put a pillow under it, and covered it up, to make the soldiers think that David was there, so as to let him have time to flee far away. Saul commanded his men to go into the chamber and take David, but when they reached the room they found only an image in the bed, laid on the pillow. Saul was angry with Michal for this.

69

The story of Jonathan and David

DAVID FLED TO RAMAH, WHERE SAMUEL LIVED, and told Samuel of all that Saul had done. Afterward David went to Naioth. Someone told Saul of this, and Saul sent men to take David, but the Lord saved David out of their hands.

Then David fled from Naioth and went to see Jonathan. He said to Jonathan,

"What have I done? Why should your father want to kill me?"

Jonathan had not heard that his father was trying to kill David. He said to David,

"You will not be killed; my father will do nothing without first telling me of it." But David said it was true that Saul wanted to put him to death, and Jonathan promised to do whatever David asked of him.

The next day was to be a feast day, when Saul would expect David to come to his house and eat of the feast. David was afraid to go, and he begged Jonathan to let him stay away for three days.

"When Saul asks why I am not at the feast," David said to Jonathan, "answer that you gave me permission to go to Bethlehem, where my father lives, so that I might be with my family when they offer up their yearly sacrifice. If Saul is angry when he hears this, it will show that he is determined to do me evil."

Jonathan gave David permission to be away for three days. Then David asked,

"But who will tell me what your father says, when he hears that I have gone?"

Jonathan answered, "Come out into the field." They went out together into the field, and there Jonathan told David that after the three days were past, David should come and hide in the field behind a rock that was there. Then, Jonathan said, he would come into the field, pretending no one was there, and he would shoot three arrows from his bow, as if he were shooting at a mark, and would send a lad after the arrows to pick them up. If Jonathan should call out to the lad, "The arrows are on this side of you," David would know that Saul was not displeased with him and would do him no harm. But if Jonathan cried out, "The arrows are beyond you," David would know that he must flee, because Saul meant to kill him.

Jonathan adopted this plan because he was afraid he would be watched and would not be able to speak with David.

So David went away from Saul's house, the day before the feast. The next day Saul sat down to eat at the feast on a seat by the wall. His son Jonathan, and Abner, his captain, sat near him; but David's seat was empty. Saul asked nothing about David that day, for he thought something had happened to keep him away, but the next day David's seat was empty again and Saul said to Jonathan,

David is absent from the feast

"Why has not David come to eat, yesterday or today?"

Jonathan answered, "David asked my permission to go to Bethlehem, for his family has its own feast and his brother had asked him to be there."

Saul was very angry with Jonathan for allowing David to go; he told Jonathan that he ought not to love David. Saul told him this because he wanted Jonathan to be king after he himself should die. Now he feared that Jonathan would never be king as long as David lived. Saul said.

"Send for David and he will be put to death."

Jonathan asked, "Why should he be put to death? What evil has he done?"

Then Saul cast his javelin at Jonathan. From this Jonathan knew that his father was determined to kill David. So he rose up from the table in great anger, and would eat no food, because his father had said these things about David.

Jonathan signals with an arrow

The next day was the day on which David was to hide out in the field, behind the rock that Jonathan had shown him. Jonathan went out at the time he had said, and a little lad went with him. He sent the lad on before him to find the arrows he would shoot.

Jonathan shoots an arrow as a signal and warning to his friend David.

Jonathan shot an arrow that passed over the lad. Jonathan cried out loud, "The arrow is beyond you."

David heard Jonathan's words, in the place where he was hidden, and he knew from those words that he must flee, because Saul meant to kill him.

The lad gathered up the arrows and took them back to Jonathan. He did not know why Jonathan had shot them, or why Jonathan had called out after him. Jonathan gave his bow and arrows to the lad, and said,

"Go, carry them to the city."

As soon as the lad was gone, David came out from his hiding-place.

He bowed down with his face to the ground, before Jonathan, three times. Then they kissed each other, and wept, because they had to part. Jonathan told David to flee, and he helped David to escape from Saul, because he loved David and because they had made an agreement together that they would be kind to each other, and to each other's children, forever.

So David fled from Saul, and Jonathan went back to the city.

70

The story of David's flight from Saul

David went first to the city of Nob, where the tabernacle was at that time, for the people had moved it from Shiloh after the ark was taken by the Philistines. Ahimelech, the high priest in Nob, asked David why he had come. David was afraid to say that he had fled from Saul, for someone might send word to Saul to come and take him; so he was tempted to tell an untruth. He said,

"The king has sent me on a secret errand, but he commanded me to tell no one what it is."

David sinned when he said this. The Lord who had saved him from the lion and the bear, and from Goliath the Philistine, was able to save him from Saul. David should have spoken the truth and trusted in God.

Some young men who were friends of David's had come with him. For their sake David asked Ahimelech for five loaves of bread, so that they might have something to eat. Ahimelech answered that no bread was there excepting the shew-bread, which, as we have been told, the priests placed each week on the golden table, but Ahimelech gave this bread to David.

At the tabernacle there was a man named Doeg. He was not an Israelite but had come from the land of Edom. He had been hired by Saul to take care of Saul's cattle. Doeg saw David while he talked with Ahimelech. David was afraid and said to Ahimelech,

"Is there a spear or a sword here that I may have? I have not brought my sword or my weapons with me."

The high priest answered,

"The sword of Goliath, the Philistine giant whom you killed, is here, wrapped in a cloth; if you want it, take it. There is no other."

"Give it to me," David said, "for I would rather have that sword than any other."

David immediately fled from the tabernacle, because he feared that Saul would find him. With Doeg's help, soon David came to the capital city of the Philistines, called Gath. The king of that city was named Achish.

When Achish's men saw David, they knew him and took him to the king. They said,

"Is not this David? Did not the women of Israel sing to each other, saying, 'Saul has slain thousands, but David has slain ten thousands of the Philistines?' "

David was afraid the Philistine king would take revenge on him, so David pretended he had lost his senses: He scrabbled on the doors and behaved strangely. King Achish saw him do these things and said to his ministers,

"You can see the man is mad; why, then, have you brought him to me? Do I need madmen?" So they let David go.

David receives the sword of Goliath from Ahimelech.

David hides in the cave

David then fled from Gath and went into a great cave, called the cave of Adullam, and lived there. When his brothers and his parents heard of it, they came to visit him, and others who were willing to help him came, until he had with him about four hundred men. David's father and mother were old, and he wished them to be in a better place than the cave where he was hidden, but he would not send them back to their home in Bethlehem because the Philistines were there. Therefore David went to the king of Moab, and said to him,

"Let my father and my mother come and stay in your land, until I find out what God will do for me." The king said they might live in his land, so David's father and mother stayed with the king of Moab as long as David was in the cave.

David remembered the time when he used to live at Bethlehem, when he was a boy, tending his father's sheep, and before all his troubles had come upon him. And he thought of the well by the gate, where he used to drink water. He longed for it, and said,

Saul orders the killing of the priests.

"I wish someone would give me a drink from the well by the gate of Bethlehem."

Three of his men heard him say this, and they loved him so much that they went and broke through the Philistine army and drew water from the well and brought it to David. When David realized that they had risked their lives to bring him water, he would not drink the water but poured it out on the ground as an offering to the Lord.

A prophet named Gad then went to David and said to him,

"Stay no longer in the cave, but go back into the land of Judah."

David obeyed the prophet and went to Judah, where he lived in a wood. Saul was in the city of Gibeah; he rested there under a tree, with his spear in his hand, and his followers were standing about him. Saul scolded them, saying that they were not his friends any longer, but his enemies, because they would not tell him what David and Jonathan were going to do against him.

Then Doeg, the Edomite, spoke to Saul, and said that he had seen David at the tabernacle, and that Ahimelech, the high priest, had given him bread and the sword of Goliath the Philistine. The king sent for Ahimelech, and for all the priests who were with him; and they came to the king. Saul asked Ahimelech why he had helped David and had given him bread and a sword. Ahimelech answered that he had not helped David to rebel against Saul; for he did not know, when David came to the tabernacle, that he was fleeing from Saul.

Saul has the priests killed

But Saul was very angry, and said,

"I will put you to death, Ahimelech, you and all your relations." And Saul turned to the soldiers that stood near him, and said,

"Kill the priests, because they are on David's side, and when they knew where he had fled, they would not tell me."

But the soldiers refused to obey Saul, and Saul said to Doeg, the Edomite, "You kill them." And that wicked man obeyed, killing eighty-five men who were priests. Doeg went to the city of Nob also, where the tabernacle was, and where the priests lived, and killed all the priests he found there.

David and his men (there were, by this time, about six hundred with him) went out of Keilah, to flee to any place they could find where they might hide from Saul.

When Saul heard that David had fled, he did not go to Keilah after him. Saul tried every day to find David, but God saved David from Saul.

David hid in a wood. One day Jonathan came to him there, and spoke to him as a friend, saying,

"Do not fear, for Saul, my father, will not find you, and you will yet be king over Israel." And again David and Jonathan made an agreement together, promising never to harm each other. Afterward Jonathan went away to his own home, but David stayed in the wood.

A tribe called the Ziphites went to Saul and said they would show him where David was. Saul and his men went with the Ziphites to seek David, but when they had almost taken David, a messenger came to Saul and said,

"Come back at once, for the Philistines have invaded your land." Saul had to go to fight against the Philistines, so the Lord saved David this time also; and David fled into the desert.

When Saul returned from following the Philistines, he was told where David had gone. He chose three thousand of his soldiers and took them into the desert to hunt for David among the rocks, where the wild goats lived. And he came to a cave.

Saul's life is spared by David

David and his men were hidden in the sides of the cave, but Saul could not see them, and Saul walked alone into the cave. While he was there, David's men wanted him to kill Saul, but he would not, for although Saul wanted to kill David, David did not want to kill him. Instead of this David was willing to obey Saul, because Saul was still king.

Therefore David would not kill Saul, but he went up softly behind Saul, while Saul was in the cave, and cut off a piece of Saul's robe and took it away in his hand, and Saul did not know it.

When Saul went out of the cave, David followed him and shouted,

"My lord, the king."

Saul looked around to see who it was. Then David bowed down with his face to the earth before him, and asked why Saul listened to the wicked men who told him that David wanted to do him harm. On that day, David said, he might have killed Saul, and some of his men wanted him to do it, but he told them he would not kill his master, whom the Lord had made king. Then David held up the piece of robe that he had cut off, and said,

"See this piece of your robe in my hand! Since I was so near you as to

David proves to Saul, by the piece of Saul's robe, that he has spared his life. David is shown below, holding up the proof; Saul and his men are on the cliff above. The cave is below the cliff. This is one of the Gustave Doré engravings.

cut it off, but did not kill you, you may know that I would not do you evil. Yet you are hunting me to put me to death. Let the Lord judge between us, and see which one is doing wrong, and let him punish you for your cruelty to me, but I will not do you any harm."

When Saul heard David speaking so kindly to him, the feeling of hatred went out of his heart, and he said,

"Is this your voice, my son David?" and he wept.

Then Saul said to David, "You are more just than I, because you have done good to me, but I have done evil to you, and you have shown me kindness today, for when I was in your power you did not kill me. May the Lord reward you for the good you have done. And now I know that you will someday be king over Israel. Promise me, therefore, before God, that you will not slay my children after I am dead." And David promised that he would not.

Then Saul went away to his own home, but David and his men stayed in the desert.

At this time Samuel died, and all the people of Israel gathered together to mourn for him. They buried him at Ramah, the city where he lived.

71

The story of Abigail

After Samuel was dead, David went down to the desert of Paran. In that country there was a very rich man, who had three thousand sheep and a thousand goats; his name was Nabal, and his wife's name was Abigail. She was a kind and beautiful woman, and acted wisely and prudently; but Nabal was ill-natured and foolish and did what was evil.

David and his men had their camp near the place where Nabal's flocks were feeding, and David's men were very good to Nabal, for although they wanted food to eat, they never took a sheep or a goat from him, nor allowed others to do so; nor did they harm his shepherds.

One day Nabal went to shear his sheep at Carmel. When David heard of it, he said to ten of his young men,

"Go up to Carmel and speak kindly to Nabal, and ask if he will not give us some food."

They went and spoke as David had told them. But Nabal answered,

"Who is David? There are many servants nowadays that run away from their masters as he has done. Why should I take my bread, and the meat that I have killed for my shearers, and give it to men I do not know?"

David's young men went back to him and told him what Nabal had said. Then David said to his men,

"Gird on your swords," and David also girded on his sword, and took with him about four hundred men, leaving two hundred men to guard the camp. David was very angry and told his men that he had kept Nabal's flocks safe all the time they were out in the desert, so that none of them were lost; but now, when he spoke kindly to Nabal and asked him for food, Nabal would give none, but returned only evil for the good that had been done to him. David said he would go to Carmel and punish Nabal.

Abigail welcomes David and feeds him and his men.

So David started to go to Nabal's house. But before he had reached there, one of Nabal's young men went to Abigail, Nabal's wife, and told her how David had sent messengers to Nabal, and how unkindly Nabal had treated them.

"Yet David's men were very good to us," the young man said, "when we were out in the desert. We were not harmed by them, and they stole nothing. They kept us safe by night and by day, all the time we were near them keeping the sheep." The young man told Abigail to think what she should do, because David would surely come and punish them for Nabal's unkindness.

Abigail hastily took two hundred loaves of bread, and two bottles of wine, five sheep that had been butchered, and five measures of parched corn; one hundred clusters of raisins, and two hundred cakes of figs, and put them on asses. She said to her servants,

"Go on before me, and I will come after you." But she did not tell her husband Nabal.

As she rode forward she came to a shady place on the hill, and there she met David and his men coming toward her. When she saw him, she got down from the ass, and bowed before him with her face to the ground.

Abigail saves her husband

"I pray," she said, "let me speak, and hear what I say; pay no attention to the evil words that Nabal has spoken. Let this present, which I have brought, be given to your men." And she begged that David would forgive her for coming to him. The Lord would certainly bless him, she said, and save him from Saul. And when the Lord did as he promised, and made David king over Israel, Abigail said, David would not be sorry that he had listened to her and let her persuade him to stay away from Nabal's house, and not go there to put Nabal to death.

David listened to her, and when she had finished speaking he thanked the Lord for sending her to meet him and for the good advice she had given him, because it had kept him from going on in his anger to kill Nabal. So he took the present which Abigail brought, and spoke kindly to her, and sent her safely away; and he and his men went back to their camp.

When Abigail returned home, her husband Nabal was holding a great feast there and was drunk. Therefore she said nothing to him until the morning. Then when she told him of the danger he had been in, he was greatly afraid, and all his strength went from him, so that he lay helpless and without moving, like a stone. About ten days afterward he died.

David takes Abigail as his wife

When David heard that Nabal was dead, he thanked the Lord again for keeping him from going to Nabal's house in his anger. David said,

"Blessed be the Lord, who has kept me from doing evil."

David loved Abigail, and sent messengers to ask her to be his wife. When the messengers arrived at her house, they said,

"David sent us to you, to take you to him to be his wife."

She bowed herself with her face to the earth, and said,

"Let me be his servant." Then she rode to David's camp, taking five of her handmaidens with her; and, following the messengers of David, she came to him and became his wife.

72

The story of the Witch of Endor

THERE WERE AT THAT TIME IN THE LAND OF ISRAEL persons who had evil spirits that would come when they called them. Then they talked with the spirits, and questioned them about what would happen in the future, and asked the spirits to help them to do things that were wicked. These spirits were often called *familiar spirits* (meaning that they were attached to a particular person or family) or *divining spirits* (meaning that they could foretell the future). It was a great sin to have such a spirit. The Lord commanded that all persons who had such evil spirits should be put to death, and He forbade the people to go to such persons to ask any questions. Saul had sent many who had evil spirits out of the land.

But now Saul was in great trouble. He had asked the Lord what he should do against the Philistines and the Lord would not answer him. So Saul said to his men,

"Find me a woman that has one of these spirits and I will go to her and ask my question."

His ministers answered, "At Endor there is such a woman."

Saul disguised himself, so that no one would know him, and he took two men with him and went to the woman at night. She did not know that it was Saul, the king, and he asked her to let the spirit bring up for him a man who was dead, but whom he wanted to speak with.

Saul should have known that an evil spirit cannot bring up a man from the dead; God alone can do that. But Saul said,

"Bring up the man I will name."

The woman asked, "Whom shall I bring up?"

Saul answered,

"Bring me up Samuel."

Then Samuel, who had been dead and buried for years, rose up before them. But it was not the evil spirit that brought him up; the Lord sent him to speak with Saul. And Saul stooped with his face to the earth, and bowed himself down to the ground.

Samuel said to Saul,

"Why have you disturbed me?"

Saul answered,

"I am in great trouble, for the Philistines are making war against me and God has gone away from me and will not answer me; therefore I have called on you to tell me what I should do."

"Why do you ask me," said Samuel. "The Lord has done to you what I told you He would do; He has replaced you as king, and has made David king, because you did not obey him. Now He will give the Philistines the victory over you, and over the army of Israel; tomorrow you and your sons shall be with me among the dead."

Then Saul fell down to the earth, and was greatly afraid, because of the words that Samuel had spoken; and there was no strength left in him, for he had eaten nothing all that day, nor all the night before. The woman saw his distress and said,

"Let me put food before you, so that you may eat and gain strength before you go on your way." Saul refused at first, but his attendants and the woman begged him until he consented. So he and his attendants ate. Then they went away.

On the next day, the Philistines gathered all their armies together at Aphek. Achish, the king of Gath, went there and took David and David's followers with him.

The lords of the Philistines were angry at Achish for bringing David. So Achish called David and told him,

"Go back, so that you will not displease the lords of the Philistines." David and his men went away from the camp the next morning.

When David and his men arrived back at their homes, which were in a place called Ziklag, they found their houses burned, for the Amalekites had been there and had destroyed the city and carried away their wives and children as captives. Then the men of Israel wept till they could weep no more.

David called Abiathar, the high priest, and told him to ask the Lord,

"Shall I go after the Amalekites, and will I be able to catch them?"

The Lord answered, "Go after them; you will surely catch them and get back all they have taken."

So David went with his six hundred men, till they came to the brook called Besor. There two hundred of the men stayed, because they were so tired they could go no farther. David followed on, he and four hundred men, until they reached the camp of the Amalekites.

When they came there, the Amalekites were scattered over the ground, eating, and drinking, and dancing. David and his men attacked them and killed them, so that none of them escaped except four hundred young men who rode on camels and fled. The men of Israel got back their wives and their children, and all the spoil that the Amalekites had taken, as the Lord had said they would.

David and his men returned to the brook Besor, and the two hundred men whom they had left there came out to meet them. Then some of David's men, who were selfish and wicked, said,

"Because these two hundred were not with us, we will not give them any of the spoil we have taken." But David told his men that all must share alike—those who were left behind and those who went down to the battle.

David and his men attack the Amalekites as they eat and drink.

73

The story of how David became king

THE LORDS OF THE PHILISTINES, after David had left their camp, went out and fought against Saul and the men of Israel. They won, and the men of Israel fled from them, and many Israelites were killed on Mount Gilboa.

The Philistines followed Saul. They killed Jonathan and two other of Saul's sons, and the battle continued to go against Saul. The archers with their bows and arrows hit and wounded him.

Saul said to his armor-bearer,

"Draw your sword and put me to death, because I fear the Philistines may take me and treat me cruelly." But his armor-bearer was afraid, and would not.

Then Saul took his own sword and stood it on the ground with its point upward; and he fell upon it, on purpose, so that it ran into his body and killed him. When Saul's armor-bearer saw that Saul was dead, he also fell upon his sword and died.

So Saul died, and his three sons and his armor-bearer, and great numbers of his men, on that day. The Philistines gained the victory as Samuel had told Saul they would.

As soon as the people of Israel who lived in that part of the land heard how their army had fled, they fled also, and the Philistines came and lived in the cities they had left.

The next day, when the Philistines went to take the possessions of the men whom they had killed in battle, they found Saul and his three sons lying dead on Mount Gilboa. They cut off Saul's head and took off his armor, and sent word through the land of the Philistines, so that all their people might hear of it and know that Saul was dead and that David was still at Ziklag. David did not know that the Philistines had fought with the men of Israel and gained the victory over them. But there came to Ziklag a man with his clothes torn and his face dirty, as though he were in great distress. When he saw David he bowed down to the ground before him.

David asked him from what place he had come. The man said,

"From the army of Israel. I have escaped."

David next asked him how the battle had gone. He answered, "The men of Israel have fled and many of them have been killed, and Saul and Jonathan are dead also."

David said to the young man,

"How do you know that Saul and Jonathan are dead?"

The young man answered, "As I happened, by chance, to be upon Mount Gilboa in the battle, Saul stood there leaning on his spear, while the Philistines with their chariots and horsemen were coming to kill him. When he looked behind him he saw me and called me; he said, 'Put me to death, for it makes me unhappy that I am still alive.' So I went to him and killed him, because I was sure that he could not live. And I took the crown that was on

Saul dies (foreground, with the sword through him); his armor-bearer is dying.

David orders the death of the man who tells him of Saul's defeat.

his head, and the bracelet that was on his arm, and I have brought them to you."

But what the young man told David was not true; for, as we have read, Saul had killed himself. The young man said that he had killed Saul because he thought it would please David, and that David would reward him for saying so.

David was not pleased. He took hold of his clothes and tore them to show his sorrow, and all the men who were with him tore their clothes. They mourned and wept for Saul, and for Jonathan his son, and for the men of Israel, because so many of them had been slain.

David asked the young man where his home was, and to what country he belonged. The young man answered that he was not one of the people of Israel, but an Amalekite. Then David asked him why he was not afraid to kill Saul, whom the Lord had chosen to be king over the Israelites. And David said that the young man should die for his sin, and that the fault was his own, because he had confessed with his own mouth that he had killed the king of Israel.

So the young Amalekite was put to death, by David's order; and David sang a sad song to mourn the death of Saul, who had been king of Israel, and the death of Jonathan, who had been David's dearest friend.

After this David asked the Lord whether he should leave the land of the Philistines and go back to the land of Israel. The Lord said he should go. Then David asked,

"To what part of the land should I go?"

The Lord told him,

"To the land of Hebron."

David belonged to the tribe of Judah, and Hebron was one of the cities of that tribe; for, as we have read, Joshua gave to each of the twelve tribes a part of the land for its own, and Hebron was in the part that he gave to the tribe of Judah.

So David, who was now thirty years old, went to the city of Hebron.

The chief men of the tribe of Judah came to Hebron and made David king over the tribe of Judah. But the other tribes did not come, because one of Saul's sons, whose name was Ishbosheth, and who was not slain in the battle, still ruled over them.

Ishbosheth ruled over the other tribes for seven years after Saul was dead. Then one day, as Ishbosheth lay on his bed, about noon, two of his captains came into his house, pretending they wanted only to bring in some wheat, but when they had come into his chamber, they killed him.

Then they cut off Ishbosheth's head and fled away with it all night to Hebron, where David was. They showed the head to David, saying,

"We have brought you the head of Ishbosheth, the son of Saul, who was your enemy and who wanted to kill you."

David was greatly displeased. He told them that when he was living at Ziklag, and a young man came to him and said that he had killed Saul, thinking that David would reward him for it, instead of rewarding the young man David had put him to death. So now, David said, these two men who had killed Ishbosheth, Saul's son, when he was doing no wrong, should be put to death for their sins, and he commanded that they should be killed. He sent away the head of Ishbosheth to be buried in a sepulchre.

When the other tribes of Israel saw that Ishbosheth, who had ruled over them, was dead, they sent overseers to David in Hebron, and made him their king. So, at last, David was king over all the tribes of Israel.

74

The story of the ark's return to Israel

Now David went with his army to the city of Jerusalem. The men of Israel had, before this time, taken a part of that city from the people who originally lived in that land, but not all of it. There was a strong fort, or castle, on the mountain called Zion, in which those people still lived. David took this castle from them, and then he went and lived in the castle, calling it the city of David. David came to be a very great man, for the Lord helped him in all that he did.

The king of a city called Tyre was David's friend. This king's name was Hiram. His people were skilled workers in wood and stone. Hiram sent builders and carpenters to David, and they built a house for him in Jerusalem.

Once he was established in Jerusalem, David wanted to bring back the ark of the covenant, which once had been stolen by the Philistines and which had now been in the house of a man named Abinadab for more than seventy years. So David had the ark loaded on an oxcart to be brought to Jerusalem.

The ark was a very holy thing. We have read that when it was first brought inside the tabernacle, God came in a cloud, into the tabernacle, above the ark, and there He stayed in the cloud, over the Mercy Seat. We have read also that when the people of Israel went on their journey through the desert, and took the ark with them, they were not allowed to put it into a cart, but it was carried on the Levites' shoulders. And the Levites themselves were not allowed to come near it until the priests had covered it with the curtains of the tabernacle. For none but the priests were permitted to touch the ark or even to look upon it uncovered. All other persons were forbidden to do so, lest they might die.

Therefore David made a mistake when he had the ark put on a cart. This proved to be a fatal mistake for a man named Uzzah, a son of Abinadab. While Uzzah was driving the oxcart, the oxen stumbled. This shook the ark, and Uzzah reached out his hand to steady it. The minute Uzzah touched the holy ark, he died.

At once David knew he must no longer let the ark be carried on a cart. For three months he left the ark in the house of a man named Obed-edom. Then David and a great party of his followers went to take the ark to Jerusalem; but this time David took with him Levites to carry it on their shoulders. David was clothed in a robe of white linen, and so were the Levites who carried the ark and the priests who were chosen to sing praises to the Lord. They brought the ark to Jerusalem with shoutings, and the sound of trumpets, and cymbals, and harps.

David dances before the ark

As soon as the Levites who carried the ark had started and gone a few steps, David offered up sacrifices to the Lord. The Bible tells us that he danced before the Lord with all his might; that is, he was so glad in being allowed to bring up the ark that he felt as though he could not walk quietly along, but must leap and dance for joy.

Michal, David's wife, looked out of a window and saw him leaping and dancing, and she despised him for it. She told him that he, who was king, made himself look mean and humble by doing so. David said it was before the Lord that he had danced, and that he was willing to make himself more humble and mean before the Lord.

David went out to war against the heathen kings around him, and gained the victory over them, and took from them great numbers of horses and chariots, and much gold and silver. Of the gold and silver he gave a part into the treasury of the Lord. The Lord helped him to prosper, wherever he went; and David ruled justly over all his people.

David keeps his promise to Jonathan

Now that he was grown so rich and great, David remembered how Jonathan, Saul's son, had loved him when he was poor and in trouble, and how they had made an agreement together to be kind to each other's children. One of Jonathan's sons was still living, but he

David dances when the ark is returned to Jerusalem.

was lame in his feet. On the day that Saul and Jonathan were killed in battle, when word of it came to Jonathan's house, the little boy's nurse took him up and fled. As she made haste to flee away, he fell out of her arms and was hurt, so that ever since he had been lame. Now he was grown to be a man, and his name was Mephibosheth.

David sent for this man and when he came to the king he bowed down to the ground. David said to Mephibosheth,

"Do not fear because I have sent for you. I will be kind to you for your father's sake and will give back to you all the land that belonged to Saul, your grandfather; and you shall come and eat at my table."

Then David gave to Mephibosheth all the land that had belonged to Saul, and from that time on Mephibosheth lived with David.

75

The story of David and Bathsheba

THE CAPTAIN OF DAVID'S ARMY WAS NAMED JOAB. David sent Joab with his soldiers to fight against the Ammonites, but David stayed in his house at Jerusalem.

One day when David had finished a midday rest and went to walk along the roof of his house, he saw, a little way off, a beautiful woman. David sent a messenger to ask who she was, and someone told him that she was Bathsheba, the wife of Uriah, a Hittite, who had gone with Joab to fight against the Ammonites.

David sent word to Joab, saying,

"Send Uriah, the Hittite to me."

Joab sent Uriah to David. When he had come, David asked him about the war, and spoke kindly to him, pretending to be his friend. But after three days David sent Uriah back to the army with a letter for Joab. In the letter David told Joab that when the men of Israel went into battle, Joab should send Uriah with them and put Uriah in the most dangerous place. As soon as the Ammonites came out to meet the Israelites, all the rest must flee and leave Uriah alone to be killed. David did this so that after Uriah was dead, he might take Uriah's wife to be his wife.

Uriah went back to the army and gave Joab the letter that David had sent, not knowing what was in it. When the men of Israel went out to fight, Joab did as David commanded. He sent Uriah to the front of the battle, and the Ammonites killed him. Then Joab sent word to David that Uriah was dead.

David brought Bathsheba to his house and took her for his wife.

The Lord was displeased at what David had done. The Lord sent Nathan, the prophet, to tell David so.

Nathan went to David and said,

"There were two men in one city. One of them was rich and the other poor. The rich man had many flocks and herds, but the poor man had nothing except one little lamb, which he had bought and taken care of; it grew up with his children, he fed it from his table, it drank out of his cup and lay in his bosom, and it seemed to him like a daughter.

"There came to the house of the rich man a traveler, who rested there from his journey. Then the rich man would not take a sheep or a goat from his own flocks, though he had so many of them, but he took the poor man's lamb and killed it for the traveler to eat."

When David heard the story Nathan told him, he was very angry, and said,

"The man who has done this thing must be put to death, and he must give to the poor man four lambs for the one he took from him."

But Nathan had told this story to show David his own wickedness. Nathan said to David,

"You are the one who has done like the rich man. For the Lord chose

David sees Bathsheba in her garden and covets her.

you to be king over Israel, and has given you wives and children, and has made you rich and great. Yet you have caused Uriah, who was given so much less, to be killed by the Ammonites so that you might take Uriah's wife to be your wife.

Nathan tells of David's punishment

"Therefore," Nathan said, "the Lord will send a dreadful punishment upon you."

When Nathan spoke these words, David knew how wicked he had been. He said, "I have sinned against the Lord."

After this, God gave a son to David and Bathsheba, and David loved the child; but the Lord sent a great sickness upon the child. David prayed that he might not die; David fasted and ate no food; he lay down on the ground all night, crying to the Lord. The chief men of the city came to David to persuade him to rise, but he would not; nor would he eat with them as he used to do at other times.

On the seventh day the child died. David's officials feared to tell him that the child was dead. They said to one another,

David grieves for the death of his son.

"While the child was alive we spoke to the king and he would not listen to us; how much greater his sorrow will be if we tell him that the child is dead."

But when David saw his servants whispering, he knew that the child was dead. He said to them, "Is the child dead?" and they answered, "He is dead."

Then David rose, and washed and dressed himself, and went out to the tent where the ark was kept. There he worshiped the Lord. Afterward he returned to his house and told his servants to bring food; and when they set it before him, he ate.

His servants were surprised and asked him why he did these things.

"You wept and would eat nothing," they said, "while the child was alive; but now that it is dead, you can eat."

David answered, "While the child was alive, I fasted and wept, for I said, 'Who can tell whether God will be kind to me and let the child live?' But now that he is dead, why should I fast any more? Can I bring him back again? I shall go to him when I die, but he can never return to me."

Later God gave to David and Bathsheba another son, whose name was Solomon (which means "peaceable"), and the Lord loved him. He was to be a great king one day.

76

The story of Absalom's revolt

DAVID HAD OTHER WIVES BESIDE BATHSHEBA. In those times a man could have more than one wife and kings usually had many wives. One of his wives had a son named Amnon, who was David's oldest son. Another of David's wives had a son named Absalom and a daughter named Tamar. Amnon was their half-brother, the son of the same father but a different mother.

Absalom was more admired for beauty than any other young man of Israel. From his feet to his head there was no fault to be seen in him. Especially admired was his long, thick hair. He cut his hair once each year, and the hair he cut off weighed "as much as two hundred shekels of silver" —that is, more than six pounds.

His sister Tamar was beautiful too, and that was unfortunate because it caused her half-brother Amnon to fall in love with her. She resisted Amnon, because he was her brother, and this caused enmity to arise between Absalom and Amnon.

Absalom did nothing to Amnon for two years. Then he gave a feast and invited his father, King David, and all his brothers. David did not go to the feast, but Amnon went; and while the feast was at its height, Absalom had his servants kill his brother Amnon.

Now, fearful of being punished by David, Absalom fled to the city of Geshur, in another country, and there he stayed three years. David mourned greatly for Amnon, but also he loved his son Absalom. He wanted Absalom to come back home, but Absalom was afraid and would not do so.

Finally Joab, the captain of David's army, who knew how much David wanted his son back, contrived to have David call Absalom back home; but

The killing of Amnon by order of his brother Absalom.

though David let Absalom return to Jerusalem, David refused to see his son.

After Absalom had lived two years in Jerusalem without seeing his father, he sent for Joab. He wanted Joab to go with a message to the king. But Joab would not come. Absalom sent a second time, and still Joab would not come. Absalom told his servants to go into Joab's field, and set his grain on fire, and the servants did so. Finally Joab came. Joab asked him,

"Why have your servants set my field on fire?"

Absalom answered that it was because he would not come to take a message to the king.

"For," Absalom said, "if I may not see the king, I might as well have stayed in that land to which I fled, and not have come back to Jerusalem at all. Let me come before the king; and if I am guilty let him kill me."

Joab went to the king and told him this. Then the king sent for Absalom, and Absalom came and bowed himself with his face to the ground before his father. David did not punish Absalom for his sin, as he ought to have done; David took Absalom to him and kissed him.

Though David had been so kind and forgiving, Absalom soon began to plot ways to remove David from the throne of Israel and to become king himself. Absalom had fifty men to run before him when he rode out in his chariot, so that all the people might see him and think him a great man. He rose early in the morning and stood by the gate of the city, and when he saw any man coming into the city, to speak with the king and ask some favor of him, Absalom called the man and talked with him, and said,

Absalom's plot against his father

"If I were only ruler over the land, you would have all you want." And whenever any man bowed down to him, because he was the king's son, Absalom put out his hand and took hold of him, and kissed him. Absalom did this to all the people who came to ask help of the king, and he made them think much of him, not because he was a good man, or really cared for them, but to deceive them and make them believe he was their friend.

Soon afterward Absalom went to the king and said,

"I beg that you let me go to Hebron and worship the Lord." Absalom pretended that he had made a vow to offer up a sacrifice at Hebron, and that now he wanted to go there and do it.

The king told Absalom he might go, so he went; but it was not to serve the Lord that he went, it was to have himself made king instead of his father. He sent spies through all the land to persuade the people to put his father away, and make him king. The spies told the people that, on a certain day, as soon as they should hear the sound of trumpets, which Absalom's friends would blow, they should cry out,

"Absalom is king in Hebron!"

Absalom took two hundred men with him out of Jerusalem to help him, and sent also for a great man named Ahithophel, who was David's counselor, or adviser. Ahithophel and many of the people turned against David and took the side of Absalom.

Soon a messenger came to David and told him how the men of Israel were following Absalom. David was afraid, and said to his own followers,

"Come, let us flee; make haste, for Absalom may come suddenly and attack the city with the sword."

David's men answered,

"We are ready to do whatever the king commands."

The priests and Levites brought the ark, to carry it with David.

So the king fled in haste from Jerusalem, he and his soldiers and many of the people of the city, and they crossed the brook Kidron and went toward the desert.

The priests and Levites brought the ark, to carry it with David wherever he should go; but David told them to take it back into the city again. He said that perhaps the Lord would be kind to him, and bring him back also; if not, he was willing to have the Lord do to him as He saw best. For David felt how wicked he had been in causing Uriah to be slain, and in taking Uriah's wife to be his wife. He remembered how the Lord had said that a great punishment would come upon him. And now a great punishment had come upon him, and David knew he deserved it, and he was willing to bear it. He went out of Jerusalem over the mountain called Olivet, weeping as he went, with his head covered and his feet bare. And all the men who were with him covered their heads; and they also wept as they went.

Ahithophel joins with Absalom

Someone told David that Ahithophel, who had been his counselor, had gone with Absalom, to help him and advise him what he should do to make himself king. David prayed that Ahithophel's advice might be turned into foolishness, so that it would not do Absalom any good.

When David had gone a little way out of the city, Hushai, one of his friends, came to meet him and go with him, for he loved David and was not willing to leave him. But David told him to go back to Jerusalem and stay there till Absalom came. Then, David said, Hushai could watch and see what Absalom would do, and send word secretly to him; and so he would do David more good than if he went with him.

Therefore Hushai went back. As you will see, David was right. Hushai was able to do him much good in Jerusalem.